THE BAVARIAN ROCOCO CHURCH

KARSTEN HARRIES

THE BAVARIAN ROCOCO CHURCH

Between Faith and Aestheticism

YALE UNIVERSITY PRESS
NEW HAVEN AND LONDON

Published with assistance from the Graham Foundation for Advanced Studies in the Fine Arts and from the Whitney Humanities Center of Yale University.

Designed by Nancy Ovedovitz and set in VIP Goudy Old Style type by The Saybrook Press, Inc. Printed in the United States of America by The Murray Printing Co., Westford, Mass.

Library of Congress Cataloging in Publication Data

Harries, Karsten.
The Bavarian rococo church.
Includes bibliographical references and index.
1. Church architecture—Germany (West)—Bavaria.
2. Architecture, Rococo—Germany (West)—Bavaria.
I. Title.
NA5573.H37 1983 726′.5′09433 82-11168
ISBN 0-300-02720-6

10 9 8 7 6 5 4 3 2 1

In memory of my father
Wolfgang Harries

Die Herrlichkeit der Erden
Muss Rauch und Aschen werden,
Kein Fels, kein Erzt kann stehn.
Dies, was uns kann ergetzen,
Was wir für ewig schätzen
Wird als ein leichter Traum vergehn.

Andreas Gryphius

CONTENTS

ILLUSTRATIONS

Plates

Unless otherwise noted, all color photographs were taken by the author.

Figures

ACKNOWLEDGMENTS

Ever since a teacher in Munich's Maxgymnasium led my twelve-year-old classmates and me through the Benedictine abbey church of Andechs, I have been fascinated by the architecture and culture of the Bavarian rococo. The present study gave me an excuse to give in to this fascination. I am grateful to the John Simon Guggenheim Memorial Foundation for its support, which ten years ago allowed me to get started seriously on a project I had long played with, and to Yale University for its generous leave policy.

I owe thanks to those many persons with whom I visited and discussed these churches. Special thanks are due to Standish and Ursula Lawder and to Dr. and Mrs. Hubert Endres, who not only extended the hospitality of their home in Erding, but introduced me to many of the delightful churches in Munich's northeast.

A study such as this depends on illustrations. Yale University's Whitney Center for the Humanities provided financial support that helped me to assemble the needed visual material. Frau Irmgard Ernstmaier of the Hirmer Fotoarchiv, Dr. Annemarie Kuhn-Wengenmayr of the Bayerisches Landesamt für Denkmalpflege, Dr. Burkard von Roda of the Bayerische Verwaltung der Staatlichen Schlösser, Gärten und Seen, Frau Ursula Meier of the Bildarchiv Foto Marburg, Rektor Franz Eberl of Erding, Professor S. Lane Faison of Williams College, and Professor John Cook of the Yale Divinity School helped and granted permission to draw on their collections. The Graham Foundation for Advanced Studies in the Fine Arts made it possible to include the colorplates. I am especially indebted to Susan Murray: without the Leica she gave me I could hardly have kept track of the many churches I visited and revisited.

I wish to thank Judy Metro, Anne Lunt, Lawrence Kenney, and Nancy Ovedovitz of Yale University Press for the caring attention they have given to this book. I owe special thanks to S. Lane Faison, who more than twenty years ago visited many of these churches with me, and gave an earlier version of this book an unusually thorough, sympathetic, yet critical reading. I have accepted many of his suggestions. My wife, who shared in this book from beginning to end, deserves more than thanks.

INTRODUCTION

In our approach to art we are the heirs of the Enlightenment. The "aesthetic" treatises of the eighteenth century helped to establish a distinctly modern understanding of works of art as occasions for an enjoyment that is its own justification. Beauty is divorced from truth, art from the sacred. Only as long as the work of art is governed by the demands of its own aesthetic perfection does it remain pure: art, earlier in the service of religion, morality, or society, becomes "art for art's sake."[1] The term *aesthetics* itself belongs to this period, for we owe it to Alexander Gottlieb Baumgarten's *Reflections on Poetry* of 1735.

Speculations, however, did not cause the shift to the aesthetic approach. The aesthetic literature of the eighteenth century is part of a transformation that is more immediately grasped in the changes of the art of the period. In this study I examine only one example of these changes: the evolution and eventual disintegration of the Bavarian rococo church, more especially of its style.[2] Yet this transformation sheds light on both the essence and the origin of the aesthetic approach and on the confused situation of the arts today.

Given my interest in the emergence of the aesthetic attitude, why the Bavarian rococo church? Why indeed the rococo at all? Why not turn to the work of late eighteenth-century architects like Ledoux or Boullée? As Emil Kaufmann has shown, a distinctly modern approach does indeed govern the architecture of the French Revolution.[3] But just because it does, we have to look back further to understand the transformation that this approach presupposes.

What attracted me to the rococo was the fact that, as the last of the great period styles, it occupies the threshold to our own aesthetic culture. Yet many of the points that matter most to me could have been made equally well discussing some other aspect of eighteenth-century art—ornamental engravings, for example, or garden architecture. I chose the Bavarian rococo church because of its precarious position between the Italian baroque and the French rococo, between the enduring culture of the Counter Reformation and an already quite modern aestheticism. Tinged with skepticism, the Bavarian rococo is no longer able to take quite seriously the pathos and rhetoric of the baroque, yet refuses to give them up; so it plays with them.

The playful character of the rococo church manifests itself above all in its borrowed ornament. Nowhere did rocaille, defined by the asymmetry of its shell forms, develop more exuberantly than in Bavaria, until finally it emancipated itself from its merely ornamental character, shed its subservient role, and approached the status of an autonomous abstract art. But autonomous ornament would seem to be a contradiction in terms. Where ornament strives for autonomy, it dies as ornament. It is precisely its tendency toward aesthetic autonomy that makes rocaille an ornament to end ornament. Just as there is a sense in which style can be said to have died with the rococo, so is there a sense in which ornament can be said to have died with rocaille. With it died also the traditional approach to architecture and to art.[4]

It is all too easy to make such assertions. They must be supported by an examination of the buildings themselves. Careful description should yield those features of the Bavarian rococo church that determine its particular style and help us to relate it to and at the same time to distinguish it from both the French rococo and the Italian baroque.

But how do we determine a style? The concept of style is problematic. We speak of the style of an artist, a group, a school, a country, a period. In each case to speak of a style is to suggest that different works of art are related, not as parts of a larger whole, but as variations on an unknown theme,[5] originating in the same force or feeling, which in turn manifests itself in a common formal "language." To call the Bavarian rococo a distinct style is to suggest that its creations refer us to something like a distinct artistic intention. Following Alois Riegl, we may want to speak of a distinct *Kunstwollen*. But the concept of a *Kunstwollen* is even more problematic than that of style. Riegl's term is of course a metaphor. Human beings intend or will; but how can we understand the artistic intention manifesting itself in a period style? Who or what intends? To speak of a *Kunstwollen* suggests an ideal artist who haunts and allows us to understand the work of particular artists. Our construction of such ideal types is always governed by our presuppositions. Depending on their interests and prejudices, different interpreters will arrive at different determinations of the artistic intention and thus at different classifications of artistic phenomena.

Consider the term *baroque*.[6] Burckhardt still saw in the baroque little more than a late and degenerate phase of Renaissance: baroque architecture speaks the same language as the Renaissance, but in a crude dialect that overturns the established grammar. And Burckhardt was not alone with his estimate. Only in the last decades of the nineteenth century, beginning with such works as Cornelius Gurlitt's *Geschichte des Barockstils in Italien* (1887) and Heinrich Wölfflin's *Renaissance und Barock* (1888) was the baroque recognized as a style of its own. Even Wölfflin set out to show that baroque was a late and corrupt form of Renaissance art, and to use this story of decline to demonstrate the laws governing art historical development. Instead he discovered that the baroque was an independent style, a style that no longer obeyed Renaissance norms. The baroque was governed by a *Kunstwollen* of its own.

But to what extent do the examined works of art yield such a *Kunstwollen* and to what extent is it read into them? We should not forget that the discovery of the baroque by art historians followed its discovery by the public at large. The neobaroque castles of Ludwig II at Linderhof and Herrenchiemsee, the architecture of the French Second Empire, and similar developments in Vienna and elsewhere show that the writing of the history of art followed a general change of taste. It was this change that enabled art historians to look at long-familiar phenomena with fresh vision.

The discovery of the specific unity, first of the rococo, then of the Bavarian rococo, rests on similar shifts in point of view. Like *baroque* and *Gothic*, the term *rococo* long suggested disapproval, implying artificiality and decadence. It shed such negative connotations only slowly and established itself, first in Germany, "as a formal designation of the general period and style of Louis XV, both in France and elsewhere under French influence."[7] Yet this formal designation often continued to carry disparaging overtones. The definition of *rococo* offered by the *Oxford English Dictionary* is quite in accord with common usage: "Having the characteristics of Louis Quatorze or Louis Quinze workmanship, such as conventional shell- and scroll-work and meaningless decoration, excessively florid or ornate." But what criteria allow us to judge an ornament meaningful or meaningless? How is excess measured, and by what standard of taste is the rococo found tasteless? More often than not such objections are not simply to an aesthetic phenomenon, but to this phenomenon understood as an expression of a decadent age. Arnold Hauser is not alone when he interprets the art of the rococo as the art of "a frivolous, tired, and passive society,"[8] a last expression of the disintegrating old order. As we shall see, there is much that supports such an interpretation, although it is difficult to reconcile with that side of the rococo that suggests the innocence of spring.

The rehabilitation of the rococo is inseparable from the rehabilitation of the baroque. Walter Hausenstein's influential *Vom Geist des Barocks* (1921), which, very much in the spirit of expressionism, celebrated the baroque as a metaphor of the organic, is also a celebration of the rococo, especially of the South German rococo. In this it reflects a tendency, still widespread, to interpret the rococo simply as the last phase of the baroque. This measures the rococo by criteria derived from an examination of developments in Italian art. As Fiske Kimball rightly emphasizes, such criteria are unlikely to do justice to the specifically French character of the rococo. But if, with Kimball, we emphasize the originators of the *style rocaille* and identify the rococo as a French style of decoration, the Bavarian contribution must be taken as secondary. The gloriously spontaneous decorations of such native Bavarians as Johann Michael Feichtmayr or Johann Georg Üblhör would have to be judged coarse imitations lacking in elegance and refinement.[9]

Challenging Kimball's definition of the rococo as a French style of decoration, Hermann Bauer points out that, while its origins lie in France, it reached its greatest height in Germany, in good part because there it was able to make its way into the religious sphere.[10] Bauer does not claim that the South German rococo church originated only in the French tradition; he insists on the importance of Italian illusionism. But his suggestion that the Bavarian rococo church be understood as an original synthesis of Italian baroque and French rococo makes it difficult to accept his other claim that, despite obvious differences, the *Kunstwollen* of the *style rocaille* and of the rococo church are one and the same, that both are variations of the same style. Bauer examines rocaille as the "critical form" that reveals the essence of this style, a style that he also finds in such superficially different forms as the English park—with its picturesque ruins, temples, and pagodas—and the romanticizing classicism of the eighteenth century. But is he justified in calling these different expressions of the same style?

Bauer also suggests that the French rococo was, if not a sufficient, at least a necessary condition of the Bavarian rococo church. Can we say that there would have been no Bavarian rococo church without the *style rocaille*?[11]

Not surprisingly, many German historians of eighteenth-century architecture have objected to interpretations of the Bavarian rococo church that emphasized the French origin of rocaille and have insisted that the Bavarian rococo be understood in terms of its own artistic intention. But what is this intention? What we take to be the *Kunstwollen* of the Bavarian rococo church depends very much on what examples we see as decisive. This again presupposes that we already know what is to count as a Bavarian rococo church. How are we to enter this circle? Fortunately there is considerable agreement: no determination of the essence of the Bavarian rococo church is likely to be taken seriously that would not allow us to consider Dominikus Zimmermann's pilgrimage church at Steinhausen (1729–33) and Die Wies (1745–54) as major rococo churches.

Yet if these churches can serve as paradigms, we have to question the dependence of the Bavarian rococo church on rocaille. Steinhausen was built a number of years before rocaille was introduced into Bavaria in the mid-1730s. It thus has become common practice to give a somewhat earlier date as the beginning of the Bavarian rococo. Norbert Lieb's date of 1730 is supported by the often-repeated suggestion that Steinhausen be considered the first real rococo church. This early rococo is preceded by a proto-rococo that can be pushed back to the beginning of the century, although new impulses make themselves felt toward the middle of the second decade, so that in Bavaria, too, we can speak of a French-inspired *régence* style beginning at that time.[12]

To assert that rocaille is not essential to the Bavarian rococo church is not to claim that the enthusiastic reception that this ornament received in Bavaria was an accident: there must have been something about the intentions of those who commissioned and built the churches of the Bavarian rococo that made them particularly receptive to the new style of ornamentation. Still, given the nonessential, if very important, role of rocaille, it seems questionable whether an analysis of its essence can do full justice to the Bavarian rococo church. Bauer's proposal that the French *style rocaille*, the English park, and the Bavarian rococo church are governed by the same *Kunstwollen* invites challenge.

Perhaps the most adequate interpretation of the Bavarian rococo church is provided by Bernhard Rupprecht in *Die bayerische Rokoko-Kirche*. Given Rupprecht's choice of paradigms—Steinhausen, Die Wies, and Johann Michael Fischer's Zwiefalten (1744–65)—there is no need to quarrel with the criteria he establishes for the Bavarian rococo church:

1. A central space is formed, illuminated by mostly indirect light.
2. The boundaries of this space remain indefinite.
3. Traditional architectural forms are transformed, isolated, and displaced.
4. An ornamental stucco zone is placed between fresco and architecture.
5. A point of view near the entrance is the most important; it determines the perspective of the main fresco; at the same time it lets us see the space in its entirety as a pictorial whole.[13]

Henry-Russell Hitchcock's *Rococo Architecture in Southern Germany* questions these

1. Johann Michael Fischer, Zwiefalten, Benedictine abbey church, interior

criteria. Hitchcock rejects one of Rupprecht's paradigms, Fischer's Zwiefalten (fig. 1). Of course, Hitchcock too recognizes rococo elements in this church. These, however, are said to be contradicted by a strong tectonic emphasis. Caught between baroque and rococo, the interior has a broken character. Like Rupprecht, Hitchcock calls our attention to the striking pairs of columns on the wall-pillars (fig. 2). But while both insist on the crucial importance of this column motif, they offer very different interpretations of it. According to Rupprecht it has a primarily pictorial function; together with the high altar the paired columns help to establish the interior as a coherent picture. Hitchcock, on the other hand, makes little of this pictorialization of architectural space, which is perhaps the most important theme of Rupprecht's analysis. He sees the columns as having a tectonic significance that remains essentially baroque.[14]

What matters here is not who is right—I only want to show how the interpreter's preconception of the essence of the rococo guides even his description of what is seen. Hitchcock seems to think that we can escape from such controversy by adopting a mode of analysis that is, as he puts it, "not inductive, from supposed principles to more or less perfect examples, but deductive." He claims to seek the essence of South German rococo architecture in what is common in the major works of its major architects.[15] But that Hitchcock himself cannot proceed in this way is shown by his claim that the prolific Johann Michael Fischer, perhaps the greatest of Bavaria's architects in the eighteenth century, belongs less obviously to the rococo than Dominikus Zimmermann. I do not want to deny this. The point I want to make is only that we cannot arrive at a conception of the Bavarian rococo by what Hitchcock calls deduction. Only if from the very beginning we question the rococo character of Fischer's interiors, that is to say, only if we have already decided what is to count as rococo, is it possible to select those works that will allow us to "deduce" the essence of the rococo. Our approach can in fact be neither deductive nor inductive; some circularity cannot be avoided. We sense a certain unity in the churches that were built in Bavaria throughout the better part of the eighteenth century. Interpretation seeks to articulate principles that will allow us to understand this unity, the structure of this style.

One goal of this book is to determine what we can call the essence of the Bavarian rococo church, but I am more interested in its origin and eventual disintegration. Why do forms change? To say that the *Kunstwollen* changes is to offer not an explanation, but a tautology. Although the history of forms is in some sense autonomous, a formal approach cannot do justice to the history of art. Art must be placed in a wider context. The history of art must be understood against the background of the history of ideas and, beyond that, of history. This claim may seem questionable to someone who, committed to an aesthetic approach, thinks of art as an autonomous realm ruled by its own laws. Yet such a commitment is not based on a timeless truth, but must itself be understood historically. "The miracle of creation" may indeed, as Kimball claims, be "wrapped up in the mystery of personal artistic individuality."[16] To speak of supraindividual forces may seem to violate this mystery. But the importance of the individual is not a constant in the history of art. Only when we keep in mind the limitations placed on an artist's creativity by his historical situation can we gain an understanding of what really is his own.

2. Zwiefalten, abbey church, north side of nave

The limits of an approach that neglects the history of ideas become particularly evident when we are dealing with religious art. A church must be understood as an answer to the task of building a church. But what is a church? We might answer by pointing to the activities that take place in the church building, yet such an appeal to function would not do justice to the way the Bavarian architects of the eighteenth century understood their task. Thomas Aquinas's often-cited definition of the church building is a better guide: *Domus in qua sacramentum celebratur, ecclesiam significat et ecclesia nominatur.* "The house in which the sacrament is celebrated signifies the Church and is called 'church.' "[17] The Bavarian rococo marks a last successful attempt to build churches as signs of the invisible Church. The playful way in which this sign character is established shows that this is indeed a last attempt.

Although the history of ideas cannot be reduced to an epiphenomenon of social history, political and social factors do nevertheless play an important role in the evolution of style. The influence of the Italian baroque and the French rococo on the Bavarian rococo church cannot be adequately understood without some understanding of the politics of the Bavarian electors. Even more important, although less easy to trace, is the relationship between economic and social conditions and the flowering of the Bavarian rococo. It is remarkable that its centers include not only Munich, the capital, and Augsburg, long a center of the arts, but also Wessobrunn, a village, or rather a collection of scattered farms assembled around an important monastery. The artist-craftsmen from Wessobrunn made a decisive contribution to almost all the masterpieces of German eighteenth-century architecture.

How was it possible to draft much of the male population into the building trades and yet to preserve a level of accomplishment that would fill one of our schools of art and architecture with envy? What were the conditions that transformed peasants into artists? Why did this happen not only here but also in other places in or close to the Alps? (Together with Wessobrunn, Roveredo in the Swiss Grisons and Au in the Austrian Vorarlberg are the best-known examples.) I have hunches, but no adequate answers. The art of the Bavarian rococo cannot be associated with a particular class; it unites all segments of society. This genuinely popular character of the Bavarian rococo contrasts with the urban and courtly art of the Renaissance that preceded it and with the bourgeois neoclassicism that was to follow, introducing a rift between popular art and high Art that is still with us.

The popular character of the Bavarian rococo is linked to the piety and backwardness of the Bavarians—proverbial in the eighteenth century. Compared to Saxony or Prussia, let alone England or France, eighteenth-century Bavaria was an unenlightened country. The church remained the leading cultural force, more important than the court, far more important than the bourgeoisie. The country continued to be very much a land of peasants, whose situation had changed little since the Middle Ages. This backwardness is closely connected with the baroque character of the rococo church. In it the Counter Reformation found its last convincing architectural expression. When the Enlightenment did come to Bavaria, late and as a foreign import, it had to place itself in opposition to the forces that had sustained the rococo church. Newly "enlightened" officials issued decree after decree in an attempt to drag the reluctant population into the modern age. One of their targets was the rococo church. The old and the new clash here with particular vehemence and clarity.

Long before this attack from without, the precarious synthesis on which the Bavarian rococo church depends had begun to disintegrate from within. The source of this disintegration cannot be separated from the specific beauty of the rococo church. The rococo church dies as the aesthetic sphere claims and gains autonomy. A once coherent value system splinters. One of the splinters is modern art.

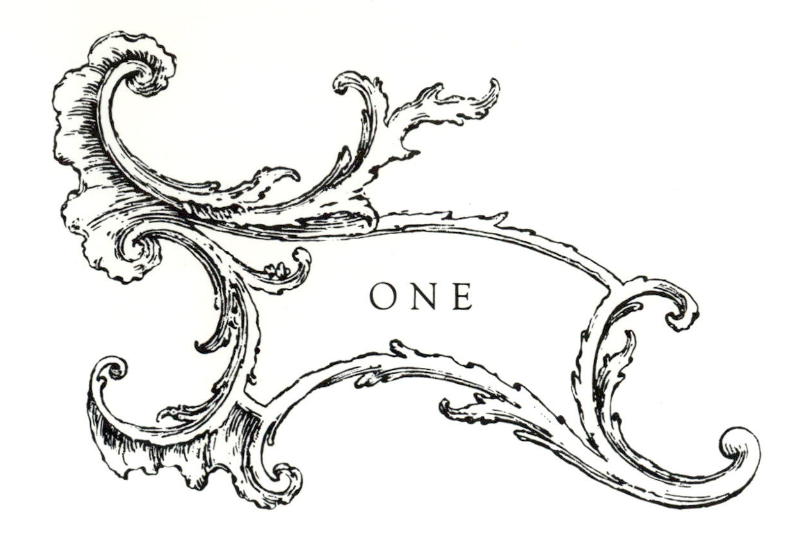

THE PICTORIALIZATION OF ORNAMENT

French Origins

Labels are both helpful and dangerous: while they let us look in certain directions, revealing aspects and connections that might otherwise have remained hidden, they can also cover up what may be more important. Such a label is "Bavarian rococo." The term *rococo* is, of course, not derived from a study of Bavarian art or architecture, but refers us to France, first of all to a French mode of decoration: rococo is that style which makes use of rocaille or shell work. Shells and shell patterns had long been popular with decorators, and in the first half of the eighteenth century the shell motif gained central importance as it was developed by such French designers as Nicolas Pineau, Juste-Aurèle Meissonier, and Jacques de Lajoue into a new ornamental vocabulary, into "rocaille."[1] An important event in the evolution of this *goût nouveau* or *genre pittoresque* was the appearance in 1734 of Meissonier's *Livre d'ornemens*. The shell is here transformed into an almost abstract, endlessly malleable material, out of which the artist molds landscapes and fantastic architectures. In these engravings of the 1730s the *forme rocaille* has been said to have its origin (fig. 3).

Today *rococo* is often given a wider sense. Its origins are sought not with Pineau or Meissonier, but at the very beginning of the century with Pierre Lepautre, designer in the office of Louis XIV's *premier architecte* Jules-Hardouin Mansart. Characteristic of his ornaments are flat bands that cross and interweave in delicate patterns, the so-called bandwork.[2] But however the term is used, to speak of *Bavarian rococo* is to suggest a local variation on an eighteenth-century French theme.

Against this it has often been urged that what is called Bavarian rococo architecture is fundamentally just baroque. This position claims that the undeniable dependence of the

Bavarians on French models was comparatively superficial: rococo ornament was applied to an architecture that remained baroque. Just as "rococo" points toward France, "baroque" points toward Italy, toward Rome and Venice. Both labels thus lead away from the at times quite different intentions of the Bavarians; yet both labels are indispensable. The rococo label in particular enables us to sketch some decisive developments of Bavarian architecture in the eighteenth century.

One such sketch is provided by Henry-Russell Hitchcock.

> Provided Rococo architecture in southern Germany is granted to have had at least quasi-independent existence, it is not difficult to outline its history. After the initial importation of the new French decorative mode into Germany in the second decade of the eighteenth century, there followed in the early and mid-twenties a short period of regional interpretation—acclimatization, one might call it—after which an increasingly autochthonous development began. That development led during the thirties to stylistic maturity, a maturity that lasted with little loss of vigour at least through the fifties and even into the early sixties.[3]

Although this is quite plausible as a brief summary, one point especially invites questioning. Hitchcock speaks here of "the new French decorative mode," referring of course to that mode of ornament initiated by Pierre Lepautre; François de Cuvilliés's introduction of rocaille into Bavaria, which occurred only in the thirties, goes unmentioned. Still, the influence French ornament had on Bavarian art in the second decade of the eighteenth century is so striking as to suggest that we should look here for the origins of the Bavarian rococo (fig. 4).

A glance at contemporary political events suggests an even more precise date. Dreams of becoming emperor and an unfortunate alliance with Louis XIV had led the Bavarian elector Max Emanuel into the War of the Spanish Succession. In 1704, after Prince

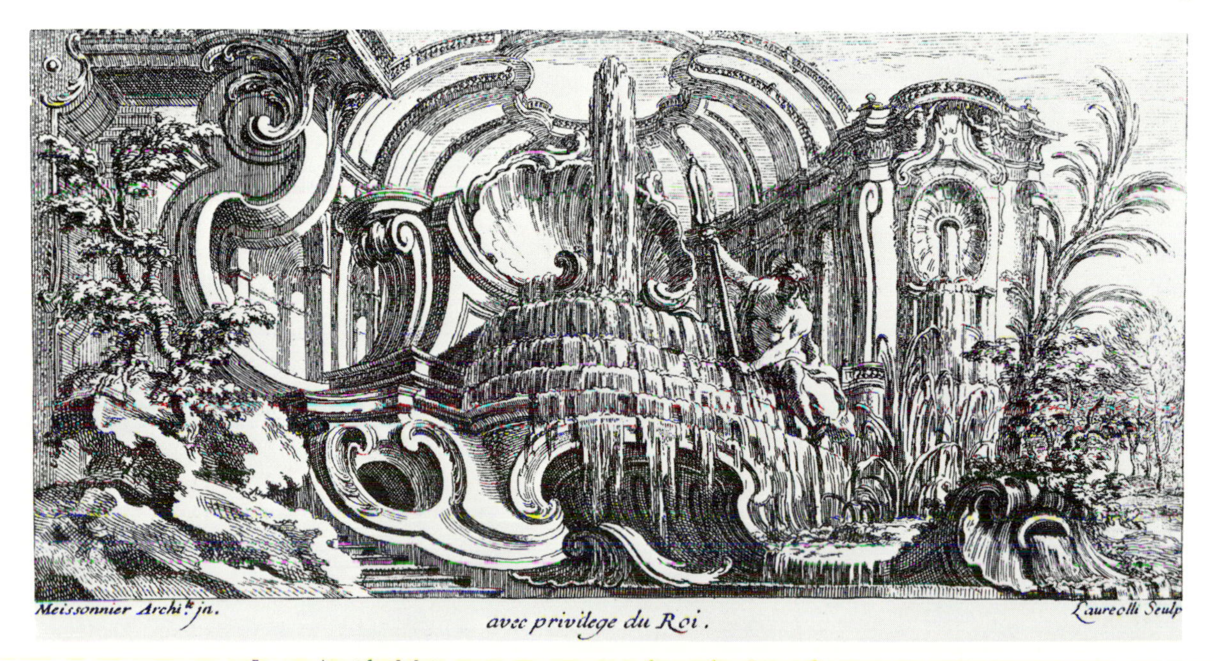

3. Juste-Aurèle Meissonier, engraving from the *Livre d'ornemens*, 1734

4. Nymphenburg, Pagodenburg, upper cabinet with *boiseries* by Johann Adam Pichler

Eugene of Savoy and the duke of Marlborough had defeated the allied French and Bavarians at Blenheim, the elector had to flee Munich, which like all of Bavaria came under Austrian administration. Only in 1715 was Max Emanuel to return home from his French exile. With him came French-trained artists: above all the architect Joseph Effner, who had been sent to Paris in 1706 to study gardening, but had soon shifted to architecture, studying and working with Germain Boffrand. Although nominally still subordinate to the aging Enrico Zuccalli, it was Effner who was in charge when building activity resumed at the elector's palaces in Nymphenburg and Schleissheim. In 1724 he succeeded Zuccalli as the elector's chief architect (*Oberhofbaumeister*). In matters of decoration the highest authority was the Flemish sculptor and decorator Wilhelm de Groff. He, too, had worked in Paris, but left the service of Louis XIV to accept the offer of the Bavarian elector.[4] In Munich he headed a large workshop, which included such French-trained artists as the Tyrolean Johann Adam Pichler, whose *boiseries* form an important part of many of the interiors created for Max Emanuel, and the sculptor Charles Dubut.

The renewed building activity in Munich soon attracted many local artists who were to mediate between the Paris-oriented artists at the court and more traditionbound artists of city and country. Thus since 1715 the young Johann Baptist Gunetzrhainer from Munich was working as *ingenieur* under Effner; in 1721 he was appointed assistant court architect (*Hofunterbaumeister*). Gunetzrhainer provided an important link between the court and a group of Munich architects that included his stepfather Johann Mayr, his brother Ignaz Anton, and the great Johann Michael Fischer, who was to marry one of Mayr's daughters.

Effner's choice of the stuccoer Johann Baptist Zimmermann to decorate the great stairhall at Schleissheim (1720) proved even more fortunate. Zimmermann's association with the court was to last until his death. As the same time he remained in close touch with his native Wessobrunn, a small community southwest of Munich, whose decorators and builders by that time had already come to dominate much of South German architecture. In the same stairhall another Bavarian, Cosmas Damian Asam, painted the fresco *Venus in the Forge of Vulcan*. At Schleissheim the two artists, who as we shall see were most responsible for the emergence of a distinctly Bavarian rococo, were thus brought together. In view of such connections, one is tempted to consider Max Emanuel's return to Munich the real beginning of the Bavarian rococo.

Unfortunately this account is just a little too neat. Everywhere in Bavaria the first decades of the century see a move toward sparser, more delicate ornament. Johann Baptist Zimmerman's decoration of the parish church in Schliersee, dating from 1714, is a particularly good example of an early rococo, antedating the elector's return (fig. 5). The stuccoed foliage of the severies and rib-bands still betrays its origin in the baroque acanthus ornament that had come to be identified with the decorators from Wessobrunn, but the leafy vines of 1700 have flattened out and become bandlike. Zimmermann's subtle deployment of yellow, green, and gray compensates for the diminished relief of his stuccowork and reasserts the contrast between ornamental figure and supporting ground; at the same time it integrates his frescoes into the ornamental scheme. Especially forward looking are the cartouches that mediate between the severies and the frescoes of the choir vault.[5]

5. Schliersee, parish church St. Sixtus, decoration of choir vault

The claim that it was only with the return of Max Emanuel that the French influence made itself clearly felt in Bavaria also makes it difficult to explain why this happened not only in Munich, the capital, but at just about the same time in other places as well, for instance in the Swiss abbey church of St. Urban, presumably decorated by Franz Schmuzer, another Wessobrunner. Hitchcock credits him with having been the first one to have adapted French rococo decoration to "large-scale church architecture, since Lepautre's work in France was restricted to accessories."[6] Where did Franz Schmuzer gain his familiarity with the new style emerging in France? Hardly in Munich, where he never worked, and where the elector's artists were just beginning their work in 1716. Clearly, the artists from Wessobrunn did not depend on the court art of Munich for their knowledge of the new French style. They must have had independent access. We do indeed know of artists from Wessobrunn active in Paris in the seventeenth century. These contacts were never broken off. "When Effner was sent to Paris to study modern French art, he met there already the Wessobrunners. Wessobrunn gained the decisive impulses for the transformation of late baroque forms into the rhythms of régence and rococo in Paris."[7] The latter seems to me a dubious claim. Far more important than such direct contacts were the models provided by publications like Paul Decker's *Fürstlicher Baumeister* (1711). The publishing houses of Augsburg played an important role in spreading the new French style[8] (fig. 6).

Munich, too, had opened itself to French art long before the return of Max Emanuel.

Already at the court of his mother, Adelaide, we meet with French artists, such as the painters Paul Mignaud, "Adelaide's Apelles," and Jean Delamonce.[9] As early as 1684 Max Emanuel sent his chief architect Enrico Zuccalli to Paris to acquaint himself with the newest fashion, and in 1703 the French architect René Alexis Delamaire was projecting interior decorations for the elector; it was hoped that he would replace Zuccalli, and only the war prevented him from coming to Munich.[10] In the same year the Italian Pietro Francesco Appiani decorated a number of rooms in the palace of Nymphenburg with "leaf-work in the French manner."[11] It is therefore misleading to distinguish an Italian phase of stucco decoration, initiated by the decorative scheme of Munich's Theatinerkirche (1663–88), from a French phase, starting with the early rococo interiors created under Effner's direction beginning in 1715. The two phases cannot be separated so easily. By the 1680s both French and Italian influences make themselves felt, and not only in Munich, but in Augsburg and Wessobrunn as well.[12]

Influences are difficult to trace, especially when they are creatively transformed rather than faithfully copied. In this connection it is interesting to consider in more detail the ways in which St. Urban anticipates the rococo architecture to come. Hitchcock points to the pilasters,

> which are coupled rather than single as at Rheinau, are neither plain nor fluted as in earlier churches but are decorated, rather like those in many French secular interiors of the previous ten or fifteen

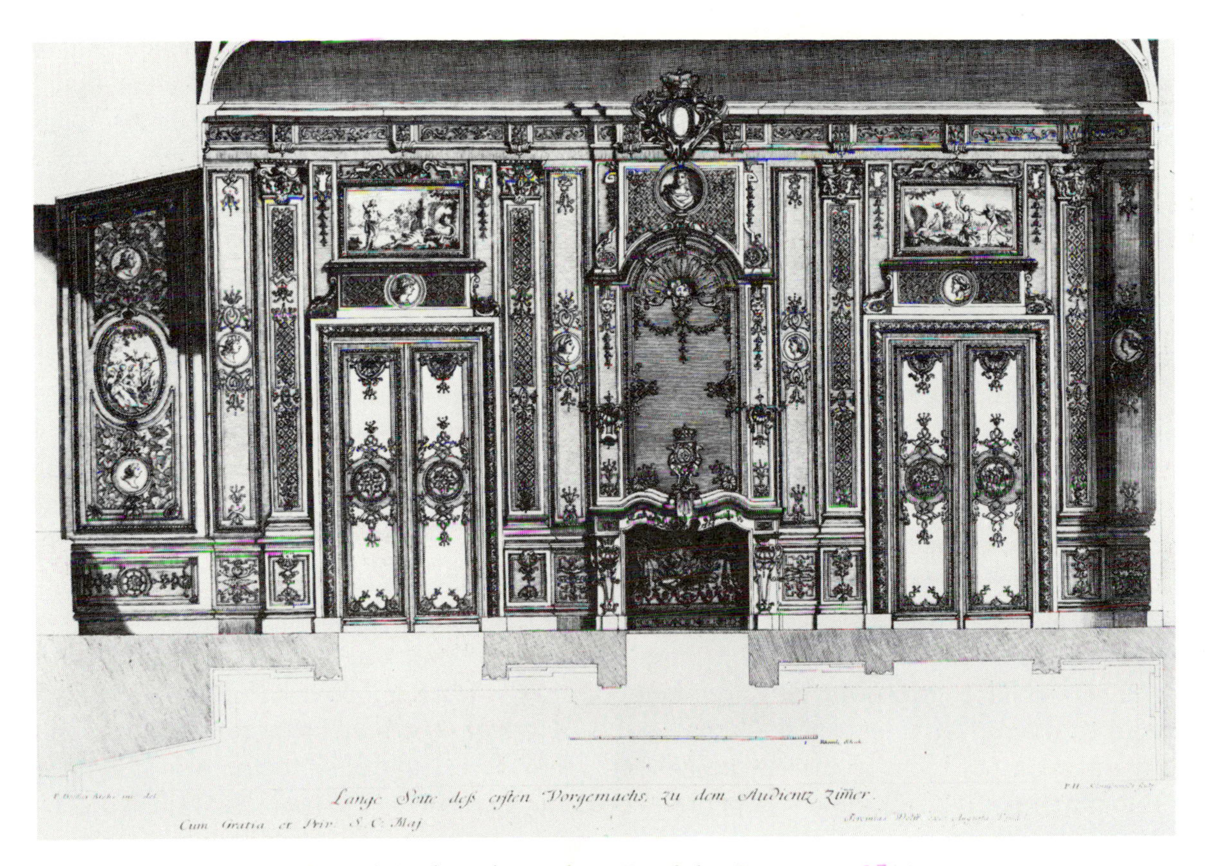

6. Paul Decker, design from *Fürstlicher Baumeister*, 1711

> years, with panels outlined by mouldings ending in a scroll decoration at top and bottom and framing blank oval cartouches at mid-height. . . . The doubling of the pilasters, with the consequent widening of the solid areas walling the nave, taken together with their surface decoration . . . reduces notably the tectonic importance of the order.[13]

But how much of an innovation was this? The doubling of pilasters—which at any rate would have to be credited to the architect Franz Beer rather than to the decorator—is not at all unusual with the architects from the Austrian Vorarlberg, of whom Beer was one. We find it in the very first church with which Beer is associated, the pilgrimage church on the Schönenberg near Ellwangen (1682–86). And even then it was hardly a novelty. Like so many features of Vorarlberg architecture, it can be traced back to the church of St. Michael in Munich (1583–97). Similarly, the decoration of pilasters with stuccoed panels was quite standard in Bavarian architecture before it succumbed to Italian influences in the decades following the Thirty Years War. We find it at Polling (1621–26) and Weilheim (1624–31), and after the war again at Niederschönenfeld (1658–62) and Kempten (1651–56). In none of these churches do we find both the doubling of pilasters *and* their decoration with stuccoed panels and, of course, in these early examples a different ornamental vocabulary is being used. Nevertheless Franz Schmuzer's pilaster decorations seem as much a renewal of a tradition with which he must have been very familiar—both Polling (fig. 62) and Weilheim (fig. 69) are within two hours' walking distance from his native Wessobrunn—as an imitation of French models. The encounter with the French rococo not only brought the Bavarians something new; in this case, at least, it freed for them a strand in their own tradition that had largely been covered up by the dominant influence of Italian decorators and architects after the Thirty Years War.

Régence and Rococo

While these observations establish that the rococo has its prehistory in Bavaria, they do not challenge the assertion that it really begins only with the importation of a new ornamental style in the second decade of the eighteenth century. That view is challenged, however, by the narrower definition of the rococo as the rocaille style, which would force us to date its beginnings in Bavaria in the 1730s.[14] At this point Hitchcock's failure to emphasize the distinction between two quite different importations of French ornament becomes important. His neglect of the introduction of rocaille might still be justified if one could show that what we have here are closely related phases of what is fundamentally one and the same French development, which sent different ripples into Bavaria.

But do these two styles, characterized by *régence* bandwork and rocaille respectively, in fact stand in so close a relationship? Are they even born of the same *Kunstwollen*? And even if such a relationship holds for France, does it hold for Bavaria? That there is a decisive difference, at least in the latter case, is suggested by even a brief comparison of the Bavarians' use of rocaille and the earlier ornament. The difference in the way in which ornament relates to ornament support is evident. Early rococo ornament remains subservient to the decorated surface. Kimball's characterization of Pierre Lepautre's creation of the new style stresses this:

> In all his work one of the most striking qualities was the abandonment of plasticity: in architectural members and decorative motifs alike. The column soon completely vanished from his work, the pilaster, greatly attenuated and reduced in relief, survived only as a strip, its cap and base dissolving. The wall panels, increased in height, had their mouldings likewise diminished in projection. At focal points their outline was further etherealized by taking on the swing of arabesque bandwork with its adjuncts of acanthus. Interlaces and scrolls of these elements invaded the panels themselves at top and bottom and around the central rosette. Not the plastic baroque cartouche, which survived only as a shield of arms, but a smooth surface with surrounding bands and scrolls became the typical field for decorative enrichment.[15]

This affirmation of wall or ceiling surface links the French rococo to the coming neoclassicism.

While at the beginning and especially toward the end of the Bavarian rococo we find the same tendency to subordinate ornament to ornament bearer, at the peak of the style the relationship is often inverted: ornament attacks its support almost aggressively; it becomes three-dimensional and plastic. Consider a doorframe (1755) from Maria Medingen by the Wessobrunner Anton Landes, a nephew of Johann Baptist Zimmermann (fig. 7). Landes plays with traditional architecture: the door's frame is crowned with a stuccoed entablature. But normally rigid architectural forms seem to have become malleable; the entablature foams upward into a wavelike rocaille on which a putto is gaily riding. As it rises it becomes more sculptural and freer. Rocaille is brought into a curious proximity to water.

Nothing comparable is found in the Paris-inspired interiors created under Effner's direction for Max Emanuel. Compared with Landes's creation, the rooms in the Pagodenburg in the park of Nymphenburg (1716–19) seem almost classically simple. The doors are

7. Maria Medingen, Dominican convent church, doorframe (detail)

simply framed. Pichler's *boiseries* (fig. 4) remain securely in the fields assigned to them. Nothing suggests the revolt of ornament against its merely ornamental status that marks the work of Anton Landes and is so characteristic of the mature Bavarian rococo. The sculptural three-dimensionality of Landes's rocaille allows it to approach the status of a self-sufficient aesthetic object; the flatness of Pichler's *boiseries* stands in the way of such self-sufficiency.

French architects never used rocaille with the enthusiasm and abandon of the Bavarians; ornament retained its ornamental, that is to say dependent, status. Bavarian *régence* decorations show similar reticence; but the mature rococo abandons it and delights in rocailles that oscillate between two roles—that of mere ornament, dependent on the ornament bearer, and that of an independent sculptural object. The three-dimensional plasticity of this ornament recalls the overrich decorations which threaten to flood the architecture of such late baroque churches as Kaufering or Holzen.

Ornamental Metamorphoses

That it is misleading to draw too sharp a line between the free approach to ornament taken by the mature rococo and the more purely ornamental approach associated with *régence* is shown by a comparison of the decorations Johann Baptist Zimmermann created for the libraries of Ottobeuren (1715–16) and Benediktbeuern (1724). In both cases Zimmermann faced a similar task (fig. 8). Given the boxlike space and its function, the decorator's work had to concentrate on the ceiling, a large, flat, rectangular area. In both cases this expanse is interrupted by frescoes (in Ottobeuren not by Zimmermann himself but by the comparatively unknown Elias Zobel—an indication that Zimmermann had not yet established his reputation as a painter). The later date of Benediktbeuern shows itself not only in the greater elegance and lightness of the decoration and in such new motifs as grillwork and *mosaïque*,[16] but also in the more irregular outlines of the frescoes—in Ottobeuren they are still framed by straight lines, circles, and circle segments. More important, however, is a changed approach to the function of ornament.

In Ottobeuren rather plain frame moldings contrast with delicate vines, still deriving from the acanthus ornament that had become a trademark of the decorators from Wessobrunn. These vines cover most of the area not occupied by the frescoes. The stucco thus appears in two quite different forms, as frame or molded border and as fillwork. No attempt is made to integrate the frescoes, which illusionistically break open the ceiling, and the ornament, which confirms the ceiling's two-dimensionality. The tension between ornament and picture remains unresolved.[17]

By contrast, the ceiling of the library at Benediktbeuern is an integrated whole. No longer do we meet with the division between frame and fillwork. In part at least this is the result of a reinterpretation of the frame. Somewhat like a late Gothic rib, it has become the generative center of the ornament, now flattening out into grillwork or brocaded areas, now rolling up in scroll patterns that like buds generate delicate leafy vines or bandwork. Besides such abstract motifs Zimmermann also uses more pictorial elements: balconies, fountains, figures, and birds (fig. 9). These changes betray a changed attitude to the ornament-support, here the flat ceiling still separated from the walls by a strongly articulated molding. At Benediktbeuern we no longer experience the ceiling as an area to be filled with decorations. It has become more like the paper that supports an ornamental fantasy. The advanced nature of the decoration of the library of Benediktbeuern is therefore not simply a matter of the more advanced vocabulary Zimmermann is now employing. Inseparable from this vocabulary is the treatment of the ceiling as an empty, inactive foil for the exuberant play of the decorations.

The shift from Ottobeuren to Benediktbeuern is so startling that one has to assume outside influences. Zimmermann's own contemporary decorations in Schleissheim, where he was executing designs by Effner and his French-trained staff, tell us where to look: to French ornamental engravings. The metamorphosis of band into vine, of flat two-dimensionality into the illusion of three dimensions is quite characteristic of grotesques and arabesques by Watteau and Bérain (fig. 10). Consider how, at Benediktbeuern, two-dimensional ornament turns pictorial and three-dimensional in the little balconies before the charming illusionistic frescoes representing allegories of the sciences. In the library of Ottobeuren, too, the illusionism, especially of the corner frescoes, is heightened by a painted balustrade; but the ornament has no part in this, while in the library of Benediktbeuern

8. Ottobeuren, Benedictine abbey, library

9. Benediktbeuern, Benedictine abbey, library, ceiling decoration (detail)

10. Jean Bérain, arabesque, ca. 1690

ornament denies its two-dimensionality and deceives us into thinking that the stuccoed balconies actually bulge toward us. Ornament has become picture.

The Turn to Rocaille

This pictorialization of ornament, dependent on the model provided by French grotesques, links Johann Baptist Zimmermann's decoration of the library of Benediktbeuern and the work of Francois de Cuvilliés. Since 1706 the young Walloon had been part of the elector's entourage, at first only as a page. But his gifts were soon recognized. By 1716 the former court dwarf was working as a draftsman under Effner; four years later he was sent to Paris to familiarize himself with the newest trends in French decoration. Shortly after his return in 1724 he was appointed architect to the court (*Hofbaumeister*), soon to be given a position equal to that of the older Effner. By 1730 Cuvilliés's was the decisive voice in architectural matters. Just as the young Effner had pushed the older Enrico Zuccalli into the background, Effner in turn had to give way to Cuvilliés.

A comparison of Cuvilliés's creations of the thirties, especially the Reiche Zimmer of the Residenz in Munich and the somewhat later Amalienburg in the park of Nymphenburg, with roughly contemporary interiors by Bavarians emphasizes the French character of his work (fig. 11). Fiske Kimball goes so far as to suggest that Cuvilliés's best creations are little more than imitations of French models—the Spiegelsaal (hall of mirrors) in the Amalienburg, for example, mimicking Boffrand's Salon de la Princesse in the Hôtel de Soubise. As Hitchcock points out, a simple consideration of the dates casts considerable doubt on this thesis. Construction of the Hôtel de Soubise was begun in 1735; the paintings in the Salon de la Princesse were completed only in 1739 or 1740. Work on the Amalienburg started in 1734, and finished in 1739. This makes the Amalienburg almost exactly contemporaneous with its supposed Parisian model, making it "extremely unlikely, if not, indeed, impossible that the Amalienburg Spiegelsaal derives from the *executed* rooms in Paris."[19] A comparison of the two works bears out Cuvilliés's originality. Hitchcock lists a number of differences, not all of which are important in this context. But his analysis of the differences between Boffrand's and Cuvilliés's treatment of the ceiling should be noted.

> Above the cornice-line the ceiling of the lower salon in Paris is quite flat and decorated only with a central ornament; the upper salon has radial open-work bands linking the central medallion on the very slightly concave surface with the cove at its edge. At the Amalienburg, however, the ceiling is much more domical. Moreover, the putti and other figures that perch on the cove-cornice, somewhat as in the Salon de la Princesse, are provided with rocky seats and backed by naturalistic trees rising . . . against the plain plaster of the vault which tells as an illusionistic sky [fig. 12].[20]

The pictorialization of ornament leads to a pictorialization of architecture: the supporting ceiling becomes a sky.

Cuvilliés's reliance on French models is apparent, but these models did not include Boffrand's Hôtel de Soubise (fig. 13). As Hermann Bauer has shown, we have to look to French publications of ornamental designs, such as Meissonier's *Livre d'ornemens*, Jean Mondon's *Premier livre de forme rocquaille et cartel* (fig. 14), or Lajoue's three *Livres de*

11. Nymphenburg, Amalienburg, bedroom, looking into the Spiegelsaal

12. Amalienburg, Spiegelsaal

13. Paris, Hôtel de Soubise, Salon de la Princesse

cartouches. But "what French ornamental engravings accomplished only on paper now appears in real decoration. This is the decisive deed of the German rococo."[21]

This characterization of Cuvilliés's role invites reconsideration of his French antecedents. Bauer ties the origin of rocaille to the development of French grotesque ornament, a characteristic of which is the joining of two different spatial logics, one ornamental, the other pictorial. The grotesque depends on that oscillation between picture and ornament which we find in the library of Benediktbeuern and which is so essential to the decorations of the Amalienburg. The *forme rocaille* arises when the shell motif, a common element of the edges and frames of grotesques, becomes the center of the composition, as happens with Meissonier, whose *Livre d'ornemens* constitutes an important step beyond Bérain, Marot, and Watteau (figs. 15 and 3).[22] Only with Meissonier does rocaille ornament become an independent object that is depicted as if it were a house or a tree or a rock. His fantastic designs are ornamental representations of ornament. Similar efforts soon followed, including Jacques de Lajoue's *Livre nouveau de divers morceaux de fantaisie* (1736) and Cuvilliés's *Livre de cartouches* (1738), created in obvious dependence on Lajoue. Bauer's comparison of a war cartouche by Lajoue with one by Cuvilliés is particularly striking (figs. 16 and 17). He goes on to suggest that to arrive at Cuvilliés's decorative system in the Amalienburg we only have to imagine one of his cartouches cut open and stuccoed out along the cornice.

14. Jean Mondon fils, Chinese ornament, 1736

15. Juste-Aurèle Meissonier, engraving from the *Livre d'ornemens*, 1734

16. François de Cuvilliés, war cartouche, 1738

17. Jacques de Lajoue, war cartouche, ca. 1735

> The stuccoed ceiling decoration of the Amalienburg is inverted cartouche. . . . Just as the war cartouche stands before and at the same time in a landscape, so here the ceiling ornamentation makes of the ceiling a landscape-like background. The ceiling becomes air, water, space. A tree growing out of the rocaille cartouche edge stands in a pictorial atmosphere.[23]

This thesis that Bavarian rococo ornament has its origin in the *frames* of Cuvilliés's and Lajoue's cartouches becomes especially interesting when compared with Kimball's observation that the decorative style initiated by Pierre Lepautre turned away from the plastic cartouche of the Italian baroque.[24] Again one senses the difference between early rococo ornament and rocaille.

It would be a mistake to place too much emphasis on the part played by the Amalienburg in the progressive pictorialization of ornament. In this respect the decorative scheme of the Amalienburg is not too different from Cuvilliés's own somewhat earlier work in the Schatzkammer (1731–33) and the Reiche Zimmer (1730–37) of Munich's Residenz.[25] The beautiful scenes of evening, night, and morning on the ceiling of the elector's bedroom offer good examples (1731), although the greater degree to which the pictorialization of ornament has been carried in the Amalienburg is shown by the fishery group in the Spiegelsaal (figs. 18 and 19): the garland of shells held by the nymph, her leg, and the way she watches the putti below who are drawing in their net, create a picture that plays over and helps to negate the division of wall and ceiling. Nowhere in the Reiche Zimmer did Cuvilliés go so far.

But we need not confine ourselves to Cuvilliés. The pictorialization of ornament had

18. Munich, Residenz, decoration of the bedroom *(Diana Appears to Endymion)*. Reconstructed after World War II

19. Amalienburg, Spiegelsaal, *Amphitrite*

played an important part in the work of his collaborator Johann Baptist Zimmermann long before Zimmermann executed the stuccoes of the Residenz and the Amalienburg after Cuvilliés's designs.[26] Consider once more the stuccoed balconies on the ceiling of the library at Benediktbeuern. The differences between Zimmermann's decorations at Benediktbeuern and those he executed more than a decade later in the Amalienburg are striking enough. The bandwork and grillwork of Benediktbeuern belong quite obviously to an earlier period. More important, however, is another difference. In Benediktbeuern it is not the empty ceiling that is transformed by the pictorial quality of the stuccoed decoration into the sky; rather, the stuccoed balconies are placed before a *painted background* that on the one hand helps to reinforce their pictorial quality, but on the other creates the illusion of real balconies. Zimmermann's balconies possess an architectural quality lacking in Cuvilliés's ornaments. Participating in both the architectural and the pictorial mode, they effect a mediation between the two. In this respect the library of Benediktbeuern is a far more typical example of Bavarian developments than the Amalienburg.

Provincial Rococo?

A revealing example of the way Bavarian decorators adapted and transformed Cuvilliés's decorative scheme is provided by five rooms decorated in the thirties in the Residenz of the prince abbot of Kempten. Compared to these rooms, Cuvilliés's somewhat later decorations in the Amalienburg seem very French indeed. The use of paintings alone would give the rooms at Kempten a very different tonality: warmer, darker, and more colorful than the restrained yellow and silver or light blue and silver of the Amalienburg; and the colors of the ceiling paintings are picked up by the decoration. This use of color to bind architecture, fresco, and ornament into an organic whole recalls the decoration of Schliersee. By this time it had become quite common in Bavaria.

Equally significant is the way the decorations at Kempten play over and conceal the separation of wall from frescoed ceiling. Something like this also occurs in the Spiegelsaal of the Amalienburg, but there it only slowly discloses itself as we explore the subtleties of the decoration; the first impression we receive is that of a rather clear separation of wall and ceiling marked by the undulating cornice. At Kempten, on the other hand, the decoration attacks and submerges this demarcation (fig. 21). In the prince abbot's bedroom, for example, a Wessobrunner created a stucco zone that mediates effectively between the architectural quality of the walls and the frescoed ceiling.[27] An even more convincing solution to the same problem is provided by Johann Georg Üblhör's decoration of the Throne Room (1740–42). Here an ornamental entablature helps to articulate the fairly large space; but its cornice functions also as the base of a stuccoed balustrade. Because ornament here possesses both an architectural and a pictorial quality, it is able to draw together architecture and fresco. Johann Baptist Zimmermann's balconies in the library of Benediktbeuern provide an obvious antecedent, although, as Hugo Schnell points out, the motif goes back to Bernini and even Holbein.[28]

Compared to the elegant decorations Cuvilliés created for the Bavarian elector, those at Kempten may seem provincial; yet their greater vigor is undeniable (fig. 20). Noteworthy

20. Kempten, Residenz, throne room, cartouche on the west side

is the different handling of doors. Cuvilliés's doors are framed by light, inobtrusive moldings, those at Kempten by heavy pilasters; but their tectonic weight is lifted by their ornamental treatment. Thus, in the prince abbot's bedroom traditional architectural forms become unexpectedly soft and malleable. Consider the way the sharp points of the door frames's cornice are echoed by the lower frame of the medallion, which at the same time furnishes the base for a new ornamental structure, including curtain and baldachin, which becomes part of the fresco frame. Playfully architectural elements are transformed into ornament; ornament in turn assumes a pictorial quality or claims for itself the part of architecture.[29] Such playful metamorphoses joining architecture, painting, and ornament are among the most characteristic features of the Bavarian rococo.

Because the stuccoes at Kempten mediate between painting and architecture, they cannot approach the status of the independent pictures as do the decorations in the Amalienburg. Bavarian ornament comes closest to such independence where the task of mediation is unimportant or does not exist, as for example in Anton Landes's doorframe in Maria Medingen or in Johann Anton Bader's astonishing pulpit in Oppolding (fig. 124). There is little in eighteenth-century art that matches its fragile strength. Ornament here has shed its servitude and become a self-sufficient work of art.

Abstract Rocaille

Both similarity and distance between the Bavarian and the French rococo are demonstrated by the corner cartouches in the prince abbot's bedroom in Kempten (fig. 21). Here we already find the almost doughy plastic rocaille forms that were to become perhaps the most characteristic expression of the Bavarian rococo. Dating probably from the mid-thirties, they force us to question Bauer's claim that it was only in 1738, when Cuvilliés's first series of engravings was published, that rocaille appeared in Germany.[30] But the exact date matters little. The cartouches at Kempten suggest familiarity with Cuvilliés's work. Even greater is their similarity with the roughly contemporary, perhaps slightly later, cartouches that Johann Baptist Zimmermann created in the now-destroyed convent church St. Jakob am Anger in Munich (1737). Compared with the ornamental vocabulary used by Cuvilliés, the cartouches in Kempten are more abstract. The part ornament has been assigned does not permit it to become as pictorially independent as in the interiors created by Cuvilliés. Characteristic of the Bavarian rococo is the way these cartouches frame small pictures, bracket together walls and ceiling fresco, spreading into the fresco and violating its frame, and spill over the molding separating walls and ceiling. At the same time each cartouche helps to fill and obscure the corner in which it has been placed. Rocaille has here at least a threefold function: it frames, it mediates between picture and architecture, and it obscures tectonic features.

Even before the mid-thirties we find rocaillelike forms, usually generated by the frames of cartouches or frescoes, as for example in St. Emmeram in Regensburg. Closer anticipations of rocaille are found at Diessen (ca. 1736). Especially interesting is a comparison of the stuccoed "clamps" that seem to bracket the fresco to the arches of the nave with the frames of the cartouches that decorate the pendentives of the choir dome, where rocaille-like forms seem more expected (figs. 22 and 115). In their light the "clamps" can be seen as truncated cartouches that were somehow forced open. We should recall Bauer's thesis that it was by breaking open and stretching the cartouche frame that Cuvilliés arrived at the ornament of the Amalienburg.

Plate 1

The responsible master at Diessen was, however, not Cuvilliés but Franz Xaver Feichtmayr from Wessobrunn, then in his early thirties, who was joined by his younger brother Johann Michael and by the somewhat older Üblhör. Given the prior Herkulan Karg's ambitious plans, the choice of Feichtmayr may seem somewhat surprising. Together with Üblhör, the two Feichtmayr brothers were to establish themselves as the leading church decorators of the forties and fifties, but at this time they hardly had the reputation of the other artists associated with the church, who included the architect Johann Michael Fischer, Cuvilliés, who seems to have been responsible for the design of the high altar, and the painter Johann Georg Bergmüller, director of the Art Academy in Augsburg. Feichtmayr's just-completed decoration of the Cistercian abbey church in Stams in the Tyrol may have called the prior's attention to the young decorator, whose independent career had begun just a few years earlier with his very successful refurbishing of the late Gothic parish church in Walleshausen (1732).[31] The decoration of these early rococo interiors has its center in large cartouches with vigorous frames that may broaden into rocaillelike forms.

21. Kempten, Residenz, bedroom, cartouche on the west side

Successful as they are, there is little about these interiors that would lead one to expect the brilliance of the achievement of Diessen. Perhaps Üblhör, whose work at Kempten shows him to have been, together with Dominikus Zimmermann, the most imaginative Wessobrunner working at that time, deserves credit for the advanced character of this decoration; we should not forget, however, that he had been associated with Cuvilliés, who was just then exhibiting the possibilities of his new decorative style in the Amalienburg. For the development of the Bavarian rococo church Diessen had far greater significance. It demonstrated how ornament could be used to provide effective mediation between a large fresco and the architecture of the church. Once again this mediating role prevents ornament from becoming as fully pictorial as the ornament of the Amalienburg. As already mentioned, Cuvilliés's decorations in the Amalienburg are themselves so pictorial that a fresco not only seems superfluous but would destroy the essence of his ornament. In a church such as Diessen the stuccoer has to establish a modus vivendi with the painter. This demands a more abstract ornament.

The success of Diessen was such that the artists associated with it came to be in constant demand. The mature style of the Feichtmayr circle is marked by a more complete domination of plastic organic rocaille forms than that of other leading artists from Wessobrunn, such as Joseph Schmuzer and the Zimmermann brothers. Compared to their work the Feichtmayrs' seems abstract. Evident is the influence of Augsburg engravers—both Feichtmayrs chose to settle in Augsburg rather than in Munich.[32]

A good example of this style is provided by Johann Michael Feichtmayr's decorations of the Benedictine abbey church at Zwiefalten (1747–58), one of the greatest, and at the same time most characteristic, achievements from the middle of the century. As at Diessen, the architect was Johann Michael Fischer, who here created what is, together with Ottobeuren, his largest interior. Much more than at Diessen, the decorations of Zwiefalten are dominated by cartouches that mediate between the vertical thrust of the wall-pillars, here faced with paired scagliola columns, and the frescoes above. Such mediating cartouches had already appeared at Walleshausen and again at Diessen, but at Zwiefalten the individual cartouche has become asymmetrical, although symmetry is reestablished when a cartouche is seen together with the corresponding cartouche on the other side of the nave (figs. 2 and 23). Such asymmetry is often seen in Bavarian rococo churches: some element of the decoration, here a cartouche, points beyond itself; an answer is demanded and given by a complementary asymmetrical form. Asymmetry thus becomes a powerful device against a compartmental or additive approach to ornament and spatial organization. It serves the organic unity desired by the Bavarian rococo better than more symmetrical forms can. Toward the middle of the century we thus meet with an increasing tendency to keep not only ornament, but furnishings, such as side altars, asymmetrical: the open form of one object demands a complementary open structure across the nave (fig. 152).

Even compared with the ornament of Diessen, the mature rocaille work of Zwiefalten seems ephemeral, as if it could maintain these particular shapes only for a moment (fig. 24). Along with this goes an organic or dynamic quality no earlier ornament had matched. Rocaille hints not only at shells, but now at water, now at flames, then again at never-seen plants or coral. Where rocaillelike forms do appear at Diessen they look as if they had been generated by a flattening out of the cartouche frame; at Zwiefalten rocaille has emancipated itself from this origin. Now the cartouche frames appear as almost incidental by-products of the play of rocaille. The importance of frame and ornament has been inverted. Although ornament still tends to form cartouchelike patterns, it has become independent enough to strike out on its own. Thus it envelops and obscures much of the frame of Spiegler's gigantic fresco over the nave, invading even the fresco itself and appearing to curve beneath the frame.

The decoration of Zwiefalten marks the high point of the development of rocaille. Already in the fifties we meet with a tendency to limit its exuberance and autonomy. Ornament is used more sparingly. Individual rocailles become first thinner, then anemic. Cartouches return to symmetry. But we shall consider this decay of rocaille in a later chapter.

Frames and Frescoes

The tension between architectural space and the illusionistic space created by the ceiling fresco helps to determine the style of the Bavarian rococo church. The Bavarians' enthusiastic adoption of rocaille has one root in their attempt to mediate between the two. To achieve such mediation a third term was needed, not simply a frame, but a framelike ornament capable of becoming either architecture or picture. Rocaille filled this need

Plates 1, 2, 3

22. Diessen, Augustinian priory church, main fresco

23. Zwiefalten, abbey church, northern transept

24. Zwiefalten, abbey church, stucco of southern transept

admirably. Although working only on paper, its originators showed how the new ornament could expand into "architecture" or "picture." Recognizing this potential, the Bavarians developed rocaille into a stucco zone that lies, both essentially and literally, between architecture and frescoed ceiling. The most important function of Bavarian rococo ornament is the mediation, not the dissolution, of the tension of architecture and picture.

The significance of this function remains obscure. Why insist that the tension between architectural and fresco space be mediated? Why not resolve it by bringing the two into complete fusion, as the illusionism of the Italian baroque attempted to do; or by rejecting illusionism altogether, thus cutting the bond between architectural and pictorial space, as neoclassicism was to do?

I shall return to these problems in later chapters. But a more easily answered question poses itself. Only in the thirties did rocaille come to Bavaria, offering a convincing answer to an already existing problem. Should we not, then, expect earlier attempts pointing in the same direction? Many such attempts were indeed made. The most successful is Dominikus Zimmermann's pilgrimage church at Steinhausen (1730–31). Here, as Bernhard Rupprecht points out, we find for the first time a fully developed stucco zone that both separates and links fresco and architecture.[33] This zone is made up of a number of quite different elements (fig. 42). Most important are the stuccoed gables that crown the arches joining the ten pillars that carry the oval vault. Especially in the east and west they have a tectonic quality that joins them to the architecture below. At the same time these gables project into the fresco, painted by the architect's brother Johann Baptist, that appears to lie behind them. This effect is supported by the stuccoed balustrades to the north and south, through which we see the fresco continuing. Like the later balustrade in the Throne Room of the Residenz in Kempten or the balconies in Johann Baptist Zimmermann's earlier library at Benediktbeuern, they are thus seen as a pictorial foreground. Yet they also belong to the ornamental zone framing the picture; they are both part of the picture and part of its frame. The latter aspect is strengthened by the more free and elaborate balusterlike forms given to the gables adjoining the balustrades. They help to establish a smoother transition from architecture to picture. At Steinhausen the quite traditional gable motif shows itself to possess the same potential of transformation into architecture and picture that characterizes rocaille.[34] This analogy forces us to agree with Rupprecht's conclusion that the Bavarian rococo *did not originate with the introduction of rocaille*, but only adopted rocaille out of an essential affinity.

The mature solution to the problem of mediation offered by the brothers Zimmermann at Steinhausen is not without antecedents. Johann Baptist Zimmermann's use of balconies in the library of Benediktbeuern has already been discussed, although in Beneditkbeuern no real effort was made to integrate the stuccoed balconies into the surrounding ornament. The balconies remained just one motif among others, unable to transform the total space. The same is even more obviously true of the choir fresco in Buxheim, where we find Johann Baptist using this device for the first time (1711).[35]

But there are more significant antecedents by other artists. Hitchcock points to Metten, where the fresco is by the Austrian Wolfgang Andreas Heindl, the stuccoed decoration by Franz Josef Holzinger; both began work in 1722.[36] As at Steinhausen, the fresco fills most of the nave vault; the stucco forms a zone mediating between fresco and architecture. The mediation achieved, however, is far less successful: for the most part the stucco remains merely ornament, too weak to mediate between architecture and picture. Holzinger does not hit on anything nearly as effective as Dominikus Zimmermann's use of the gable motif.

That Holzinger's intentions were related to Zimmermann's, however, is suggested by the somewhat awkward stuccoed putti that play in the valleys of the frame. Like the putti in the Hôtel de Soubise, these could perhaps be considered mere ornament—were it not for the clouds on which they play, which relate them, if not altogether convincingly, to the painted clouds of the fresco (fig. 25). The use of stuccoed clouds is particularly interesting at the eastern end of the fresco, where they connect with a mass of similar clouds that spill over and conceal (somewhat ineffectively) the architectonic quality of the choir arch. To these clouds correspond painted clouds that spill over the fresco frame in its western corners. But while a first step is thus taken toward the mediation between architecture and fresco, at Metten it is no more than that. The too purely ornamental character of most of the stucco work and the smaller frescoes set into the stucco of the pendentive zone, which are seen very much as framed pictures in the traditional sense and in turn render the surrounding stucco pure frame and ornament, prevents it.

25. Metten, Benedictine abbey church, interior

Especially when looking at the choir fresco, one has the feeling that a vocabulary is being used that has not quite been mastered. Here, too, the fresco spills over its frame and is in turn invaded by stuccoed angels and clouds. But these mediating devices are countered by a rather rigid handling of the frame, which traces a form suggested by the architecture instead of becoming its full partner, as is the case in Steinhausen. Metten thus presents us with a curious mixture of progressive ideas and conservatism.

Perhaps the former can be tied to Cosmas Damian Asam, who had been approached to fresco the church. A plan of his, dating from ca. 1715, has survived although it was never executed.[37] Asam did some work for the church: the painting of the high altar is by him, as is the choir fresco (1718), or at least its design. Thus, even if Asam was succeeded by Heindl, it seems likely that his association with the church left its traces. At any rate, the cloud motif in its twofold form, as fresco spilling out of its frame and as stucco becoming picture, had for some time been characteristic of the Italianate approach of the brothers Asam.[38]

A more interesting approach to the problem of mediation is taken in Aldersbach (1720–21), reflecting perhaps the influence of Cosmas Damian's young brother, the sculptor Egid Quirin Asam. Here, as at Metten, stuccoed clouds spill out of the fresco. In their pasty heaviness they contrast with much of the stucco, which is comparatively flat in the then newly popular *régence* mode. But they do relate quite directly to the four cartouches that "support" the fresco, and in their pink pastiness help to establish a transition between ornament and picture (fig. 26). This is done more effectively by the riband weaving in and out of the picture, twining itself around the frame, and by the putti that carry it, riding on stuccoed clouds. Both share in that ambivalence between ornament and picture that Bauer takes to be essential to rocaille. Our sense of ambivalence is further strengthened by the scalloped frame, which is not only frame, weakened as such by its form, but at the same time the *pictorial base* of the scene presented in Cosmas Damian's fresco. Again a balustrade, here painted, helps to facilitate the transition from framing ornament to picture.

All of these devices deny closure to the fresco and open the realm of St. Bernard's Christmas vision to the space below in which we ourselves stand. Pozzo's illusionism has been translated into Bavarian. Because Egid Quirin Asam's stuccoed clouds are not only obvious downward extensions of his brother's painted clouds, but at the same time bear a close resemblance in consistency and color to the stuccoed cartouches, they possess not only pictorial but also ornamental status. The illusionism of the fresco is threatened by these clouds, which at first seem only an extension of it. Their ornamental status is transferred to the fresco itself, which functions as ornament as much as it provides a pictorial illusion. This ornamentalization of the fresco is strengthened by the way the colored stucco of the church picks up the colors of the fresco. The Asam brothers were too free, too playful, to take Pozzo's illusionism altogether seriously. Nor were they alone in this: such play with baroque conventions helps to define the style of the Bavarian rococo.

What makes Aldersbach so significant for the subsequent development of the Bavarian rococo is the Asams' treatment of the stucco zone framing the fresco. More effectively than at Metten, it begins here to function as a third mediating reality between illusionistic

26. Aldersbach, Cistercian abbey church, nave vault

SIC
ENIM
DILEXIT
MUNDUM
UT
FILIUM
SUUM
UNIGENITUM
DARET

fresco and architecture. In effecting this mediation Egid Quirin's pasty clouds play an important part, anticipating, not so much in form as in function, the rich rocaille work of later rococo churches. As we shall see later, this emergence of the stucco zone mediating between pictorial and architectural space is itself inseparable from innovations Cosmas Damian introduced in the fresco. The Bavarian rococo church developed as an original response to the illusionism of the Italian baroque.

Ornament and Architecture

Hitchcock, too, discusses Aldersbach as a precursor of the Bavarian rococo church, but has something quite different in mind: the Asams' increasing appropriation of French *régence* forms, an appropriation that translates this vocabulary into a more robust idiom. At Aldersbach, for example, we can point to "the decorative panel-heads on the sides of the wall-pillars; the treatment of many of the transverse severies of the nave vaults; and, most conspicuously, that of the eastern wall above the choir arch."[39] Next to the elegance of these French-influenced forms—only a little earlier Cosmas Damian Asam had been working under Effner's direction at the Neues Schloss in Schleissheim—the putti-carrying clouds seem not so much anticipations of the rococo as rather heavy, almost embarrassing offsprings of the Asams' Roman training. The contrast between the delicacy of French *régence* forms and the pasty robustness not only of the pink clouds but also of the cartouches is disturbing. In each case ornament seems to follow very different laws. While the *régence* forms subordinate themselves to the architecture, the pink clouds and the associated ornament show much greater independence. Thus, the latter can play over the former, but never the reverse.

This distinction between two modes of ornament, one serving the architecture, the other more closely tied to painting, can also be drawn in the Asams' roughly contemporary churches in Rohr and Weltenburg.[40] With this tension between two very different modes of ornament the Asams' churches of about 1720 show themselves to belong to a period of transition. Ten years later at Steinhausen we no longer find such tension, nor do we find it in the rococo churches following its example. Only an echo of it remains in a tendency to continue to use *régence* forms where the architecture demands a subordination of the ornament to it, as for instance in the decoration of intrados, while rocaille is generally used to effect the mediation between fresco and architecture. At Aldersbach the Asams did not quite achieve such mediation. Their clouds and other similar devices play over the architecture, which beneath it remains intact. While at Steinhausen ornament becomes inseparable from architecture, at Aldersbach the stucco finally is too weak to really mediate between fresco and church. We are left with an uneasy tension between the Asams' brilliant decoration and a rather uninteresting wall-pillar church that cannot fully maintain itself in this competition and yet is not really transformed either (fig. 27).

That the Asams were moving in the direction of Steinhausen is shown by their redecoration of the cathedral of Freising (1723–24). At Freising, too, the Asams had to accept the space they were given—here a five-aisled basilica, fundamentally Romanesque, altered in the fifteenth century and again in the seventeenth. Indeed, the problems they faced

27. Aldersbach, abbey church, interior

were greater than at Aldersbach, for the length of the nave made it impossible to unify the space by means of one dominating fresco, while the repetitive rhythm of the nave arcades provides a tectonic emphasis at least as strong as that provided by Magzin's wall-pillars at Aldersbach. Given the Asams' earlier work, Cosmas Damian's contribution is hardly surprising. More violently than in his earlier churches, but in the same Bacciccian manner, the frescoes overflow their borders (which here are only painted, not stuccoed), and in places also the rib-bands separating the different frescoes. No use is made of the stuccoed clouds we find at Aldersbach.

More significant is the contribution of Egid Quirin. The renovation of 1619–22 had already decisively altered the medieval space; tribunes were built over the inner aisles. To lighten the tectonic weight of the shallow pilasters of the nave wall, Egid Quirin covered their surface with tripartite stuccoed marble panels, visually not so much supported by the pilasters that bear them as floating between and held in place by the arches of the double arcades, as are also Cosmas Damian's frescoed panels, separating or rather joining the two series of arcades (fig. 28). Thus while at Aldersbach the wall-pillars seem active and define the spaces between them, at Freising the relationship seems inverted: it is the empty spaces of the arcades that seem active and assign to the panels on the pilasters their place. The supporting pilasters remain white and almost immaterial.

Hitchcock points out that similar treatment of tall, narrow surfaces had been a characteristic of French secular interiors for a decade or more, although by no means on so monumental a scale.[41] Thus, as the Asams were decorating Freising, Effner was using similar panels at Schleissheim. Earlier such panels had appeared both in the Pagodenburg in the park of Nymphenburg and in the main castle. But the way in which these panels relate to their supporting surfaces has become very different. Consider how the galleries at Freising, together with Cosmas Damian Asam's frescoed panels, form another row of tripartite structures, echoing the narrower verticals of the pilasters. Read horizontally, the frescoed panels form a band that has its place between the band formed by the pilaster's pink bases and the greenish frieze of the entablature. The long arcaded walls are thus held together and unified by a grid of vertical and horizontal bands that are made up of elements contributed by stucco, fresco, and architecture. Their different modes are not respected. In just this respect the Asams' ornamental approach at Freising provides an antecedent to the Zimmermanns' decorative scheme at Steinhausen (fig. 29).

Because of their different dimensions and greater intimacy, the upper galleries demanded a very different approach (fig. 30). Egid Quirin makes use of three distinct vocabularies. The basic accents are set by the heavy molding, following the frames of the frescoes, sometimes marking, sometimes disguising the arrises of the severies. Asam develops here a curiously hybrid form, somewhat in between rib and frame, not unlike the ribs of late Gothic net vaults. Again we have an ornament that mediates between architecture and fresco. The field created by this molding that is not covered by frescoes is decorated with very delicate bandwork—one is reminded of Rohr, where the large field left vacant by the unexecuted fresco is filled with ornament of similar delicacy. "This inner bandwork," Hitchcock suggests, "is the most distinctly rococo element of the entire decorative scheme."[42] The suggestion can be accepted only with reservation: this bandwork is indeed

28. Freising, cathedral, interior

29. Freising, cathedral, northern nave wall

30. Freising, cathedral, looking into the north gallery

closest to French ornament, but given the goals of the Bavarian rococo, the ambivalence of the heavy molding seems more decisive.

Yet a third element plays an important part: a leafy ornament somewhat in between the heavy molding and the delicate elegance of the French-derived bandwork. Here we find foliage reminiscent of the acanthus ornament of the Wessobrunners. Visually this foliage belongs most to the surface; it is closest to us. Thus, it can cover up both bandwork and molding. The molding in turn can generate the leaf ornament, which in places becomes altogether independent of the supporting ceiling, assuming a fully three-dimensional sculptural existence. Whenever the framemolding is interrupted as it curves toward the center of the vault, the scrolls in which it ends become like buds, breaking forth into leaves (fig. 31). The molding is thus given something of the quality of living wood. This device, employed again and again by the Asams, derives from French grotesques, but it also recalls late Gothic developments—the almost frightening way in which the ribs of two side chapels in the Marienkirche in Ingolstadt become independent of the vault, for instance, forming a thorny thicket above us (fig. 32). At Freising it is this foliage that is least bound to the architecture, anticipating the freedom of much rocaille, but even closer to the preceding acanthus ornament of the Wessobrunners.

31. Freising, cathedral, south gallery, stucco detail

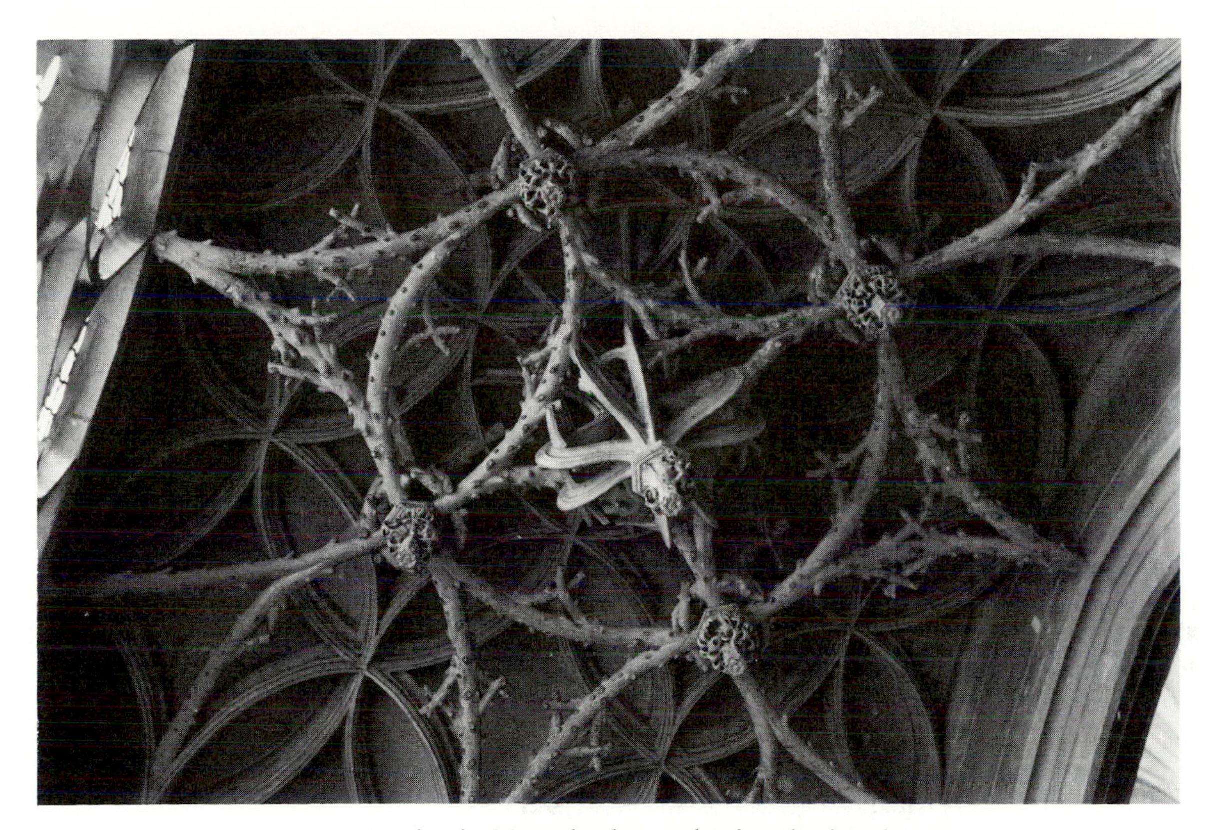

32. Ingolstadt, Marienkirche, vault of a side chapel

The history of the Bavarian rococo is the history of a continuing adaptation of French forms to at times very different ends. When these ends are kept in view it becomes difficult to speak of a beginning of the Bavarian rococo. Various beginnings can be suggested, and in each case something significant is brought into view, yet they don't lead us to what is most essential. To understand the Bavarian rococo church—and the term itself may be unfortunate, since it leads almost inevitably to the application of a measure that finally cannot do justice to what the Bavarians were after—we have to place it in a different context.

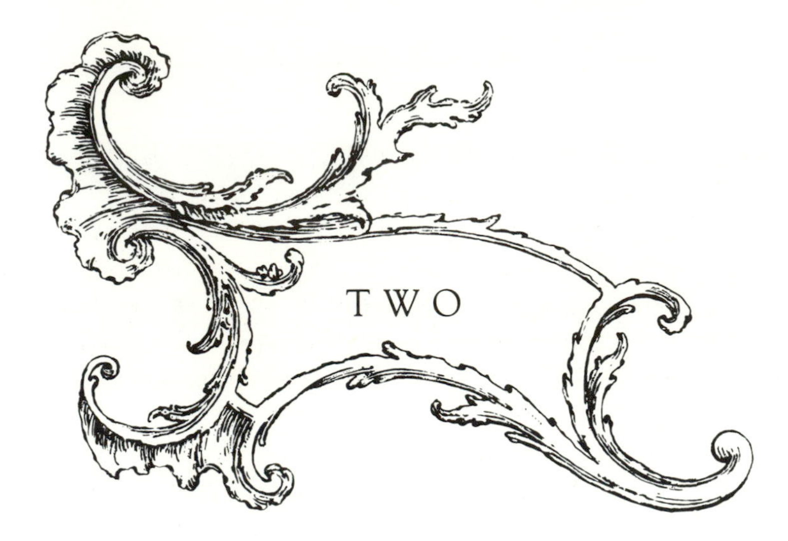

TWO

SPACE AND ILLUSION

A Modest Beginning

In one respect there is a decisive difference between the French and the Bavarian rococo—the Bavarian rococo church demands a frescoed ceiling. Ceiling frescoes never gained the importance in France that they had in Italy and later in Germany. The French apparently had a very different attitude to the ceiling, a greater willingness to accept it and its boundary instead of trying to negate it with pictorial illusion. The point should not of course be exaggerated; frescoes do play an important part in French baroque and rococo architecture. But rarely in French rococo interiors do we find frescoes that seem to break open the ceiling, and toward the end of the seventeenth century emphasis shifts from the ceiling to the wall. The bare ceiling predominates, perhaps broken by a not-too-obtrusive central ornament.

His tendency to spurn the use of fresco makes Cuvilliés's interiors seem French in comparison with contemporary works by native Bavarians.[1] Where Johann Baptist Zimmermann and Johann Georg Üblhör, Cuvilliés's collaborators in the Residenz, worked on their own, they tended to use frescoed ceilings. In this turn to the fresco we have a decisive characteristic of the Bavarian rococo, both a turn away from the French rococo and a return to the Italian baroque.

Hans Georg Asam, the father of the more famous brothers, is often said to have been the first Bavarian to use frescoes of relatively large size to open the built church to an illusionistic space above. But we have to go back further: the first church of the Bavarian baroque in which ceiling frescoes play a significant part, although compared with later churches this part may seem small enough, is the parish church (1624–36) in Weilheim (fig. 69). Its three round frescoes occupy only small areas of the vault. For this reason alone they tend to look somewhat like accessories, like panel paintings that instead of having been hung on a wall are fixed to the ceiling, where their darkness rests somewhat uneasily in the surrounding white. Their perspective in rendering the heavenly drama above reinforces this impression. Little attempt has been made to take the spectator's point of view into account. At first glance it seems as if the frescoes could be moved to some other location, for instance to one of the walls, without too much loss; and yet the artist, the local painter Johannes Greither, must have intended something quite different.[2] Although ignoring our point of view, he does attempt to make the frescoes appear as if we were looking through holes cut into the vault into heaven above. The illusion is reinforced by dark, half-moon-shaped strips at the eastern, visually lower, edge of the frescoes, which suggest the thickness of the vault into which the "holes" have been "cut."

A few years earlier the artist's father, Elias Greither, had painted a now-destroyed fresco in the Residenz in Munich that had used the same dark half-moon to create an illusion of depth. More significant as an early attempt at illusionistic ceiling painting was Hans Werle's architectural fresco in the Schwarze Saal of the Residenz, it too a victim of World War II. Werle was following a design by Christoph Schwarz, the court painter of Wilhelm V, who, celebrated as *Pictor Germaniae primus*, appears as a key figure in transmitting Italian, especially Venetian, ideas to the north.[3]

The impact of this court art is demonstrated by a comparison of Johannes Greither's frescoes in the parish church of Weilheim with his father's decoration of the late Gothic cemetery church in the same city, an octagon with one palmlike central pillar from which ribs issue like branches (fig. 33). The older Greither's frescoes, his first major work (1591), attempt to speak the language of the Renaissance, but that language is no longer (or not yet) understood. We can detect echoes of Schwarz and Mielich, hints of the Italian Renaissance, yet all of these remain quite superficial. In the end Greither's decorative scheme remains more Gothic than Renaissance.

And yet, in spite of the more advanced nature of the son's work in the parish church, the cemetery church forms a more convincing aesthetic whole. The frescoes of the parish church continue to function much like panel paintings. But a panel painting has a certain autonomy: it is experienced as an object that has been brought to a particular place and that can be taken away again without serious damage to either painting or architecture. In turning to panel painting the Renaissance tended to make painting sufficient unto itself. The more pronounced this self-sufficiency, the greater the threat such painting posed to the unity of painting and architecture characteristic of the Gothic church. Seen in this light, the cemetery church is pre-Renaissance. The artist was content to let the ribs of the vault determine the shape of the frescoes; as a result they belong in this church as no panel paintings can, giving the Gothic interior a magical warmth. Taken out of this setting they would lose their value. Only in the eighteenth century were Bavarian architects to achieve similarly successful unions of fresco and architecture, which, however, now presupposed baroque illusionism.

The development of illusionistic devices has one root in the felt need to respond to the destruction of the unity of painting and architecture threatened by the Renaissance emphasis on panel painting.[4] The fascination of such early Renaissance painters as Masaccio and Uccello with the possibility of using their newly gained mastery of one-point per-

33. Weilheim, Friedhofskirche, decoration, detail

spective to create an illusion of space beyond the limits imposed by the walls may be understood in part as an attempt to integrate architectural and pictorial space. The younger Greither's frescoes in the parish church of Weilheim are part of this tradition, although hardly at its center. The provincial nature of Greither's art is painfully apparent when one compares the Weilheim paintings with Correggio's much earlier frescoes at Parma, where the new illusionism celebrated its first triumphs. Correggio's achievement rests on a long development that has its origin in first explorations by Masaccio and Uccello and includes Mantegna, Melozzo da Forli, and Raphael. Greither cannot draw on a similar tradition. There did indeed exist a native German tradition of illusionistic painting; Holbein was admired for his ability to create spatial illusions. But it is difficult to establish any connection between this tradition, which at any rate concentrated on exterior walls, and Johannes Greither's efforts.[5] He offers us no more than pale echoes, twice removed from their Italian originals. And yet his art marks a beginning, a first effort, significant for pointing in what, in Bavaria at least, were new directions.

Heaven Made Visible

The parish church of Weilheim found no quick successors; the second decade of the Thirty Years War had brought building activity to a virtual standstill. This makes it all the more significant that the first major church to be built after the war, the abbey church St. Lorenz in Kempten, again makes use of frescoes, perhaps in dependence on Weilheim.[6] Although the Kempten frescoes occupy a larger part of the nave vault than those in

Weilheim, the artist, Andreas Asper of Constance, was even less able than Johannes Greither to extend the architectural space below with the illusion of another space above. The frescoes look more than ever like panel paintings set into the stucco. There is no device corresponding to Greither's half-moons, and while the heavenly drama Greither unfolds at least hints at the Italian illusionistic tradition, Asper's frescoes fail to modify the space in any significant way. The same is true of the paintings, usually small, that appear with increasing frequency in church interiors during the second half of the seventeenth century. In most cases they provide little more than accents. The stuccoed decoration remains far more important.

A decisive step forward was taken by Hans Georg Asam (1649–1711), first at Benediktbeuern (1682–83) and then, more confidently, at Tegernsee (1689–94). A student of the court painter Nicolaus Prugger, Asam had learned in Italy about the possibilities of opening up architectural space by means of illusionistic frescoes. Karl Mindera points to Veronese's San Silvestro as a likely source of inspiration. But of at least equal importance seems to have been the impression made on Asam by the newly finished church at Garsten (near Steyr, Austria) which he visited on his return from Italy.[7]

The paintings at Benediktbeuern, for the most part not frescoes but done in tempera,[8] no longer appear as panels that can be moved from place to place without loss. The perspective of each painting is such that it demands to be seen from a point of view below and somewhat to the west. Considered in themselves, these paintings are hardly overwhelming. Asam is no Veronese or Correggio. And yet we can understand Mindera's enthusiasm; given their context they must have seemed absolutely astounding. "For the first time in the Bavarian baroque this world and the world above flow into each other; something known only to faith is made visible."[9] Mindera has traced both Italian and Flemish influences. The cloud podests are said to derive from Pietro da Cortona, while other details—such as the similarity of Asam's St. Cecilia to a Rubens sketch for the Jesuit church in Antwerp, the conception of Christ in the painting of the Resurrection, and the bishop of the St. Wolfgang scene—suggest that Asam must have been familiar with the Flemish painter's work in Antwerp. His son Philip was later to enter a monastery in Brussels.[10]

Yet while we can agree with Mindera that Hans Georg Asam has carried the fusion of the world below and the world above further than any Bavarian painter before him, this fusion is not without tension. In spite of the perspective, which demands that the pictures be seen from below, their very heavy stuccoed frames make them look too autonomous. This tendency is reinforced by their shape—elongated rectangles that derive from the nave's division into bays (fig. 34).

In light of the illusionistic tradition of Italy another consideration is more significant. Italian illusionism tends to follow one of two strategies: (1) The real architecture is continued into the fresco. If we place ourselves correctly, usually below or to the west of the center of the fresco, it becomes difficult to detect just where the real fresco begins and where the architecture leaves off. Through openings in this illusory architecture above the shapes of heaven, clouds, angels, and saints are allowed to enter. This type of illusionism is associated with Andrea Pozzo, whose work was made generally available by a publi-

34. Benediktbeuern, Benedictine abbey church, nave vault

cation of his designs that appeared in Augsburg in 1702. (2) A more usual strategy, employed for example by Correggio in his decoration of the cathedral at Parma, makes no attempt to continue the built architecture into the fresco. The fresco appears here much like an opening cut into the vault through which we are allowed to look into heaven. It was this strategy that Greither was trying to employ, if rather ineffectively, in the parish church of Weilheim. The first approach offers this advantage over the latter: it increases the illusion. At the same time, however, the fresco can only be seen correctly from one particular spot; the further we move away from that position the more decidedly the illusion is unmasked. Because it avoids representations of architecture, which tend to fix a particular point of view, the second approach allows more readily for a change of place. Yet for the same reason it tends to leave our sense of a solid vault untouched, suggesting at best openings cut into it. The *quadratura* of a Pozzo, on the other hand, can go a long way toward eliminating our sense of the vault altogether, achieving a genuine fusion of real and pictorial space.

In Benediktbeuern Asam follows neither tradition. Instead he offers something like a synthesis, perhaps only an unhappy compromise between illusionism and expectations tied to traditional panel painting. The result is, given the criteria of Italian illusionism, an impossibility. Illusionism demands that one point of view unite both real and pictorial space into a whole. Only what could reasonably be expected to appear above us could be allowed to appear on the ceiling; first of all, of course, heaven with its clouds, but also a more or less fantastic architecture, which could conceivably rest on the real architecture. Within these restrictions, not every theme of traditional religious painting could lend itself to such an illusionism. A representation of Christ's baptism or crucifixion, for example, requires the inclusion of landscape elements in the fresco. But a strict illusionism rules this out—a landscape in a ceiling fresco amounts to a pictorial contradiction. The artist had to look for other themes better suited to illusionistic treatment, such as the saints in their heavenly glory or the Assumption of the Virgin.

At Benediktbeuern, however, we are given representations of this world. Asam does not shy away from representing the earth with its trees and brooks. Indeed, as long as a ceiling painting is looked at as if it were a panel painting there is no reason to exclude such elements. But to illusionism they must appear an *Unding*, a visual paradox. Why did the Bavarians accept this paradox, while Italian *quadratura* found few wholehearted supporters? Why did Hans Georg Asam's impossibilities appeal to the Bavarians as Pozzo's illusionism did not? At least one reason is the Bavarians' insistence that the fresco preach to us, that it tell of events and scenes that illusionism could not handle. But besides this insistence on story there seems to be something else at work, an *unwillingness to make space comprehensible*. Perspective offers us something like mastery of the infinite. Bavarian artists tended to resist such mastery. I shall return to this point in chapter 4.

At Tegernsee Hans Georg Asam carried the achievement of Benediktbeuern a step further. In spite of the fact that Tegernsee and Benediktbeuern used to be attributed to the same architect, the spaces are quite dissimilar and present the painter with different opportunities.[11] Tegernsee is fundamentally still a Romanesque structure, which was first changed in the fifteenth century and given its present form by Antonio Riva. While

Benediktbeuern is a wall-pillar church with galleries, Tegernsee is a basilica with transept and a shallow-domed crossing. At Benediktbeuern the vault is flatter; the individual bays are rather narrow, forcing the painter to content himself with oblong towel-like areas. Tegernsee, with its wider bays, gave Asam a happier format, while the dome confronted him with a new task and provided him with a much larger area than he had had to work with up to this time. At the same time the interior of Tegernsee is more compartmentalized than at Benediktbeuern. Our attention is divided between the nave, the transept, the dome, the side aisles, and an entrance hall.

The frescoes of the nave follow the pattern set in Benediktbeuern, although the effect is generally happier. In part this is because of the changed format; more important, some of the stiffness of Benediktbeuern is gone. Like the ceiling paintings in Benediktbeuern, the frescoes in Tegernsee still recall panel paintings. Here, as there, Asam does not hesitate to paint hills, trees, and brooks on the ceiling.

Very different is his approach to the shallow dome over the crossing. More than any earlier fresco in Bavarian baroque architecture, this one affects the space. As our eye moves from the fresco's edge toward its center, we appear to leave the darker circles of clouds, supporting countless saints and angels, and rise into the light enveloping the Trinity. Only with this fresco does Asam follow the Italian tradition of Correggio. How little this tradition agrees with the approach in the other frescoes is sensed as soon as one enters the church: the Transfiguration with its hilltop appears beyond and therefore above the heaven opening up over the crossing, which is thus revealed to be just another picture. Its illusion would have been more effective had the frescoes of the nave remained unexecuted. We are left with the tension between panel painting and illusionism.

Impossible Illusions

Cosmas Damian Asam, who was to become the most important painter of the South German rococo, inherited this problem from his father. But the father only visited Italy; the son studied there. After the death of Hans Georg, abbot Quirin Millon of Tegernsee made it possible for the two brothers to complete their studies in Rome, where Cosmas Damian is supposed to have worked with Pierleone Ghezzi, although the influence of Giovan Battista Gaulli, Andrea Pozzo, and Carlo Maratti is more apparent in his later work.[12] On March 23, 1713 he was awarded first prize by the Accademia di San Luca.[13] Less than a year later we find him back in Germany, at Ensdorf, like Tegernsee a Benedictine monastery.[14] Indeed, the abbot who called Cosmas Damian to Ensdorf came from Tegernsee, where he had seen the older Asam paint his frescoes.

The tensions that mark Tegernsee are also found at Ensdorf. Here, too, the frescoes filling the three bays of the nave retain many of the panel-like qualities of the corresponding frescoes in Tegernsee, although in this first major work the son already shows himself a far more accomplished artist than the father. Gone are Hans Georg's stiffness and dull colors. As at Tegernsee the shallow dome over the crossing, here too given to a representation of saints and angels adoring the Trinity, is treated in a very different manner, closer to the illusionism of Correggio. There are, however, significant changes. The son's more dynamic approach suggests careful study of Giovanni Lanfranco's and Pietro da Cortona's

1. Diessen, Augustinian priory church, western part of the main fresco by Johann Georg Bergmüller (1736): St. Mechthild enters the priory of St. Stephan

▲ 2. Steingaden, Premonstratensian abbey church, fresco above the organ by Johann Georg Bergmüller (1751): Duke Welf VI and the abbot of Roth with a plan of the abbey they founded

3. Rottenbuch, Augustinian priory church, fresco of nave vault by Matthäus Günther (1742): angels lift the heart of St. Augustine from his grave; stuccoes by Franz Xaver Schmuzer after a design by his father, Joseph, who was in charge of the decoration of the church. A brilliant example of the use of color to integrate fresco, stucco, and architecture

4. Ettal, Benedictine abbey and pilgrimage church, detail of Joseph Schmuzer's decoration of the Gothic dodecagon. The fresco above the choir arch, representing the founding of the abbey, by Johann Jakob Zeiller (1755): a monk promises aid to Emperor Ludwig the Bavarian, should the latter found a monastery in honor of God and the Virgin; he is seen holding the miraculous image of Ettal, which also appears in the cartouche below.

5. Schäftlarn, Premonstratensian abbey church, interior. Stuccoes and frescoes by Johann Baptist Zimmermann (1745–56), high altar by Johann Baptist Straub (1756)

6. Die Wies, pilgrimage church, southern side of nave

7. Die Wies, pilgrimage church, decoration of choir (detail)

Roman frescoes. Two spiral movements lead us to the center of the fresco; greater identity is given to individual groups. While clouds are allowed to spill out of this fresco over the frame, as if to emphasize its more illusionistic character, the frescoes of the nave, dealing with scenes from the life of St. James, remain securely framed.[15] It seems that Cosmas Damian, like his father, considered Italian illusionism just one possible approach to the problem of fresco painting, to be employed only when the theme permitted it, as for instance in representations of the Glory of Heaven. When other themes were given to the painter, as in the nave of Ensdorf, another approach, closer to panel painting, was employed. In Bavaria (in Italy and neighboring Austria the situation was quite different)[16] the painter had to subordinate himself to the program furnished by the abbot or whoever else had invented it; not an artist, at any rate, but an ecclesiastic. The literary dimension of the frescoes remained more important than the requirements of illusionism. The peculiar development of fresco painting in Bavaria can only be understood if this insistence on the *priority of the word* is kept in mind; and an interesting question is why in Bavaria the demand for story was given such importance. At any rate it proved strong enough to prevent the full dominance of Italian illusionism.

Cosmas Damian Asam's next major work in the Benedictine abbey church in Michelfeld (1717–18)—here, too, the abbot had come from Tegernsee—brings some new developments. The church itself, a rather plain rectangle of four bays without either crossing or clearly marked-off choir, presented an unusual problem: if the easternmost bay was to function as a choir, the decorators had to come to the architect's assistance. Asam's fresco does just that. In Austrian or Bohemian fashion the choir vault is completely given over to painting, which raises the illusion of a dome—a real dome had originally been planned—above the choir bay (fig. 35). Perhaps it was this necessity of giving the choir special importance, but whatever the reason, never before had a German painter so effectively united real and fresco space. None had come so close to the spirit of Italian *quadratura*.

Only a narrow rib-band, and even it invaded by clouds spilling out of the choir fresco, separates choir and nave. The frescoes of the nave resemble those of Ensdorf, although here they have become almost square and take up a still larger part of the vault. From the narrow rectangles of Benediktbeuern to the squarish frescoes of Michelfeld a steady evolution leads to frescoes spanning two or more bays, such as the large fresco Cosmas Damian was to paint a little later in Aldersbach. But in Michelfeld, as in the earlier churches, we are left with the tension between illusionism and panel painting. Indeed, due to the increased illusionism of the choir fresco this tension has become even more pronounced.

From Michelfeld Cosmas Damian Asam was called to yet another Benedictine abbey, to Weingarten, to help decorate the immense church that had just been built there, a wall-pillar church with a full dome over the crossing (1718–20). The very strength of this architecture, the clearly articulated bays and the dome, make this very much a baroque—that is to say in this context backward-looking—church, in spite of many forward-looking details, such as the French-influenced delicate stuccowork by Franz Schmuzer. Given this space, it must have been difficult for Asam to push further in the direction he had pursued at Ensdorf and Michelfeld. There is little surprise in the dome fresco, another circular composition, showing the same spiral movements already familiar from Ensdorf, although here the dome's lantern poses an additional problem in that its strongly architectural

8. Rottenbuch, Augustinian priory church. The rococo decoration of the medieval basilica is the work of Joseph Schmuzer (1737–47).

35. Michelfeld, Benedictine abbey church, interior

quality breaks the pictorial illusion that the fresco is trying to create. The same must be said of the dome's drum: the brightness of Asam's frescoed heaven simply cannot compete with the bright windows below (fig. 36).

As if to compete with the architect on more favorable grounds, Asam raises a second dome above the choir, which makes comparison between the architect's and the painter's work almost inevitable. As at Michelfeld, Asam is following here a design from Pozzo's *Perspectiva pictorum et architectorum* (fig. 37).

The rivalry between architecture and painting is carried further in the nave. Given Cosmas Damian's earlier work one would expect another version of the kind of fresco first created by his father in Benediktbeuern. Instead Cosmas Damian seems here, too, to follow the example of Pozzo. The middle fresco—larger than the two adjoining frescoes, effecting a certain centralization—at first appears as just another exercise in *quadratura* painting. Indeed, the relationship between the architecture of the fresco and the real architecture in which we stand would seem to have been carried to new heights, for the former is now not simply an extension, but an imitation of the latter.[17] The massive pillars of the church with their vigorous capitals reappear in the fresco, as do the stuccoed rib-bands joining them. Not that the imitation is complete: in the fresco the very delicate concave galleries are replaced with more robust little balconies, which now curve out, into the space, while the place of the fresco itself is taken by an oval opening that plays somewhat the part of the round illusionistic frescoes of Tegernsee and Ensdorf (fig. 38). Through this opening we see with St. Benedict the Glory of Heaven. This is an important change. We see the saint seeing the Glory of Heaven; Benedict is seen by us

36. Weingarten, Benedictine abbey church, dome and choir vault

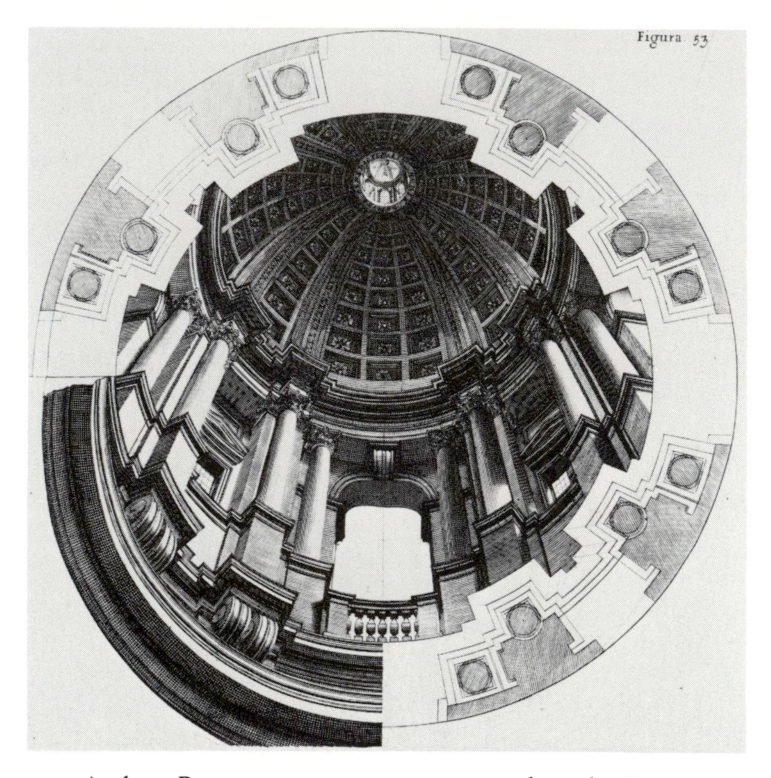

37. Andreas Pozzo, perspective construction from the *Perspectiva pictorum et architectorum*

both as the spectator of a sacred theatre and as an actor in the play the painter has staged above us. He mediates between us and heaven. Again spiral movements draw us upward on cloudy paths, through the opening in the painted architecture into the light above. Only in this fresco is the frame broken by a group of devils, cast down by the power of Benedict's cross.

What is the point of this doubling of the real architecture in the fresco?[18] Does it help to increase the illusionistic effect? Is Asam trying to outdo Pozzo? If so, the fresco must be judged a failure, for in its juxtaposition with reality imitation is revealed to be just that. The illusion that the painted architecture above has the same mode of reality as that architecture in which we stand is thereby destroyed, just as it is by the juxtaposition of the real dome above the crossing and the painted dome beyond.

But let us consider the fresco in somewhat more detail. The oval opening in the fresco is analogous to the fresco itself; the fresco is like an opening to heaven, the opening to heaven like a painting. Instead of being permitted to remain captured by the illusion created by the painter, we are reminded that it is an illusion, theatre. And yet that reality in which we stand, Franz Beer's pillars and Franz Schmuzer's stuccowork, is like that theatrical reality above, which does in fact mirror it. Our space, too, is thus rendered theatrical: theatre within theatre. (Imagine an actor who thinks his part done walking off stage, only to discover that he is still on stage, still acting, playing his part in a more encompassing play.)

The two adjoining frescoes—a representation of the Assumption of the Virgin to the east, to the west the Blood of Christ as a fountain of grace (and thus a celebration of the

38. Weingarten, abbey church, nave vault

relic of the Holy Blood that had made Weingarten an important pilgrimage place)—appear rather closer to the panel-like frescoes of Michelfeld and Ensdorf. But here, too, a decisive step has been taken. True to their origin in panel painting, the earlier frescoes demand a horizon parallel to the lower, (that is, eastern) edge of the painting. The Holy Blood fresco follows this general scheme. But in the Assumption fresco Asam attempts a very different spatial organization. Perhaps it is best understood as an attempt to fuse the kind of perspective that he had learned from Pozzo, a perspective that lent itself to the representation of interior spaces that could conceivably be above the spectator, such as a dome, with the models provided by his father.[19] In many ways the perspective of the Assumption fresco is related to that of the choir fresco. But instead of looking up into an interior space we now look up from our place on the ground into an architectonic landscape that demands a second ground above. The fresco invites us to rise, quite literally, and to step into the landscape above. Here we meet an important difference between the Bavarian rococo and the Italian baroque. The illusionism of a Pozzo leaves us secure in our point of view; the impossible illusionism of the Bavarians, with its landscapes above, *calls our point of view into question.*

We shall have to return to this difference. Here I would only like to suggest that there is a relationship between the spatial organization of the St. Benedict fresco and the Assumption. To return to the former: a doubling of the architecture suggests a doubling of the ground that supports this architecture. A second ground is thus at least implicit in the St. Benedict fresco as well. In this respect, it, too, breaks with Pozzo.

But why the doubling of this world by another? Why not simply open up the architecture to the heavenly sphere? What was Asam after? Perhaps we do have here the result of the impossible attempt to fuse Pozzo's illusionism with traditional panel painting. But such an account cannot explain the decisive importance that Asam's innovations had for the subsequent development of rococo painting and architecture. Spaces such as that first created here, extended from one to several bays, were to become characteristic of the Bavarian rococo church.

Beyond Illusionism

The step from a fresco filling just one bay to one covering three, thus uniting the bays of the nave, was taken by Cosmas Damian Asam at Aldersbach, his next major commission (1720).[20] This time it was the Cistercians who invited him. It is not St. Benedict who appears here as mediator, but St. Bernard, whose Christmas Vision is represented by the main fresco. Again the painter does not attempt to open heaven itself for us; instead he is portraying a vision. The heaven of Aldersbach is a mediated heaven, a heaven seen through the eyes of the Cistercian saint.[21]

Little remains that still recalls Pozzo: above all the heavy marble balustrade that uses the fresco frame for a base. As is usual in Bavarian churches, the point of view dictated to us is not below the center of the fresco, but near the entrance. Thus the balustrade becomes less and less visible as we look from east to west, that is, as we look up; at the top it disappears altogether. This balustrade forms something like a barrier preventing us from entering the fresco (fig. 39).

39. Aldersbach, abbey church, fresco

Only at one point, at the bottom, where the balustrade curves toward us in the form of a little balcony, is it broken. Here there is an opening that invites us to step into the fresco. But the way is blocked; the space through which we would have to pass is filled by the sleeping St. Bernard. In the cartouche below him we read: *Bernhardus Nascente ex Verbo Infante Magistro Mellifluus Ecclesiae Doctor*—"Taught by the Word become Child St. Bernard became the honey-tongued teacher of the church." His position and posture clearly separate the saint from the Christmas scene above. The scene itself uses few of the familiar conventions. The stable has become a fantastic arch. Leading up to it is a double stairway, shepherds hurrying up the steps toward the Child in the center, a source of sunlike light. This scene is tied to St. Bernard by an angel, who, "like a speaker in a play,"[22] seems to beckon him to join the shepherds and to adore the Child. The shepherds are joined by a group of angels on the right who are performing one of St. Bernard's hymns: *Nil Canitur Suavius quam Jesus Dei Filius*. This reference in the fresco to St. Bernard is somewhat surprising, another reminder that what we see here is not a representation of an historical event, but of a vision of that event. The upper half of the fresco is given to a heavenly assembly reminiscent of such compositions as Cosmas Damian Asam's glory fresco in Ensdorf; yet it also bears a relationship to the scene below: it, too, has a brilliant center, only God the Father now has taken the place of the Divine Child. Upper closure is provided by a brownish curtain carried by angels, which in its curves parallels rather closely the rhythms of the stable architecture below. The spiral movement, up the right stairway to Joseph and the Divine Child, is paralleled by another such movement above, leading from the angels carrying their *Gloria in Excelsis Deo* in a sweeping arc up to God. Above and below there are corresponding supporting movements: the group of the adoring shepherd and the Virgin below is paralleled by the two angels carrying the Cross above, while the angelic musicians to the right of the Child are paralleled by another group of angels above.

The whole fresco is thus organized around two centers that function somewhat like the foci of an ellipse. Each becomes the center of what, although oval, is seen as a circular composition. The two centers are joined by a reversed S: the C-like arc leading from the angels carrying their *Gloria* banner to God above extends in another C-like arc below and joins that group to the Christ Child.

One detail merits special attention. Why did Asam choose to bound the fresco above by the group of four angels carrying a reddish-brown drapery? Not only does it provide closure and a parallel to the architecture below, it also serves to emphasize the theatricality of this fresco: as if the curtain had just been raised to permit us to see the sacred spectacle of God in his glory. And yet this angelic theatre is itself part of a theatrical composition. Again: theatre within theatre. The four angels above stand also in a relationship to the angel below, mediating between St. Bernard and the Christmas scene. Even visually this is apparent in the green of their dress. The angels here appear as those who make St. Bernard's and our own vision possible. They are the messengers of the holy. And yet these angels are themselves part of a theatrical composition. The fresco thus operates on several planes. St. Bernard and the balustrade are closest to us. Next come the angels, clothed in the green of hope. Only through the mediation of saint and angels are we led to the twofold vision below and above.

In its treatment of perspective this fresco seems rather close to the Assumption fresco of Weingarten, although the great size of the Aldersbach fresco posed new problems. Even more pronounced is a sense that to see the fresco correctly we should rise. We seem to be in the stable's cellar. As is usual in Bavarian rococo churches, the fresco should be seen from a point of view near the entrance, but even from the most privileged point of view available to us the architecture does not quite seem to stand. It is impossible to see this fresco correctly. Following Hans Geiger, Rupprecht suggests that Asam employs here the device of the "inclined plane." Measured by the demands of Pozzo's illusionism the fresco appears tilted out of its horizontal position, as if it had been pushed upward at its western end: we sense that there is a correct point of view, but that we should have to rise, angel-like, to reach it.[23] This attributes to the painter a more careful use of perspective than the fresco warrants. The free use of multiple vanishing points leads to an architecture that, measured by the laws of geometry, simply makes no sense.

Cosmas Damian Asam's surreal perspective, his references to the theatre, his doubling of the familiar world by another above, all make it difficult to speak of illusionism. Just because the Aldersbach fresco cannot be seen correctly from any point of view, it cannot be said to extend that space in which we actually find ourselves illusionistically. If it is a weakness of Pozzo's illusionism that only from one particular place is the illusion powerful enough to take hold of us, Asam presents us with an image that can never quite convince, that will always remain theatre. The Bavarian rococo calls its *theatricality to our attention*. But an illusion that advertises its illusory character can no longer function as such. The illusion has been unmasked.

Why this tremendous production? Can it really be dismissed as just theatre? Or is it born of a more ambiguous response? No longer able to take Italian illusionism quite seriously, the artists and their society were yet not ready to give it up altogether. "Look at what I have done," the painter seems to be saying, "but don't take it too seriously; it is just play, just my attempt to render not what transpired in Bethlehem, but the vision of the event given us by St. Bernard." Notable is the stress on mediation, also a new historical awareness. We see the Nativity through the eyes of the saint. And the real Nativity? The artist has become too modest to attempt to capture it; he is content with reflections, echoes. Illusionism has given way to a play with illusion that unmasks itself.

Should we still speak here of illusionism? Rupprecht disputes Geiger's claim that in Aldersbach Asam had gone beyond illusionism with the argument that this has to be granted only as long as illusionism is identified with the *quadratura* of Pozzo. Illusionism, he suggests, has to be understood differently.

> *The illusionistic principle is fundamentally a question of the degree of reality.* In every case the illusionistic object and the illusionistic space demand to be experienced as real to the same degree as the actual space. Aldersbach shows that even without a constructive connection with the space of the church, a visible, equally real sphere in the fresco can be given.[24]

I would question "equally real." What is revealed by the Aldersbach fresco does not possess the same degree of reality as our own world. What we are permitted to see is a vision, and that vision is in one sense less real than our world; as the sleeping St. Bernard and the pictorial means chosen suggest, it has rather the reality of a dream. And yet this dream puts us into touch with what is more real than our world. Its irreality is a superreality. The art of Cosmas Damian Asam is born of the conviction that what is truly real cannot be revealed by illusionistic means, for that would make it too relative to our human point of view. If we are to point to a higher reality that human point of view has to be put into question. The Aldersbach fresco does this quite literally through its use of perspective.

The rejection of baroque illusionism in favor of the tension between our world and a double of that world above, thus threatening the unity of the aesthetic space, was to become characteristic of the Bavarian rococo church. Its frescoes therefore occupy a place somewhat in between the paintings of the older Asam, which in spite of their illusionistic perspective remain tied to panel painting, and Pozzo's illusionism. This is reflected by a new attitude to the frame, which is perhaps the most readily noted characteristic of the Bavarian rococo.

To understand this attitude a few general observations on the significance of framing a picture are in order. The frame creates first of all a barrier separating the picture from what supports it. The reality in which the observer stands, and beyond this the familiar world with its cares and concerns, are bracketed out. The frame thus has its foundation in a need for aesthetic distance; the art work is established as an *autonomous reality*.

But perhaps the word "established" is too strong here. Does the frame establish the art object as an autonomous reality? Is it not rather because the art object establishes *itself* as an independent reality that it demands the barrier represented by the frame? Many a painting is so obviously autonomous that the frame seems superfluous; the painting is composed in such a way that its borders seem inevitable. In such cases the frame is only an external expression of this inevitability. Indeed, if the autonomy of the painting is sufficiently secured from within, the frame may seem redundant. The picture no longer needs a frame, as is the case with many modern paintings.

A framed fresco cannot function illusionistically. Illusionism thus has only two options. It can try to merge the frescoed space and real space so completely that it becomes impossible for the observer to tell where one begins and the other leaves off. This, the method of Pozzo, has the already-mentioned disadvantage that the illusion works only as long as we occupy some determined point of view, usually right below the center of the fresco. When this privileged point of view is abandoned the illusion is destroyed. The results are at times grotesque, as Giovanni Francesco Marchini's fresco in Balthasar Neumann's church in Wiesentheid (1728–29), for example, shows. A second approach interprets what we see in the fresco as higher realms glimpsed through openings cut into the space that actually encloses us. Where this approach is taken we do tend to find strongly articulated frames, but these frames are experienced, not as an expression of the autonomy of the fresco, but simply as the termination of the vault, where often this termination can be read at the same time as the base of a merely painted architecture in the fresco.

The mature rococo of Bavaria tends to reject these solutions and with them illusionism. Not that it returns to the frame in its traditional sense; it chooses instead the *scalloped frame*, formed of different curved and straight line segments—which Hitchcock quite correctly makes a defining mark of the South German rococo.[25] It is impossible to credit Cosmas Damian Asam with this innovation. In tracing the prehistory of the scalloped frame Hitchcock points to Schloss Weissenstein in Pommersfelden and to the Kaisersaal in Ebrach (ca. 1718), both of which are said to reflect Viennese influences.[26] Closer to Munich, the still earlier little church in Kreuzpullach (1710) deserves to be mentioned (fig. 81). The stucco here is by Johann Georg Bader, the fresco by Johann Georg Bergmüller, who was to become director of the Art Academy in Augsburg. Since it seems somewhat unlikely that Asam knew the Franconian examples, Kreuzpullach could have occasioned the shape given to the fresco in Aldersbach. More convincingly, the scalloped frame can be traced back (fig. 40) to such publications as Paul Decker's *Fürstlicher Baumeister* (1711). But regardless of the antecedents, the scalloped frame of the Aldersbach fresco is as important for the subsequent development of the Bavarian rococo church as its playful transformation of Italian illusionism. Both are indeed closely related.

To understand this relationship we should ask ourselves, Why do frames tend to come

40. Paul Decker, ceiling decoration from *Fürstlicher Baumeister*

in a relatively limited array of shapes? Why do they tend to be rectangular, less often circular or oval? Is it not because the closing function of the frame is obscured by irregularity and complexity, robbing the painting of its autonomy? The scalloped frame is therefore a device to weaken the usual function of the frame without surrendering it altogether. The picture is framed and yet the frame is not secure. In this connection we should reconsider the already-mentioned clouds spilling over the frame of the Aldersbach fresco, as well as the riband weaving in and out of the picture. In the last chapter I discussed these as prefiguring the stucco zone that in the Bavarian rococo church mediates between architecture and painting. The Bavarians' play with Italian illusionism holds the key to their enthusiastic adoption of rocaille.

Mediating Frames

In his unwillingness to settle on a particular scheme, Cosmas Damian Asam is unique among the fresco painters active in eighteenth-century Bavaria. Every new commission seems to lead to a rethinking of the problem of the fresco's relationship to the architecture and to new solutions. I cannot begin to do justice here to the development of his art, but we must consider the Nativity fresco in Einsiedeln (1725–26).[27]

With its many different compartments, the complex space Caspar Moosbrugger had created had to resist the kind of unity at which the brothers Asam were aiming. There is therefore no unifying fresco as at Aldersbach, nor could the painter draw the vault together as Cosmas Damian had done in Freising (1723–24), with its painted clouds, spilling over the frames, trailing from one fresco to the next. And yet Einsiedeln does present us with a further development of ideas that were already present in Aldersbach and Freising.

Cosmas Damian's handling of the domed third bay especially demands our attention. The dome itself is covered almost completely by a representation of the Nativity; only the pendentives are given over to framed medallions of allegorical figures of Mercy and Truth, Justice and Peace. The fresco does not look framed; it simply ends where it meets the dome's supporting arches and the medallions. All this recalls Freising, where the frescoes extend similarly downward between the severies of the vault to almost meet the cornice. And as at Freising, where painted ornament takes the place of stuccoed decoration, so the Nativity fresco in Einsiedeln can be divided into two quite different zones: a pictorial center representing the Nativity and an outer framing zone that is less pictorial than ornamental.

Although at Aldersbach, too, Cosmas Damian Asam had painted the Nativity, there are striking differences between the two frescoes. In part they reflect the different tasks that had been set. In Aldersbach the fresco serves to unite three bays; its shape is necessarily oblong, a fact Asam exploits by organizing the fresco around two foci. In Einsiedeln he was given instead a large dome that demanded a circular composition. The western point of view so characteristic of the Bavarian rococo therefore had to be modified: it does work for the Nativity scene that occupies the area of the fresco just above the choir arch, but different parts of the fresco demand different points of view, roughly speaking diagonally below whatever part of the fresco is being observed. Although the fresco does have two scenic centers—opposite the Nativity scene the angels sing their *Gloria* to the shepherds—spiraling patterns, already familiar from other Asam compositions, establish the small lantern rising above the dome as the real center of the fresco. In this little dome we see God the Father, holding the olive branch of peace, and the dove of the Holy Spirit. Both are linked to the world below by their downward motion and by angels rushing from heaven to earth. The lantern's central importance is further heightened by the orange-golden light falling through its tinted panes, a device the Asam brothers had brought to Bavaria from Rome. The real light of the lantern appears as the origin of the painted golden light emanating from the Christ Child.

The second outer zone, which in Freising is given mostly to rich *mosaïque*, is here elaborated into a fantastic scroll architecture, far more ambiguous than the corresponding ornament in Freising in that it functions as framing ornament and yet has an architectural quality that makes it part of the depicted scene. Once again Paul Decker's *Fürstlicher Baumeister* provides an obvious source. The observer is not permitted to separate these two zones too sharply. Although in its stuccolike forms and colors quite different from the Christmas scene, the scroll architecture itself merges with the ruin in which the Holy Family has found refuge. Included in this ornamental zone are allegorical figures, which correspond to those of the medallions below and in their plaster whiteness suggest the stucco sculptures so popular at the time; but like the gesturing angel in the Aldersbach fresco, they also relate to Joseph and to the shepherd carrying his lamb to the Child, and thus become part of the picture. Similarly, white "stuccoed" foliage is placed next to green plants. But if the ornament of this framing zone thus tends to become part of the picture itself, it also resembles the stuccoed scroll ornament of the choir arch. More effectively than in any of their earlier churches, the brothers Asam have created a zone binding fresco and architecture together.

What in Einsiedeln is still a painted zone becomes stuccoed decoration in Munich's St. Anna im Lehel (1729). The architect, Johann Michael Fischer, had given the Asam brothers an ovalized, highly unified interior. The vault, tentlike in its lightness, is carried by eight fluted wall-pillars, which function much like the slightly later free pillars of Dominikus Zimmermann's Steinhausen. Before the destruction of World War II most of the vault was occupied by Cosmas Damian Asam's large, roughly oval fresco of St. Anna in Glory, framed by a vigorously scalloped molding.[28] The pendentive zone is mostly given to gold and blue-gray *mosaïque*, which mediates between the tectonic wall-pillars and the fresco. What makes this mediation so effective is the way in which segments of the frame molding are tied to the arches supporting the vault: above the cornice of each wall-pillar spirals generate stuccoed gables above the wider longitudinal and transverse arches. As in the almost contemporary Steinhausen, the gables are seen as both part of the frame and extensions of the architecture. Especially these volute gables suggest the painted scroll architecture of Einsiedeln. Only now this framing zone is taken out of the fresco: the stuccoed ornament forms a third mediating zone between architecture and fresco (fig. 80).

In St. Anna stucco is used effectively but sparingly. It becomes elaborate only in the cartouche bearing the Bavarian arms, which almost fills the stuccoed gable above the choir arch. Particularly interesting is an easily overlooked detail: the banner carried by the angel is thrust into the fresco above so forcefully that just at this point a piece of the stuccoed gable is missing. Instead we see the frescoed ground. Has the frame been pierced by the angel, or was it this opening that permitted the angel to leave the heavenly scene above and enter the nave of the church? While the stuccoed gables appear like extensions of the architecture, the angel appears more like an extension of the fresco. Architecture and picture fuse. St. Anna is the first church to show modestly, but flawlessly, that triple structure which helps to define the Bavarian rococo church: the tectonic verticals of the wall-pillars are led by a mediating stucco zone over into the fresco.[29]

An Exemplary Rococo Church

More than Cosmas Damian Asam and his students Matthäus Günther and the brothers Scheffler we associate Johann Baptist Zimmermann with the rococo. His frescoes in Steinhausen and Die Wies, incredibly light and airy with their pastel blues and grays, seem to have realized possibilities only hinted at in the work of Cosmas Damian Asam. Given this on-the-whole correct impression one is surprised to discover that Zimmermann, born in 1680, was six years older than Asam. Zimmermann was almost forty when the Aldersbach fresco was painted, and just fifty when he started on his first major fresco in Steinhausen. Although it is false that Zimmermann had taken up painting only after he had reached the age of fifty, as is reported in a recent survey of baroque architecture,[30] his earlier efforts hardly suggest that his would be a major contribution to Bavarian fresco painting.

We have no certain knowledge of where he studied painting; perhaps in Augsburg, which had become the most important center for painting in southern Germany, rivaling Vienna and Prague.[31] But in the first half of his life Zimmermann appears as a decorator who also used painting. His first frescoes function first of all as accents in a larger decorative scheme, significant only for their colors, which already at this time tend to be lighter than those of his local rivals.[32] In none of his early churches do his frescoes have the importance that they had almost thirty years earlier in Benediktbeuern or Garsten (see fig. 5).

As already mentioned, in 1720 Zimmermann was called to Munich to help with the decoration of the elector's palace in Schleissheim. His work there brought him into close contact with the two most significant and innovative painters then active in southern Germany, Cosmas Damian Asam and Jacopo Amigoni (1675–1752), a much-traveled Venetian. Like Zimmermann, Amigoni had worked in Ottobeuren before being called to Schleissheim.[33]

In Schleissheim Asam painted two major frescoes: the somewhat cramped *Venus in the Forge of Vulcan* (1720) in the dome above the Stairhall and a *Martyrdom of St. Maximilian* (1721) in the palace's Great Chapel. Amigoni's much more extensive work (1723–25) includes the large frescoes *Dido Receives Aeneas* in the Dining Hall and *Aeneas and Turnus Battle for the Hand of Lavinia* in the Great Hall (fig. 41). More than Asam, the cosmo-

41. Schleissheim, Neues Schloss, great hall

politan Venetian impressed and influenced Zimmermann.[34] New, at least in Bavarian fresco painting, is Amigoni's resolute turn toward landscape. Greens, blues, silvery and brownish grays gain a new importance. It is as if a window had been opened. By comparison Asam's slightly earlier and thematically related fresco above the Stairhall seems dense and cluttered.

The novelty of the fresco in Steinhausen is at least in part due to Zimmermann's adaptation to a church ceiling of the model provided by Amigoni's secular frescoes at Schleissheim. In Zimmermann's art the atmospheric sky above a landscape merges with the heavenly realm of God and His angels. Heaven is brought, usually quite literally, down to earth. In the church frescoes of the mature rococo the darker and warmer golden and orange tones of the baroque give way to lighter blues and grays. Again Aldersbach may be taken to anticipate this new approach, but in the Asam church blue still plays only a minor part. It triumphs only in Steinhausen. This triumph is of iconographic interest: in Zimmermann's art the idea of heaven is naturalized, which is not necessarily the same as secularized. The rococo church presupposes this naturalization (fig. 42).[35]

Unlike Cosmas Damian Asam, who never settled on any one solution, Zimmermann remained faithful to the fresco style he had worked out in Steinhausen. In his later frescoes we find the same pastel colors hinting at a sunny day in late spring or early summer. Blue is given an important role; below we find green, gray, and brown tones; groups of figures provide more colorful accents, as do architectural props. The older glory compositions have left their trace near the center of the fresco, where we often find spiraling representations of the angelic realm. There the blue changes to more golden tones. This general description applies not only to Steinhausen, but to many of the frescoes that followed it—to Prien (1738), where large ships sail across the vault (we see Don Juan defeating the Turk at Lepanto); to Berg am Laim (1743–45), where the largest fresco represents a pilgrimage to the sanctuary of St. Michael on Monte Gargano; or to Schäftlarn (1754–56), where a magically transformed Isar valley witnesses the founding of the monastery (fig. 92). Many of these frescoes attempt to represent particular places and events. I return to this in chapter 5.

What gives Steinhausen, and later Die Wies, a special place in this series is the way in which architecture, stucco, and fresco have fused, a fusion that was made possible only by the close collaboration between Johann Baptist Zimmermann and his brother Dominikus. In many ways Steinhausen recalls St. Anna. In both churches the strongest architectural accents are provided by the verticals of the white pillars—wall-pillars in St. Anna, free-standing pillars in Steinhausen. In both churches an ornamental zone, which in Steinhausen has become much more elaborate, mediates between architecture and fresco. Details such as the stuccoed gables also suggest St. Anna. The gables are most simple above the choir arch and above the corresponding arch beneath the organ. Here they only echo the outline of the arch below, a curve that is picked up again by the painted architecture at the eastern end of the fresco. The adjacent arches are crowned with volute gables that, in spite of their rich decoration, resemble those of St. Anna. As we move toward the middle of the nave these gables lose their architectural quality and begin to resemble ornamentally transformed balustrades. Both spatially and in appearance they lie halfway between the stuccoed gables and the balustrades stuccoed into the fresco. The stucco zone in its entirety thus seems to undergo a metamorphosis that transforms the architectonic into the pictorial. In the balustrades ornament becomes pictorial foreground. As such it belongs to the picture, while at the same time it continues to belong to the ornamental zone framing the picture—it is both part of the picture and part of its frame. With its gables and gablelike forms this ornamental zone also repeats and joins in the rhythm of the arches joining the pillars.

The relationship between fresco and architecture is further enhanced by the fresco's composition. Each of the pillars seems to extend itself into the fresco, most energetically in the tall trees standing in the Garden of Eden in the west, and in a corresponding garden, the *hortus conclusus* of the Song of Songs, in the east,[36] but also in the four groups of figures symbolizing the four continents. Only the two pillars in the middle of the nave have no painted extensions in the fresco; their place is taken by the already-mentioned stuccoed balustrades, which in this way, too, are brought closer to the pictorial reality of the fresco. These painted projections of the pillars, most developed in the east and west,

42. Steinhausen, pilgrimage church, nave vault

also serve to achieve a transition between the oval shape of the fresco and the more nearly circular central composition, representing Mary as the queen of heaven. It is this interplay of architecture, ornament, and fresco that makes Steinhausen an exemplary rococo church.

ARCHITECTURE AGAINST ARCHITECTURE

Indirect Light

Dependent as it is on frescoes, the Bavarian rococo church requires a great deal of light. Ideally this is an indirect light. Next to a bright window even the brightest fresco will seem dark, even the most exuberant painting of heavenly glories all too material (fig. 36). An obvious way of meeting this demand is to hide from view the exterior walls and the windows cut into them by surrounding a central space with a visually indeterminate, light-filled mantle. This is the first of Rupprecht's five criteria to determine the essence of the Bavarian rococo church.[1]

But we should not interpret the indirect light so characteristic of the Bavarian rococo church exclusively, or even primarily, in relation to the fresco. At least as important is the way in which the white walls and pillars of the interior absorb this light, become immaterial and radiant. Light and matter fuse as stone and stucco are transformed into an ethereal substance. The light of a church like Schäftlarn lets us forget the heaviness of the material with which it is built and helps to establish the sacred character of this architecture (fig. 43). Compare a typical New England church. It, too, is filled with light, but it remains a natural light. Bright as it is, it lacks the power to dematerialize the architecture. The alchemy sought by the Bavarian rococo does not take place.

Plate 5

We also cannot limit Rupprecht's first criterion to the rococo church. Bavarian builders had explored the magic of indirect light long before the eighteenth century. Instead of claiming that it is the rococo fresco that bends architecture to its demands, it is more correct to say that a characteristically, although by no means exclusively, Bavarian approach to matter, light, and space continues to shape the Bavarian rococo church and

43. Schäftlarn, Premonstratensian abbey church, interior

forces fresco and ornament into its service. The Bavarian rococo church must be understood as an eighteenth-century variation on quite traditional themes. And such understanding presupposes a knowledge of these themes.

Renaissance Interlude and Gothic Prelude

Perhaps the best way to gain an overview of the development of Bavarian art is to walk through Munich's Bayerisches Nationalmuseum. Particularly striking is the rupture that occurs in the first decades of the sixteenth century. As we leave the rooms devoted to the Middle Ages and enter the section given to the Renaissance we step into a different world, less tied to religion, less provincial, but also less sure of itself, less original. The self-confident strength of a Leinberger is gone. In the sixteenth century German artists appear to be trying to speak a foreign language that they have not quite mastered and that prevents them from expressing themselves with ease.

A good part of postmedieval Bavarian art, indeed, can be understood as the product of an ongoing struggle with imported vocabularies. To be accepted, learned, and appropriated as they were, these vocabularies must have seemed superior to what the past had to offer. The reasons for this have less to do with purely artistic considerations than with that general dislocation of which reformation and skepticism, the peasant wars and scientific discoveries were expressions. Yet native traditions continued to live, if often submerged, and more in peasant villages than in the cities and at the court, where one was more likely to measure artistic achievements by the accomplishments first of the Italians, later of the French. The Bavarian rococo church is witness to this life.

The affinity between the art of the fifteenth and early sixteenth centuries and the later baroque and rococo has long been recognized. Churches like Dominikus Zimmermann's Die Wies have been said to fulfill the promise of late Gothic hall churches, while Altdorfer's and Leinberger's art has been called Gothic baroque.[2] This suggests the possibility of viewing the Renaissance, at least in Bavaria, as an interlude, an artistic dislocation, followed by a gradual reappropriation of one's origins. At first this dislocation brought with it a new freedom, a new excitement, an up-to-then unknown openness to what others were doing; but increasingly it also brought a somewhat anxious casting about for models to follow. The religious base of medieval art had been lost.

The late fifteenth century and the first two decades of the sixteenth knew an intensity of church-building activity matched only two hundred years later. This activity ceased suddenly and almost completely in the 1530s. In Upper Bavaria more churches were built in the first two decades of the sixteenth century than in the remaining eight put together. The almost complete cessation of church building did of course not mean that art itself came to a halt. But it did mean a shift to different sources of support and to different tasks. The clergy became less important than the wealthier burghers, the nobility, and especially the court. A new self-understanding led to a new art that sought its models elsewhere.

As one would expect, the Renaissance first makes itself felt in the larger cities whose trade put them in close touch with Italy and Italian developments, above all in Augsburg, where the Fuggers aspired to Medicean grandeur. Here we find what is often considered the first monument of Renaissance architecture north of the Alps, the Fugger Chapel of St. Anna (1508–18), unthinkable without Italian models, yet still covered by a Gothicizing rib vault. The dukes of Bavaria soon followed the lead of the Fuggers. From Augsburg, from the ducal residences Landshut and Munich, and from other smaller cities and courts, a mannered renaissance spread to the country, if not to the peasants. Castles dating from the sixteenth century still dot the Bavarian countryside. But all this building activity had little impact on church architecture. The few churches that were built continued to adopt the inherited Gothic style. The cemetery church in Freising and the parish churches of Bairawies, Leonberg, and Thann offer examples. None of these are important. It is difficult to exaggerate the poverty of Bavarian church architecture between the Reformation and the building in Munich of St. Michael (1583–97). What building took place tended to follow late Gothic models; but it was completely overshadowed by the secular architecture of city and court. And yet we have to keep this decaying Gothic tradition in mind if we are to understand not only the achievement of St. Michael, but the ways in which the example it provided was received and transformed.

The difference between the secular architecture of the court and the Gothicizing religious architecture of the countryside cannot be written off as a difference in ornamental vocabularies. Presupposed are very different conceptions of the function of ornament, of the relationship of ornament to ornament support, especially to the ceiling. These again presuppose different attitudes to the boundaries of a space. Earlier, to an ornament that respects and serves the surfaces that support it, I opposed another that tends to disguise and even to dissolve them. The former is characteristic of the Renaissance and Mannerist architecture of the court, and since the renewal of Catholicism in the late sixteenth century is a renewal from above, inseparable from the confessional absolutism of the Wittelsbach rulers, it is this fundamentally Italian approach that furnishes the vocabulary for the church architecture of the Bavarian baroque; but not without undergoing modifications and transformations in which a very different, in many ways still late Gothic sense of space remains alive.

Late Gothic architecture in Central Europe took an increasingly decorative approach to the rib vault. With the proliferation of tiercerons and liernes, the ribs lose much of their structural significance and become ornament, an ornament that tends to let us forget the architecture of the vault as we become absorbed in the ribs' linear play. We are reminded of intertwining branches. This often-remarked-on turn from the tectonic to the organic finds what is perhaps its most beautiful expression in the work of Benedikt Ried, especially in the Vladislav Hall of the castle in Prague.[3] With its span of forty-nine feet, made possible by wrought-iron tension bars and bracing ribs, the vast royal hall represents an extraordinary engineering feat. Even more extraordinary is the linear play of the ribs, which lets us forget the vault and its weight. Although each bay is decorated with the same rosette pattern, the total effect is not that of different compartments strung together. The curvilinear ribs move and intertwine in a way that negates the division of the space into bays. It is indeed misleading to speak of rosette patterns; it puts at the beginning what we see as generated (fig. 44). Our attention is drawn to the treelike piers. They are

44. Prague, Vladislav Hall

the generative centers of this space, sending upward S-shaped ribs like swaying branches. Their curves reach up to the peak of the vault, only to bend back to the earth. Returning, the ribs divide; one branch terminates abruptly, as if it had been cut off with a knife. "The cut, open end of the rib bleeds lines of force from the vaulted surface. Nothing remains of static and self-contained mass."[4]

When Marc Antoine Laugier, perhaps the leading architectural theorist of the eighteenth century, emphasizes the analogy between ribs and branches, Gothic columns and tree trunks, this not only anticipates a romantic naturalism; it is another expression of a deep affinity between late Gothic and eighteenth-century architecture.[5] That the identification of rib and branch rests on more than a later misunderstanding is shown by those two side chapels of the Frauenkirche in Ingolstadt, where the ribs of the net vault generate a thicket, as a rose's old wooden branches put forth new shoots. Out of this thicket emerge strange thorny flowers (fig. 32). Although unique, these strange creations are nevertheless quite characteristic of late Gothic interpretations of the rib as somewhat like a wooden branch that can generate new growth. The common use of painted vines and tendrils to decorate the fields of a net vault points in the same direction. Especially where ribs join or cross they send forth stalks, leaves, and flowers. As shown in the first chapter, the decorators of the Bavarian rococo were to use related ornaments.

Built into this turn to the organic is a particular attitude to time. In the early and high

Middle Ages the beautiful was thought to partake of the eternal. Artists tended to avoid forms, colors, and materials that would tie their creations too closely to time. Figures that look as if constructed with compass and ruler lack the directionality, and thus the temporality, of configurations that recall handwriting. Similarly there are colors, for instance grays, greens, or blues, that hint at specific times of day or year, while pure primary colors minimize such associations, as does the gold background of medieval painting. Portrayed against such a background, events gain a timeless significance.

The discovery of the beauty of the temporal is generally characteristic of late Gothic art, and nowhere is the fascination with time more pronounced than in Bavaria. One only has to think of a drawing by Albrecht Altdorfer or Wolf Huber, of Erasmus Grasser's *Moriskentänzer*, or of Hans Leinberger's *St. James*. Enough has been said already to suggest that in this respect, too, late Gothic architecture anticipates the rococo.

Inseparable from the fascination with time is a fascination with the irrational and elusive. We can grasp only what stands still and abides; the organic will always finally escape us. A similar elusiveness marks Altdorfer's rising rocks and trees, the cascading folds of Leinberger's madonnas, and the ribs of Benedikt Ried's vaults. Where there is motion there is also a lack of closure. Only apparently do the starlike patterns of Benedikt Ried's vaults let the motion of the rising ribs come to rest. We find it difficult to remain with these stars; the motion that leads us to them also lets us return to the ground, where the play begins anew. This play is essentially a play of lines. The vault that supports it is rendered curiously insubstantial. We meet a very similar attitude toward the supporting architecture in the churches of the Bavarian rococo.[6]

St. Michael and the Wall-Pillar Church

Nothing in the small churches that continued to be built in Bavaria after the Reformation shows even a trace of the originality of a Benedikt Ried. Their net vaults offer modest and uninspired repetitions of late Gothic patterns that had come to be taken for granted. Yet when the Counter Reformation came to Germany and restored to church architecture its lost base, it was not only to Italy that artists turned, but also to their own Gothic past. This is particularly true of the Rhineland, where even the Jesuit churches follow in the tradition of the late Gothic basilica with galleries. The situation was similar in the diocese of Würzburg. Here, too, Renaissance spaces were given a Gothicizing dress.[7]

Compared to the Mannerist churches of the Rhineland and Franconia, Munich's St. Michael (1583–97) is much more of a piece. In this Jesuit church the Counter Reformation's victory in the north and Duke Wilhelm V's self-interpretation as the Catholic faith's most loyal defender found their triumphantly monumental expression. At first glance the spacious white interior with its Italianate ornament appears to have no antecedents north of the Alps. The break with local tradition seems to have been complete. Yet it would be a mistake to see St. Michael simply as a foreign import. Its originality is not diminished by a comparison with Italian examples, for instance with Il Gesù in Rome, which, as the mother church of the Jesuit order, provided an obvious model for the Munich church. When we compare the façade of St. Michael to Giacomo della Porta's slightly earlier façade we are struck more by what separates than by what links the Bavarian church to its Italian precursor (figs. 45 and 46). In both churches entablatures provide strong horizontals; but in St. Michael the broad attic of the Roman church is missing. Its place is taken by the second of three stories, the whole crowned by a steep gable, which lets the house of God look not altogether unlike an oversized burgher house. Gothic verticality triumphs over the horizontal. No attempt is made to follow the by-then-familiar scheme, first introduced by Alberti, that models the façade's first story on a triumphal arch and places on it a second story that only has the width of the nave, where large volutes are used to link the two stories and to hide the lean-to roofs of the aisles. Indeed, no such attempt could have been made in this case, for Alberti's scheme assumes a basilica. St. Michael, however, unlike Il Gesù and its predecessors, is a wall-pillar church. In this respect is takes up and transforms a native late Gothic tradition.

In the typical Gothic church the load of the vault is concentrated on the ribs and led down the piers. The thrust is spread to exterior buttresses, be they the flying buttresses of French cathedrals or the more modest step buttresses characteristic of fourteenth-century German brick churches. Brought inside the church, these buttresses become wall-pillars.[8] The most obvious advantage of the wall-pillar is that the vulnerable brick buttressing is now protected from the destructive action of ice and snow, an important consideration, given the wet, cold winters of Bavaria. If the wall-pillar is something of a constant in

45. Munich, St. Michael, façade

46. Rome, Il Gesù, façade

Bavarian late Gothic and post-Gothic architecture, it is first of all to the weather and to the building material that we have to look for an explanation. But important, too, is the way in which the wall-pillar scheme meets liturgical requirements. Just as the veneration of saints and their relics played a secondary, but nevertheless important, role in worship, the niches formed by the wall-pillars provide in a strikingly simple and effective way for side chapels, which accompany the nave focused on the high altar.

The presence of internal buttresses is not sufficient by itself to define the wall-pillar church. Wall-pillars, sometimes joined by galleries, are found in several of the large Gothic hall churches of Bavaria (fig. 47). The wall-pillar church eliminates the aisles of the hall church and thus simplifies and unifies the space, a natural step, given the quite modest size of all the late Gothic wall-pillar churches of Bavaria. A comparison of the plans of Elsenbach (late fifteenth century) and Perlach (1728–32) shows how small the distance can be between late Gothic and early rococo architecture (figs. 48 and 49).

The well-proportioned interior of St. Maria in Elsenbach reveals the essential properties of the wall-pillar church. Given a point of view near the entrance, wall-pillars projecting into the nave obscure the outer walls with their windows. The nave is provided with a light-filled mantle. Its boundary is rendered indefinite. Similarly, the play of the ribs obscures the vault, which functions as the inactive ground of the ornamental figure of the ribs. This figure counteracts the division of the nave into separate bays. Both the obscuring of spatial boundaries and the unification of the nave by the decoration of the vault remain essential features of the Bavarian rococo church. In Elsenbach the tension between the flowing pattern of the ribs and the architecture of the nave is most easily grasped in the abrupt way in which the net vault is cut off where the nave terminates and meets the choir. Just as the cut-off ribs of Benedikt Ried "bleed lines of force," this violent termin-

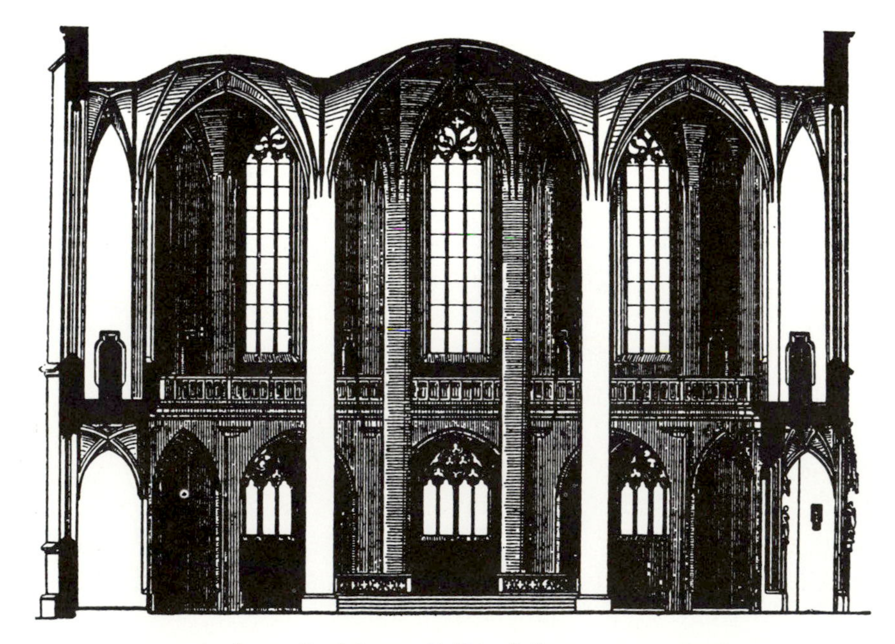

47. Amberg, St. Martin (1421–34), transverse section

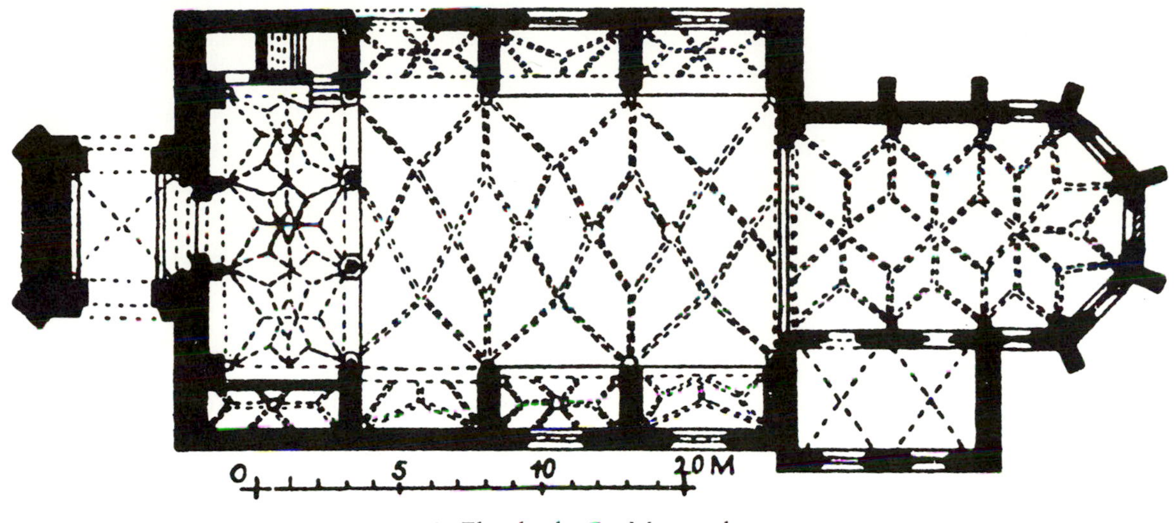

48. Elsenbach, St. Maria, plan

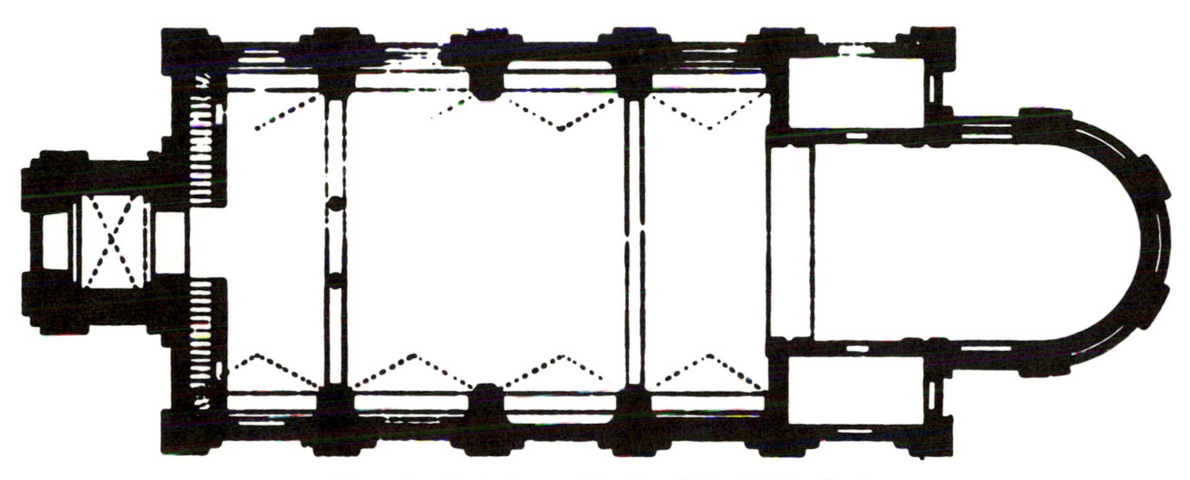

49. Munich—Perlach, parish church St. Michael, plan

ation of the vault suggests a movement that extends indefinitely beyond the choir arch. This handling of the termination of the vault returns in many churches built in the seventeenth century and even in the eighteenth.[9] It, too, gives us insight into the (in many respects) quite constant artistic intention of the Bavarians.

St. Michael is separated from such modest late Gothic precursors as Elsenbach or St. Johann in Neumarkt first of all by its much larger dimensions. The spaciousness of its nave, with a span of about sixty-five feet, had no local antecedents, and must have overwhelmed contemporaries.[10] Without precedent in Italy or Germany is the way the barrel vault rests on the transverse barrels joining the wall-pillars (fig. 53).[11] Simpler and more expected, given not only Italian practice but late Gothic tradition, would have been to lead the stress of the vault to the wall-pillars by severies cut into the barrel, a device that allows for better lighting and permits a shallower vault, but at the price of monumentality.

A glance at the floor plan suggests other obvious differences. The Bavarian wall-pillar churches of the fifteenth century join a simple choir to the nave. The same was true of the original design for St. Michael (fig. 50). But this design was changed after the collapse of the tower (1590), which the duke interpreted as an admonition by the archangel to build him an even larger, more splendid church. There is little doubt that the cruciform plan, according to which the church was finished, should be credited to Friedrich Sustris, the son of an Amsterdam painter associated with Titian. Sustris studied with Giorgio Vasari. Like so many foreign artists, he came to Munich by way of Augsburg and the Fuggers (fig. 51).[12]

Compared to Il Gesù (fig. 52) the cruciform plan, which commended itself to the architects of the Counter Reformation as particularly Christian, finds only a very modest realization in St. Michael. The transept, which does not project beyond the outer walls of the church, does not provide a very effective transverse axis. Its arms are too shallow to be experienced as much more than large niches. Similarly, the vertical provided in Il Gesù by a dome over the crossing in missing. As a result the crossing tends to become part of the nave, instead of being experienced as an independent centralized space, a third spatial unit, placed between choir and nave. In St. Michael the triumphal arch that frames the choir strengthens the bipolar character of the interior.

Curious, given Renaissance practice, is the way the pilasters of the wall-pillars reach only the height of the galleries, not much more than half the distance to the foot of the vault. The remaining part of the wall-pillars is structured by an extremely tall and quite unorthodox attica, which provides a weaker repetition of the pilaster order below and at the same time offers a transition to the vault (fig. 53). Compare the surprisingly feeble action of the cornice in St. Michael with the strength of its counterpart in Il Gesù, where it is a dominant motif, effectively separating the church into two zones (fig. 54). Given the Roman model, the handling of the cornice in St. Michael is likely to appear a somewhat awkward reminder that the Italian vocabulary had not yet been mastered; the overly tall attica seems a not quite convincing attempt to fill that part of the wall-pillars not structured by the Corinthian pilasters, which could not be stretched further without

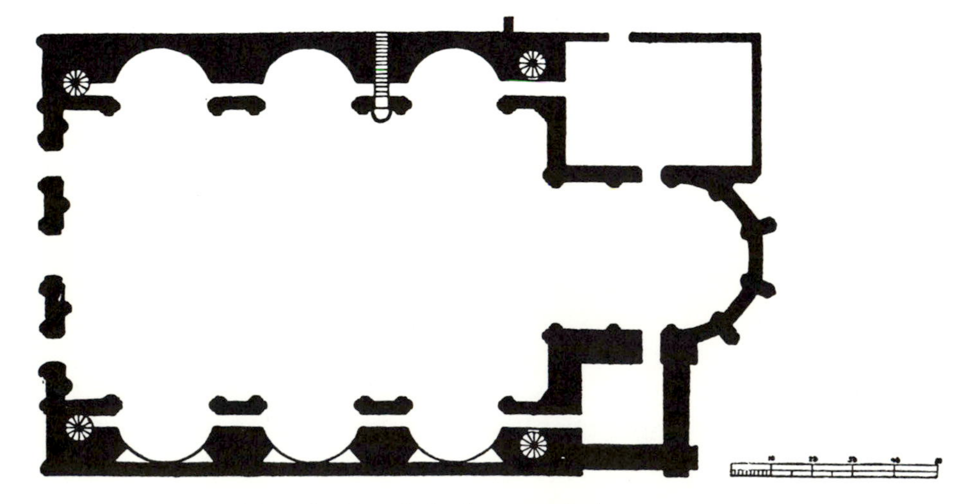

50. Munich, St. Michael, original plan

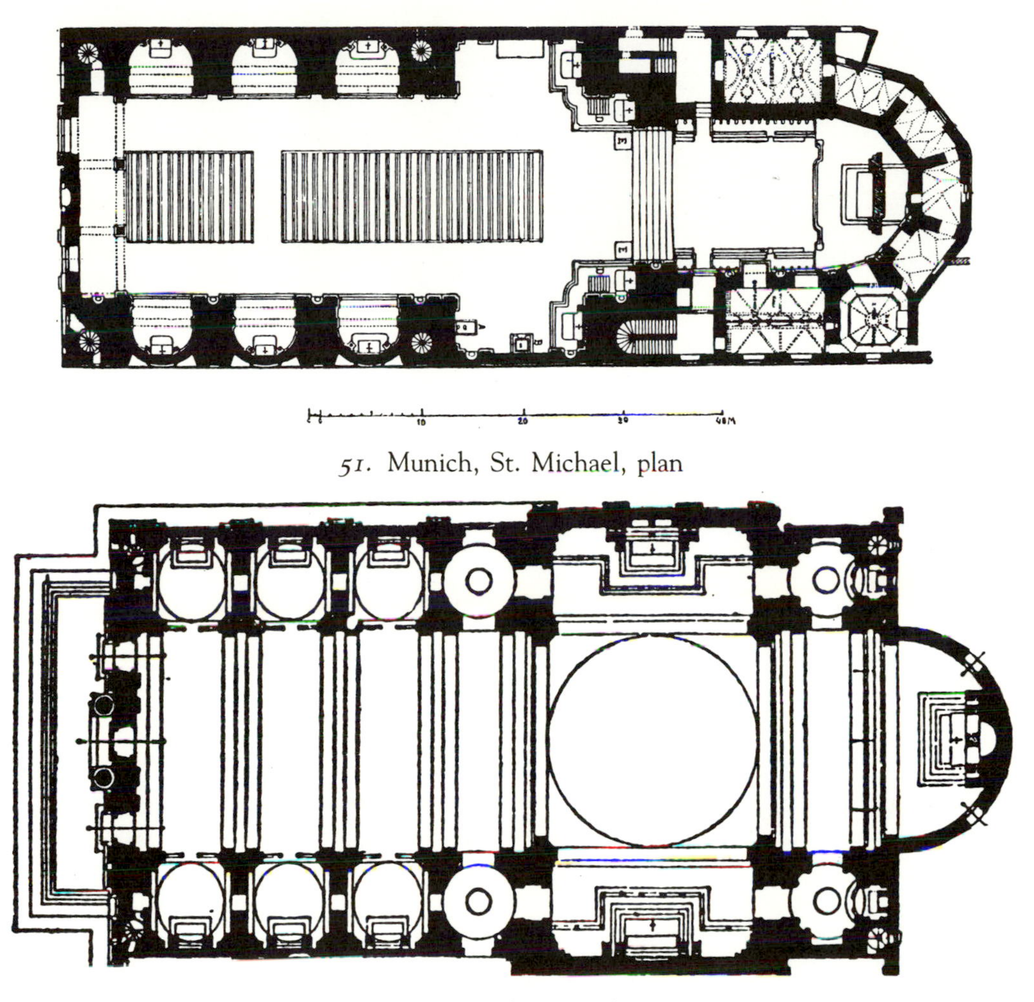

51. Munich, St. Michael, plan

52. Rome, Il Gesù, plan

losing all proportion. But to make this criticism is to do an injustice to the intention that speaks to us in this space. What links St. Michael to its Gothic precursors is above all the dynamic integration of wall-pillars and vault, which gives the church an organic quality that its Roman model does not possess.

Just as the Counter Reformation can be understood as a repetition of the old faith, but in a new key, so St. Michael repeats the traditional wall-pillar scheme, but with a difference that manifests itself both in the post-Tridentine spaciousness of the interior and in its Italianate decoration that recalls the coffered ceilings of the Renaissance rather than the flowing net vaults of late Gothic architecture.[13] In St. Michael, too, we sense something of the tension between Renaissance and late Gothic that characterizes the contemporary Gothicizing mannerism of the Rhineland and Franconia. But in the Munich church no attempt is made to clothe the space in a Gothicizing dress. Here it is the surface that is most obviously dependent on Renaissance models, while the space, especially the nave, retains something of the spirit of Gothic architecture. And yet to point this out is to do small justice to the transformation of this spirit. The originality of St. Michael invites us to forget its precursors.[14]

53. Munich, St. Michael, interior before World War II

54. Rome, Il Gesù, interior

An Influential Adaptation

The Bavarian baroque begins with St. Michael. The spacious splendor of its interior called forth numerous imitations, while its monumental scale assured that such imitations would offer reductions of the solution that had been found there; reductions in size and also, inevitably, in architectural complexity. That in these reductions the native Gothic tradition should manifest itself more strongly than in the Munich church is to be expected.

Of all these successor churches the Studienkirche in Dillingen (1610–17) is historically the most significant.[15] Its location helps to explain its importance. In 1546 the prince bishop of Augsburg, Cardinal Otto Truchsess von Waldburg, had founded here a school to better train the clergy of his diocese. Only five years later it became a university, which in 1563 was entrusted to the Jesuits. Quickly it established itself as one of the intellectual centers of the Counter Reformation, rivaling nearby Bavarian Ingolstadt. Many of those responsible for the churches that were to be built throughout Southern Germany received their education in Dillingen and carried with them the image of the church in which they had once worshiped.

More significant, however, is the way the Dillingen church simplified and reduced the model provided by St. Michael. This reduction, which is at the same time a translation into a more familiar idiom, helps to account for its impact on the church architecture of the seventeenth and eighteenth centuries in Southern Germany. Much of it can be considered a variation of the theme provided by the Studienkirche. A glance at the floor plan shows how the architect (the extent to which it is the work of Hans Alberthal has been questioned)[16] simplified the plan of St. Michael, where such simplification is also a return to the scheme exemplified by churches like Elsenbach or St. Johann in Neumarkt. Gone is even a rudimentary transept. The choir is not much narrower than the nave. As a result the Studienkirche offers us a more unified interior than St. Michael (fig. 55).

Very different in the two churches is the treatment of the wall-pillars. In St. Michael their breadth, coupled with the galleries and the expanse of the vault, provides the nave with comparatively firm boundaries. The side chapels are experienced as dark niches cut into the nave wall, while the similar niches above the gallery function as bright light cells. The *wall* remains alive in the wall-pillar. In Dillingen, on the other hand, it is once again the *pillar* in the wall-pillar, which in Gothic fashion triumphs over the wall (fig. 56). The elimination of galleries in Dillingen contributes to this effect. No longer do their horizontals impede the upward thrust of the wall-pillars. The vault of the Studienkirche is less monumental and more traditional than St. Michael's. As in countless earlier and later churches, severies cut into the barrel, which is much shallower than its Munich counterpart. Rather as in a hall church, the peak of the side chapels is not much lower than the peak of the nave vault. Proportionately much larger windows fill the church with a strong light.

The present appearance of the interior is determined by the rococo decoration of 1750. Its success shows how easily the baroque space is adapted to rococo taste. Characteristic is the elimination of the central rib-band at the later date, allowing for a fresco spanning the central two bays of the nave, which further unifies the interior. Equally characteristic

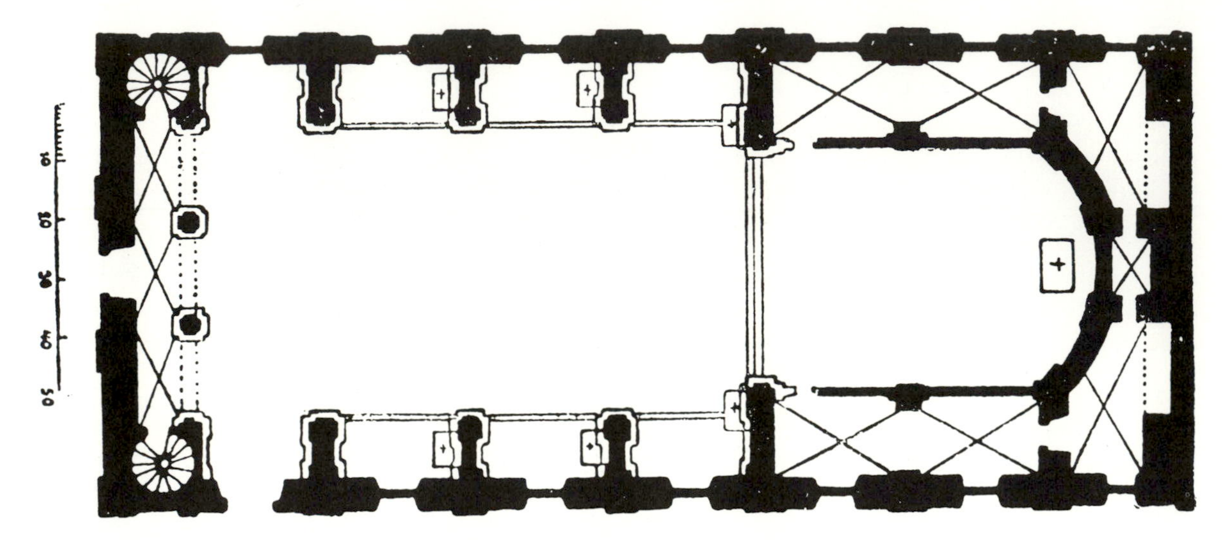

55. Dillingen, Studienkirche, plan

is the way the wall-pillars now function like the wings of a theatrical set. The effect is heightened by the side altars placed before them. Together these altars form a zone of painting, framed by sculpture and ornament, analogous to the similarly framed fresco zone of the vault yet separated from it by a white zone that has its center in the gleaming entablature. The large high altar is both focus and climax of the altar zone and at the same time furnishes a ladder linking it to the painted heaven of the vault.

Constitutive of the rococo church is the primacy of a point of view near the entrance, which allows the church's interior to be seen as a pictorial whole that has its center in the high altar. To be sure, in a church like Dillingen, this pictorialization of architecture, which lets us almost forget that the wall-pillars must have substance and solidity to bear the weight of the vault, is largely the work of the decorators of the eighteenth century. But imagine St. Michael dressed up in a rococo gown. There can be no doubt that its architecture would have resisted such transformation. The wall-pillars there, to give just one example, could never have gained the winglike appearance of their counterparts in the Studienkirche; it would have been impossible to construct a similarly effective altar zone. Not that the decoration of the Studienkirche is in any way extraordinary. Most of the larger rococo churches follow a similar pattern—a particularly successful example is provided by the interior of Diessen, which I consider in some detail in chapter 5. Here I am more interested in the common languages of Bavarian baroque and rococo architecture. By translating the achievement of St. Michael into the vernacular, the Studienkirche in Dillingen did much to establish that language.

The wall-pillar scheme continues to dominate the church architecture of the eighteenth century. Giovanni Antonio Viscardi's abbey churches in Neustift and Fürstenfeld, both begun just after the turn of the century, provide the splendid beginning (fig. 57). The festive grandeur of the latter recalls St. Michael, as do many details; the placement of the cornice and the tall attic deserve to be singled out.[17] Less imaginative architects were content to repeat with little change a time-honored model: Holy Cross in Landsberg am

56. Dillingen, Studienkirche, interior

Lech (1752–54), another Jesuit church, can serve as an example. Architecturally undistinguished, yet pleasing in its spacious harmony, its indebtedness to Dillingen is apparent. Results were much more exciting where the wall-pillar church offered only a point of departure, a basic theme that could be varied, for instance, by reintroducing galleries, a transept, perhaps even a dome; or by playing with the width of the bays or the depth of the wall-pillars. I shall have to return to some of these variations. Here I would like to recall the five criteria that Bernhard Rupprecht establishes for the Bavarian rococo church.[18] The three that pertain most directly to its architecture, as opposed to fresco and ornament, are readily met by a wall-pillar church of the Dillingen type: it provides for a central space, illuminated by indirect light; it leaves the boundaries of this space indefinite; and it gives special significance to a point of view near the entrance. All three criteria give special emphasis to the eye. In such late Gothic wall-pillar churches as Elsenbach or St. Johann in Neumarkt the observer's point of view is already very much taken into account; that theatricality, which triumphs in rococo architecture, makes an appearance (figs. 1, 27, 43, 112).

Transformations of the Hall Choir

A feature of the Studienkirche that deserves special mention is its hall choir. A radical departure from the model provided by St. Michael, it inaugurated a tradition that culminated in the choir of Die Wies.

The hall choir, too, has its origins in late Gothic architecture. It can be traced back to such Austrian Cistercian churches as Heiligenkreuz and Zwettl.[19] The choirs of Heiligkreuz in Schwäbisch Gmünd (1351–1410), of St. Sebald (1361–79) and St. Lorenz (1439–77) in Nürnberg, and of the Franciscan church in Salzburg (1408–ca. 1460) are well-known examples (figs. 58 and 59). Especially the last deserves a few comments here. This late work by Hans von Burghausen[20] reminds us once again of the extent to which the spatial imagination of the Bavarians remains constant beneath stylistic change, and raises the question of how to account for such constancy. In what way do climate and landscape shape the spatial imagination of a people? And to what extent is it possible to separate spatial and religious imagination? Are the patterns of Bavarian piety linked to this landscape before the Alps, with its wet, cold winters and that peculiar sense of distance, granted by mountains that are present even when weather conditions are such that they cannot be seen? The term *genius loci* points to a phenomenon that still awaits adequate analysis.

The Salzburg church exploits the contrast between the dark, earthbound nave, dating from the early thirteenth century and still Romanesque in feeling, and the choir, in comparison almost weightless, that attracts us with its light, beckons us forward, and yet remains visually too remote to encourage entry (fig. 60). Long before the Asam brothers' Weltenburg (fig. 99) Hans von Burghausen has pictorialized architecture; here already the altar room has become stagelike. Two motions rule this space: forward in the nave, upward in the choir. We participate in the first, horizontal motion, as we approach the high altar; vertical motion belongs to a sacred realm, which we are allowed to glimpse,

57. Fürstenfeld, Cistercian abbey church, interior

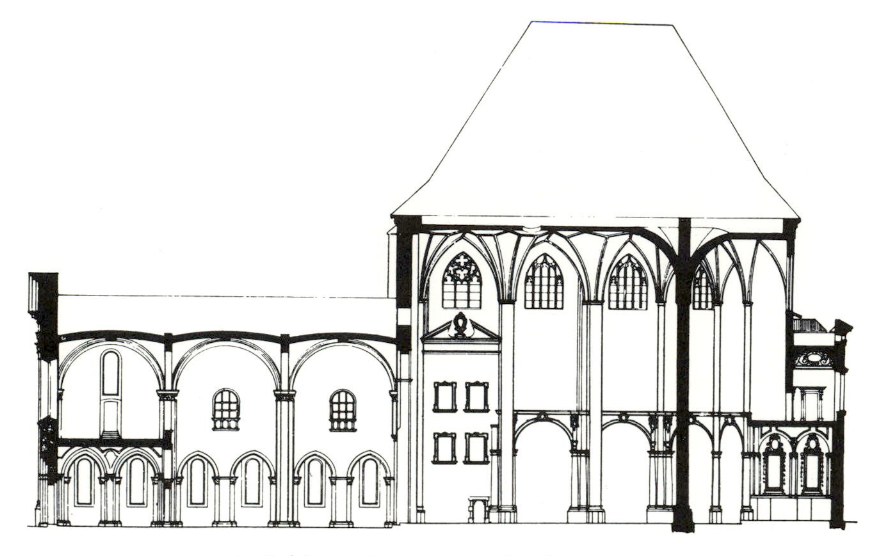

58. Salzburg, Franziskanerkirche, section

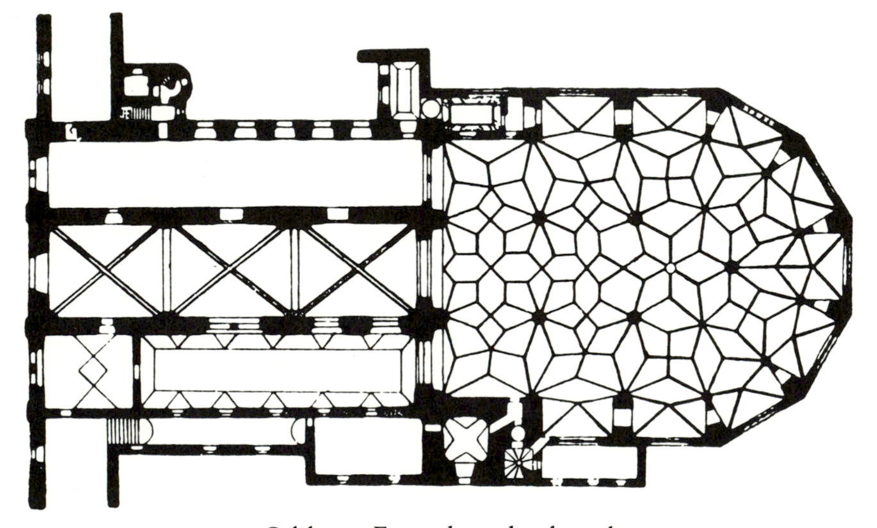

59. Salzburg, Franziskanerkirche, plan

but from which we are excluded. Drawn to the bright choir, the eye is led upward by its rising columns. The unusually tall and narrow choir arch lets us see only part of the choir. The implied whole remains hidden from view and mysterious, its boundaries indefinite. Visually the choir lacks closure. Together with its mysterious light, this lack of closure functions as a sign of transcendence. Here we have a key not only to that fascination with different possibilities of rendering spatial boundaries indefinite that is something of a constant in the sacred architecture of Bavaria, but to the way this fascination finds its natural focus in the choir, which possesses its center in the high altar—in the case of the Franciscan church in Salzburg an impressive baroque construction by the greatest architect of the Austrian baroque, Johann Bernhard Fischer von Erlach (1709)—and a spatial autonomy that establishes it as a sacred other to the nave. Within the sacred architecture of the church, the different spatial quality of nave and choir mirrors the

60. Salzburg, Franziskanerkirche, interior

distance that separates the human and the divine. The choir's numinous quality is enhanced by the choir arch, which not only limits what we can see and thus renders the architecture of the choir elusive, but, like a frame, pictorializes it and renders it unreal.

Built two hundred years after the choir of the Salzburg church, the hall choir of the Studienkirche is much more modest and less theatrical. Its width serves to assimilate it to the nave. The dramatic juxtaposition of choir and nave has been subordinated to a baroque insistence on unity. The decoration and furnishing of the rococo strengthen this unity by interpreting it in pictorial terms. Yet within the picture that presents itself to us as we enter the church the choir appears as a sacred other, distinguished from the nave by its hall form, suggested perhaps by the traditional association of that form with sacred architecture.[21] It is easy to overlook that the choir is a hall. Only as the eye travels upward toward the vault does this become apparent. While at ground level the walls joining the pillars provide for closure and darkness, above the galleries the space opens up. Bright and without definite boundaries, this inaccessible upper zone contrasts dramatically with the more confined, darker space below (fig. 61). This ascent from dark to light prepares for the upward movement of the high altar with its painting of the Virgin ascending to heaven.

The two-storied choir of the Studienkirche provides a much imitated model. We find its successors especially among pilgrimage churches, which have to furnish a path that leads the procession of the faithful around the venerated image. One solution is to exhibit the sacred image on a gallery leading around the choir. The late Gothic church of Andechs had such a gallery.[22] When the Augustinians of Polling redecorated their church in the early seventeenth century, they adopted this model. The ancient and much venerated image of the Crucified was raised above the main altar. Much more theatrical than in Dillingen is the use of light (fig. 62). Recalling the choir of Dillingen, the three bays of the old choir are transformed into a two-storied space that with its arcaded upper story opens to the sacristy and a chapel. Like a proscenium, this comparatively dark space both links and separates the nave and the new light-filled altar room (fig. 63).

Following the example set in Dillingen, the hall choir retains its popularity through the seventeenth century. We find it thus, a few years after Polling, in the nearby and also Augustinian Beuerberg (1629–35). After the Thirty Years War it returns in Gars (1661–62).[23] Especially the architects from the Austrian Vorarlberg liked to employ it. Schönenberg, Obermarchthal, and Irsee present it in particularly convincing fashion. In

61. Dillingen, Studienkirche, hall choir

62. Polling, Augustinian priory church, interior

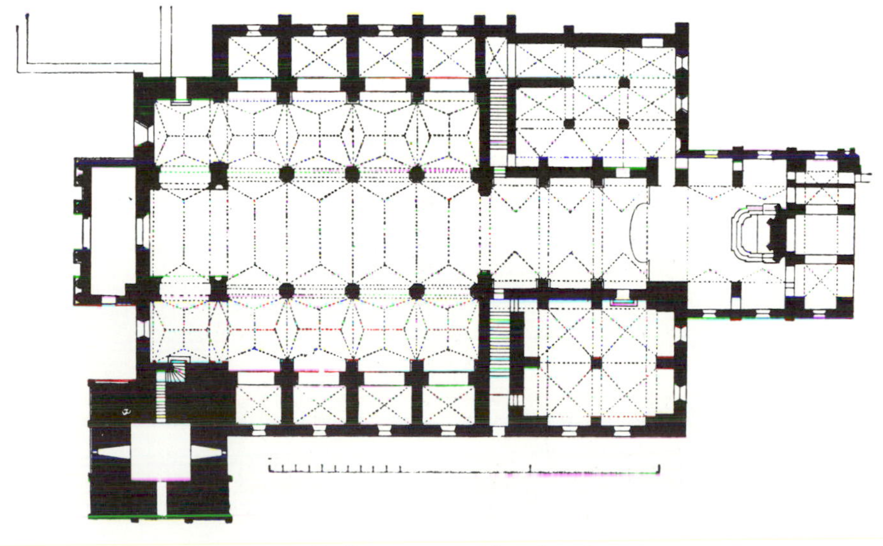

63. Polling, priory church, plan

each of these Swabian churches the hall choir is separated from the wall-pillared nave by a strongly articulated transept.[24] Spiritually and geographically closer to Polling is the pilgrimage church in Vilgertshofen (1686–92), built and decorated by the Wessobrunner Johann Schmuzer (fig. 64).[25] Dominikus Zimmermann's church in Günzburg and Die Wies demonstrate the affinity between the rococo church and the hall choir (fig. 65).

Plate 7

Despite the last two examples, the hall choir is more characteristic of baroque than of rococo architecture. What makes me dwell on it here is not so much the particular solution it provides as the intention of which it speaks: the desire to establish the sacred quality of the choir by treating it as a quasi-autonomous entity, possessing a more elusive, more pictorial spatial reality than the nave. That intention continues to shape the rococo church. To use Wölfflin's terminology, more than the nave the choir tends toward painterly, atectonic, open forms. Often, as in St. Johann in Neumarkt and again in Polling, a darker proscenium is interposed between the stagelike altar room and the nave. The former is rendered elusive by its indefinite boundaries and the mysterious presence of light. Here the vertical triumphs more completely over the horizontal than in the nave.

This bipolar conception of the church leaves little room for a strong transept, crowned by a full dome that gathers together nave and choir. Where a transept appears in a

64. Vilgertshofen, pilgrimage church, interior

65. Die Wies, pilgrimage church, choir

Bavarian church of the baroque or rococo it tends to be weakly developed, a somewhat wider bay that may function as a proscenium (see fig. 51). This helps to explain the Bavarians' resistance to the model provided by Santino Solari's cathedral in Salzburg (1614–28), a cruciform basilica with a full dome over the crossing. For the first time in the region the tradition that lead from Alberti's St. Andrea in Mantua to Il Gesù had found a convincing, if somewhat chilly, representative. After the Thirty Years War Agostino Barelli's Theatinerkirche in Munich (1663–88) confronted the Bavarians with an even stronger demonstration of the power of the dome above the cross (figs. 66 and 67). It met with the same reception.

In part, no doubt, Bavarian resistance to the dome is to be explained by the same climatic conditions that argue for the wall-pillar. But the Bavarians' bipolar and theatrical conception of the church also has to be kept in mind. This preference shows itself when we examine those isolated cases where Bavarian architects did adopt the Italian motif of the dome. We encounter a tendency to raise the dome not above the crossing, but above the choir.

An early, not altogether successful, but nevertheless revealing example is provided by the parish church in Weilheim, in many ways one of the most interesting (which is not to say most successful) churches of the early seventeenth century.[26] Once again nave and choir possess a very different spatial quality. The broad and heavy barrel vault emphasizes the horizontal, while the slender choir arch directs us toward heaven (figs. 68, 69, and 70). Its upward thrust is answered by the very modest eight-sided dome above the altar, which remains totally submerged beneath the large roof of the church and therefore lightless and ineffective. Here, too, a prosceniumlike antechoir joins nave and altar room.

A much later and stronger example of the choir dome is provided by St. Jakob (1717–24) in Innsbruck, the work of Johann Jakob Herkommer and his nephew Johann Georg Fischer, both from Füssen. The choir dome, one of the few full domes erected by a German architect in the seventeenth or eighteenth centuries, is all the more remarkable here because St. Jakob follows a cruciform plan, which leads one to expect a dome above the crossing; but there we find only a shallow saucer dome. Its darkness makes it difficult to understand the crossing as the center of this interior.[27] Although Cosmas Damian Asam did paint an illusionistic architecture in the place of the missing dome, it offers little more than a foil for the real dome beyond. Someone standing in the nave is given only hints of the latter's existence and shape. As in the Franciscan church in Salzburg or in the parish church of Weilheim, the choir is conceived as a quasi-autonomous space, governed by a vertical movement that terminates in an indefinite beyond. Standing in the nave we are allowed to glimpse this space, but are excluded from it. The light that floods the choir from above helps to enhance its sacred character.

St. Jakob is an isolated example. Especially in the eighteenth century Bavarian architects avoid the full dome. The Bavarian rococo demands less compartmentalized, more unified spaces. And yet this desire for what Wölffin calls "unified unity" had to be reconciled with the demand that the choir be established as more sacred than the nave. The attempt at reconciliation of the desired homogeneity and the heterogeneity demanded by the separate functions of nave and choir helps to define the Bavarian rococo church. The

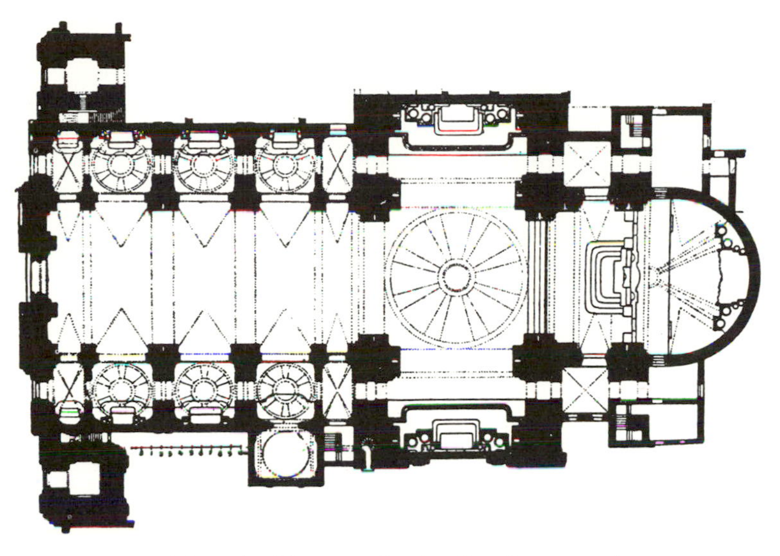

66. Munich, Theatinerkirche St. Cajetan, plan

67. Munich, Theatinerkirche, dome

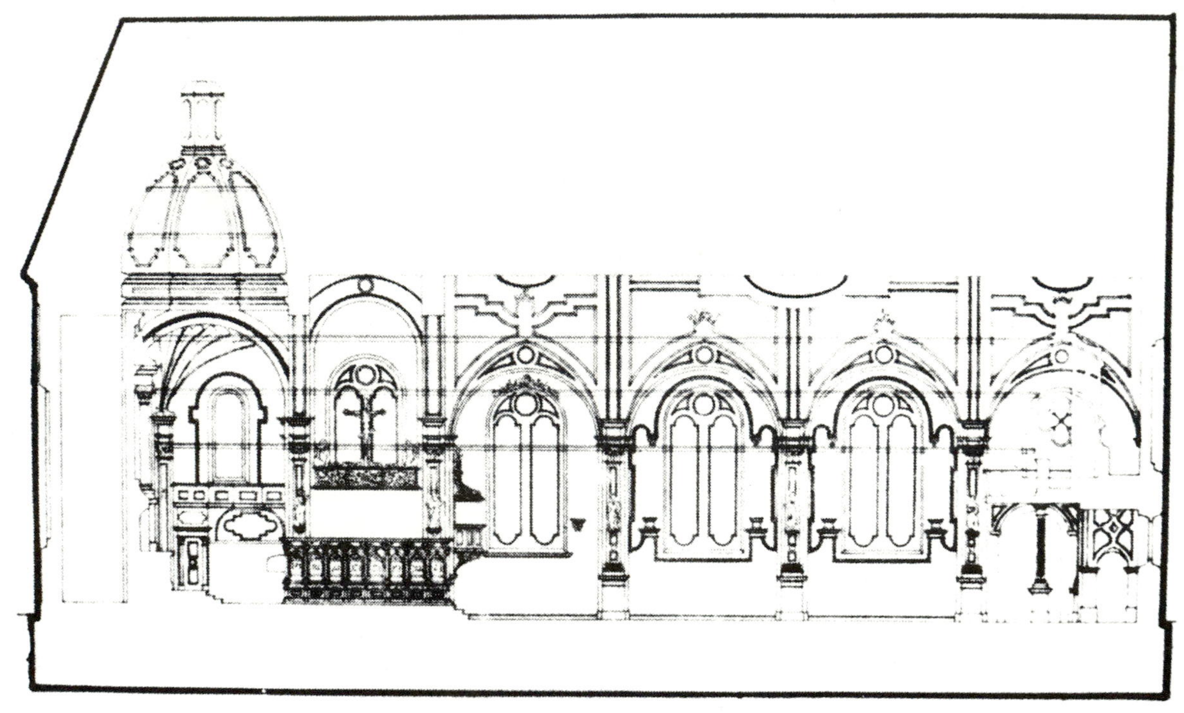

68. Weilheim, parish church St. Mariae Himmelfahrt, section

69. Weilheim, parish church, interior

70. Weilheim, parish church, choir dome

privileged point of view near the entrance easily lets us forget the tension between the two considerations: to someone entering the church the interior presents itself as a picture that has its center in the vertical of the high altar. But as we step forward this pictorial unity weakens. Especially in larger churches the choir will increasingly assert its autonomy and be experienced as a pictorial whole. The choir of the Bavarian rococo church presents itself to us as a picture within a picture.

What was said in the first two chapters about the rococo fresco and its frame of stuccoed ornament does indeed fit the large frescoes that span and help to unify the naves of the churches of the Bavarian rococo. In these frescoes we tend to find landscape elements that demand a horizon distinct from the horizon implicit in our own standpoint. The world of the fresco presents itself to us as a second world, parallel to the world in which we live. This pictorial parallel helps to support the horizontality of the nave. But the choir frescoes tend to follow a very different type. Here the more illusionistic glory compositions of the Italian baroque continue to provide the model.[28] The fresco is experienced somewhat like a hole cut into the vault that permits us to glimpse the heavenly realm, which appears, not as a second world paralleling our own, but as the extension of our world into heaven. In the choir the vertical triumphs over the horizontal. A ladder links the here and now to the beyond.

Once again Steinhausen is typical. In the choir Johann Baptist Zimmermann painted God the Father and the Holy Spirit, surrounded by archangels and a heavenly orchestra, awaiting the Son. The painted balustrade strengthens the illusionism of the fresco. In characteristic fashion it provides the terminus, itself indefinite, for the strong vertical that links the tabernacle, the much venerated Gothic Pietà, the high altar painting of the Deposition, and the smaller painting in the altar gable showing Christ rising triumphantly toward heaven (fig. 71), one of many rococo variations on the theme stated by the Franciscan church in Salzburg.

To give just one more example (to which I return in chapter 5): At Diessen the fresco of the choir's saucer dome has a strong ringlike frame. Unlike the scalloped frame of the main fresco, this lets us see the painting as a circular opening through which we are allowed to glimpse something of the glory of heaven, in this case a heavenly assembly of those members of the house of Diessen and Andechs who are counted among the blessed and saints (fig. 115).

As the floor plans of Steinhausen and Diessen make clear (figs. 72 and 113), the choir's quasi-autonomy is recognized not only by the fresco but by the architecture. In Steinhausen the oval architecture of the nave is separated by the easternmost pair of pillars from the transverse oval of the choir. In Diessen, too, the choir is treated as a centralized space that possesses its own integrity. Typical of Bavarian developments is the way the choir is divided into two parts: a square bay covered by a saucer dome is placed like a proscenium before the semicircle of the apse filled by the high altar. Like the church as a whole, the choir is articulated as a two-part structure: nave is to choir as antechoir is to altar room (fig. 73).

A glance at the floor plans of rococo churches shows that such treatment of the choir is not at all unusual; indeed it is the norm, at least in larger churches.[29] Again and again

71. Steinhausen, pilgrimage church, interior

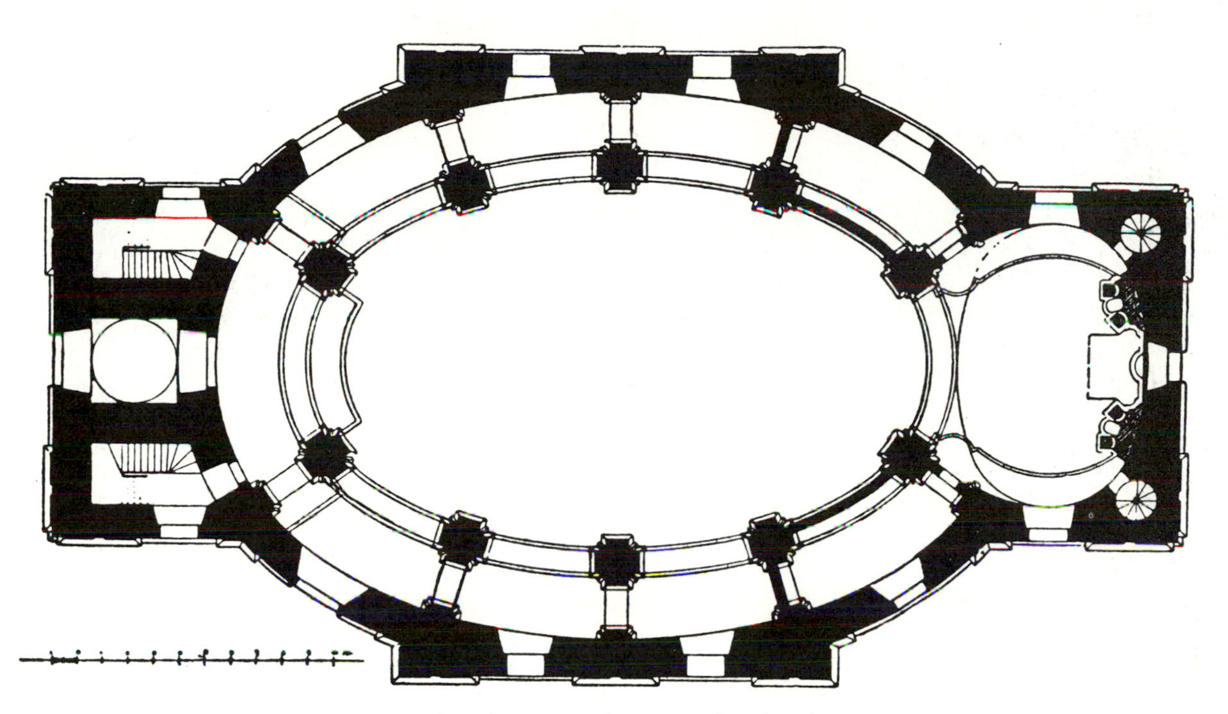

72. Steinhausen, pilgrimage church, plan

we find saucer domes or designs that exploit the centralizing power of octagon, circle, or oval. The different spatial quality of nave and choir is emphasized by the choir arch, which, like a proscenium arch, transforms the choir into a stage, the nave into an auditorium. That this reference to the theatre is intended is shown by the common practice of decorating the choir arch with a stuccoed curtain, as in Diessen. The use of indirect light and the obscuring of spatial boundaries, either by placing them in a way that hides them from someone standing in the nave or by obscuring them beneath fresco and ornament, help to transform tectonic into painterly values.

The average village church, which joins a rectangular nave to a narrower choir, does not permit such elaborate solutions. And often an older, usually late Gothic structure was redecorated. The success of many of these interiors shows that, while the Bavarian rococo has indeed produced a distinctive architecture, ornament, fresco, and furnishings are sufficient to let us speak of a rococo church. Crucial is the turn from tectonic to pictorial, or should we say to theatrical, values. The difference between choir and nave is interpreted in a manner that suggests the difference between stage and auditorium. To the choir's quasi-autonomy corresponds the quasi-autonomy of the nave.

Plates 4, 8, 13

Versions of the Centralized Nave

The desire to centralize not only the choir but also the nave is a defining characteristic of the Bavarian rococo church. It leads to the demand that the nave vault be treated as a unified whole. By itself, of course, this is hardly novel. Already the net-vaults of such late Gothic churches as Elsenbach or St. Johann in Neumarkt counteract the division of the nave into bays. And while the Italianate decoration of churches like

73. Osterhofen, Premonstratensian abbey church, interior

St. Michael or the Theatinerkirche subordinates itself to and reinforces the articulation of the nave into bays, Bavarian decorators never seem to have felt quite comfortable with such compartmentalization.

Their very different intentions become clearer when we compare the decoration of St. Michael with that of the Augustinian church (ca. 1630) in Beuerberg (fig. 74). Its dependence on the model provided by the Munich church is evident. But in Beuerberg the simple stuccoed frames spread evenly across the vault and somewhat in the manner of late Gothic net-vaults help to unify the nave. Not that rib-bands have disappeared altogether; in expected fashion they rise from the pilasters of the wall-pillars. But instead of meeting at the peak of the vault to form a series of arches, separating bay from bay, they broaden into fields that straddle and thus join adjacent bays. By their repeating rhythm these stuccoed fields create a motion that extends itself indefinitely. As already in such late Gothic churches as Elsenbach, this creates a problem where the vault terminates. Given the pattern of the decoration, there is no reason why it should end just where it does. This unresolved tension between an ornamental pattern that extends itself indefinitely and its actual termination is common in Bavarian architecture of the seventeenth century.[30] It should be noted that such tension is quite easily avoided if one is willing to subordinate the decorative scheme to the articulation of the nave into bays. The Bavarians' refusal to do so becomes intelligible only when it is understood as an expression of a different artistic intention which resists the organization of the nave imposed by a succession of clearly defined spatial compartments.

The Bavarian rococo, too, resists compartmentalization of the nave. But it goes beyond the just-mentioned example in treating the nave vault as a *centralized* whole. The large frescoes so characteristic of the rococo church provide for such centralization. But long before Cosmas Damian Asam demonstrated the centralizing power of the large fresco by spanning several bays at Aldersbach attempts had been made to effect such unification by other means. Just after 1700 the vault of the Benedictine convent church at Holzen was treated as a centralized whole. Here for the first time an attempt is made to organize the decoration around the center of the vault. A fresco, still rather small, is used to mark that center.[31]

As the conflict between the Asam brothers' decoration and the architecture of Aldersbach shows, fresco and ornament often do not satisfy the demand for a centralization of the nave (fig. 27). Beyond what the decoration can furnish this demand invites architectural solutions. One obvious response is to ovalize a rectangular nave by rounding off its corners. Hitchcock considers the ovalized rectangle a defining feature of the rococo church, and suggests that it makes what is perhaps its first appearance in Bavaria in the unusually interesting parish church (1710) in Kreuzpullach (fig. 81).[32] Hitchcock emphasizes the part played by Johann Georg Fischer "in maturing a spatial form which quite a few other Germans had for several years been approaching without as yet realizing that form in a larger church interior."[33]

But it is misleading to place too much emphasis on the ovalized rectangle. I cannot agree with Hitchcock's characterization of Johann Georg Fischer's St. Katharina in Wolfegg as "one of the finest interiors of the opening years of mature rococo architecture in

74. Beuerberg, Augustinian priory church, interior

the mid-1730's" (figs. 75, 76, and 77).[34] Yet it is easy to understand what leads Hitchcock to praise the church and its architect. If we agree that the rococo can be characterized by its tendency away from the more articulated and tectonic architecture of the baroque toward roomlike spaces, where ceilings are kept quite flat and sharp corners and harsh transitions are avoided, it seems reasonable to argue that, following his teacher and uncle Johann Jakob Herkommer, Johann Georg Fischer arrived at a rococo architecture at a remarkably early date. Given the paradigm of the French secular rococo, this seems plausible enough. But the Bavarian rococo church speaks of very different intentions. It hardly takes roomlike clarity for its ideal. Just the opposite: the room form conflicts with the intention to obscure such spatial boundaries as walls or ceilings. In spite of the profusion of ornament and the enormous size of the fresco, in Wolfegg the pictorialization of architecture that is a defining characteristic of the Bavarian rococo church does not take place. The spacious broad nave speaks too strongly for this to happen. The wall-pillars are too weakly developed to wrap the nave in a spatial mantle. This lack of an effective mantle distinguishes the church in Wolfegg most decisively from the great churches of the Bavarian rococo.

The Bavarian rococo seeks not simply the ovalization of the nave, but the creation of an ovalized central space within a larger, usually rectangular space. The difference between the two provides for the desired mantle. Johann Michael Fischer's St. Anna im Lehel furnishes a good example (figs. 78 and 79). Eight white pillars, really wall-pillars, define

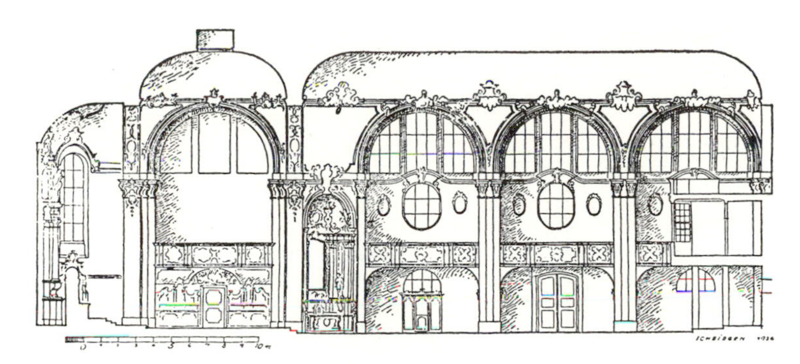

75. Wolfegg, St. Katharina, section

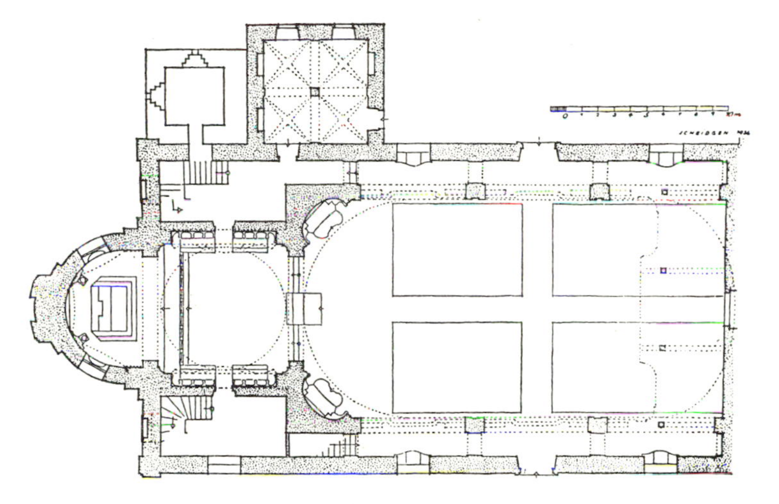

76. Wolfegg, St. Katharina, plan

77. Wolfegg, St. Katharina, interior

the central oval; they give the eye its first orientation and provide a moment of stability in an interior rendered restless by the wealth of color and indefinite by the uncertain outer boundaries. The shape of this oval is determined by two interlocking circles, their centers separated by their radius. But what determines our experience of this interior is not the simple geometry that governs it, but the way the white elements, the eight pillars and the arches joining them supported by the stuccoed frame, define a screen or figure on a much less definite ground or background. It is this pictorial figure-ground relationship that enables us to consider St. Anna im Lehel a rococo church, while in comparison the interior of Kreuzpullach, in spite of a number of striking anticipations of the rococo, seems quite baroque (figs. 80 and 81).

Dominikus Zimmermann's Steinhausen, almost exactly contemporary with St. Anna im Lehel, invites a similar analysis. Ten free-standing pillars here define the central oval, which is placed, not within a rectangle, but within a larger oval (fig. 72). If St. Anna illustrates the ovalization of the wall-pillar church, Steinhausen, and later Die Wies, illustrate the ovalization of the hall church (fig. 103).

More commonly it is not an oval but an octagon that is placed inside a larger rectangle. The parish church in Murnau offers a typical and influential early example (1717–34). Eight compound pillars carry a large saucer dome (fig. 82). The architect of the church is unknown. Enrico Zuccalli and Johann Mayr, the father-in-law of Johann Michael Fischer, have been suggested.[35] Recalling designs by Giovanni Viscardi, the interior states a theme on which such architects as Johann Baptist Gunetzrhainer and Johann Michael Fischer were to create numerous variations.[36] Fischer's churches in Ingolstadt, destroyed in the Second World War, Aufhausen (fig. 83), and Rott am Inn (fig. 84) rank with the best creations of the Bavarian rococo.

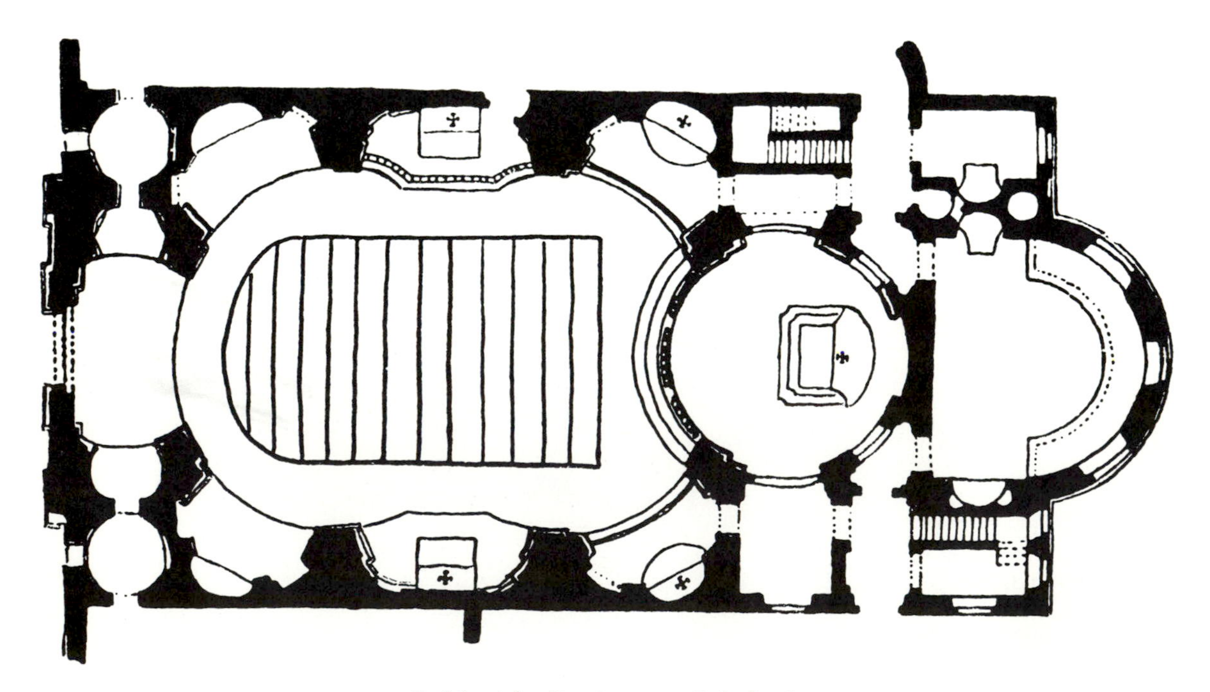

78. Munich, St. Anna im Lehel, plan

79. Munich, St. Anna im Lehel, interior as it appeared from 1951 to 1967

Fischer's work also illustrates how effectively this basic scheme could be applied to churches of very modest dimensions. The small church in Unering is particularly impressive. The plan recalls that of Murnau (fig. 85). Even the cruciform layout of the Murnau choir finds a modest echo. When we actually enter the church, however, it is not so much Murnau that comes to mind as St. Anna im Lehel. Built in 1732, the church in Unering was finished before the Munich church. Considering its much smaller dimensions and the limited means available it is astonishing how well Fischer succeeded in creating an interior that exhibits many of the key characteristics of the Bavarian rococo as well as many of the larger churches. To be sure, the fresco is rather disappointing and there is little stucco ornament. Yet I cannot agree with Hitchcock when he claims that there is little "early Rococo 'feeling.'"[37] Once again such disagreement presupposes a different assessment of what is essential to the Bavarian rococo church. It seems to me that what matters is not so much fresco or ornament as the pictorial quality of the space. Compare the way the white of the eight strongly articulated compound pillars combines with the white band of the scalloped picture frame to form an abstract ornamental figure set off against the more restless background with the way pillars and picture-frame function in St. Anna (fig. 86).

80. Munich, St. Anna im Lehel, interior before 1944

81. Kreuzpullach, Hl. Kreuz, interior

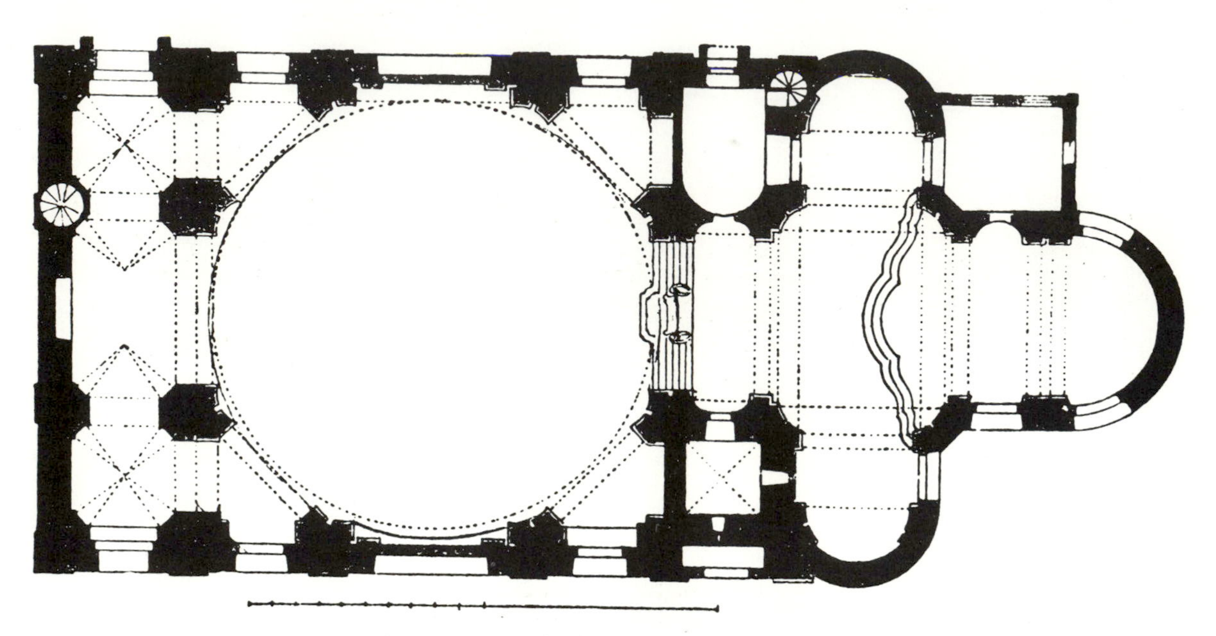

82. Murnau, parish church St. Nikolaus, plan

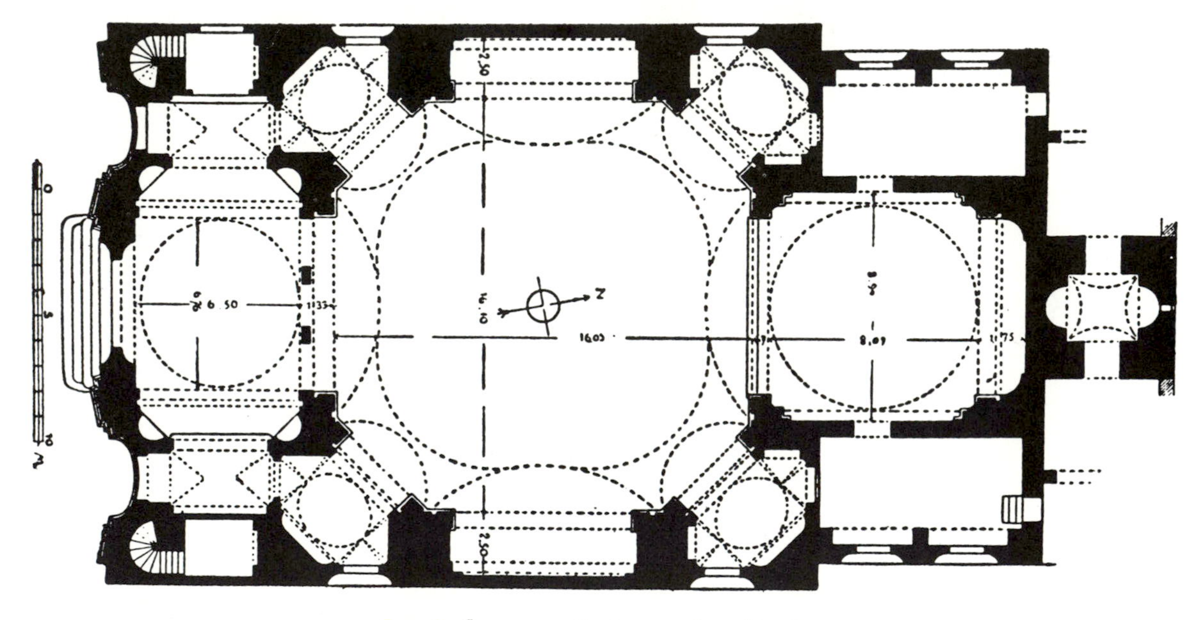

83. Aufhausen, pilgrimage church, plan

Well into the seventies many of the best churches follow this scheme of centralizing the nave by means of the octagon, often in direct dependence on the work of Johann Michael Fischer.

Yet another way of centralizing a wall-pillar nave is demonstrated in exemplary fashion by the Premonstratensian abbey church in Schäftlarn (fig. 43). Although Cuvilliés and Johann Baptist Gunetzrhainer were involved in the planning, once again Fischer's contribution would appear to have been decisive.[38] Here the centralization of the nave is achieved by varying the width of the bays and the depth of the wall pillars (fig. 87). A look

Plate 5

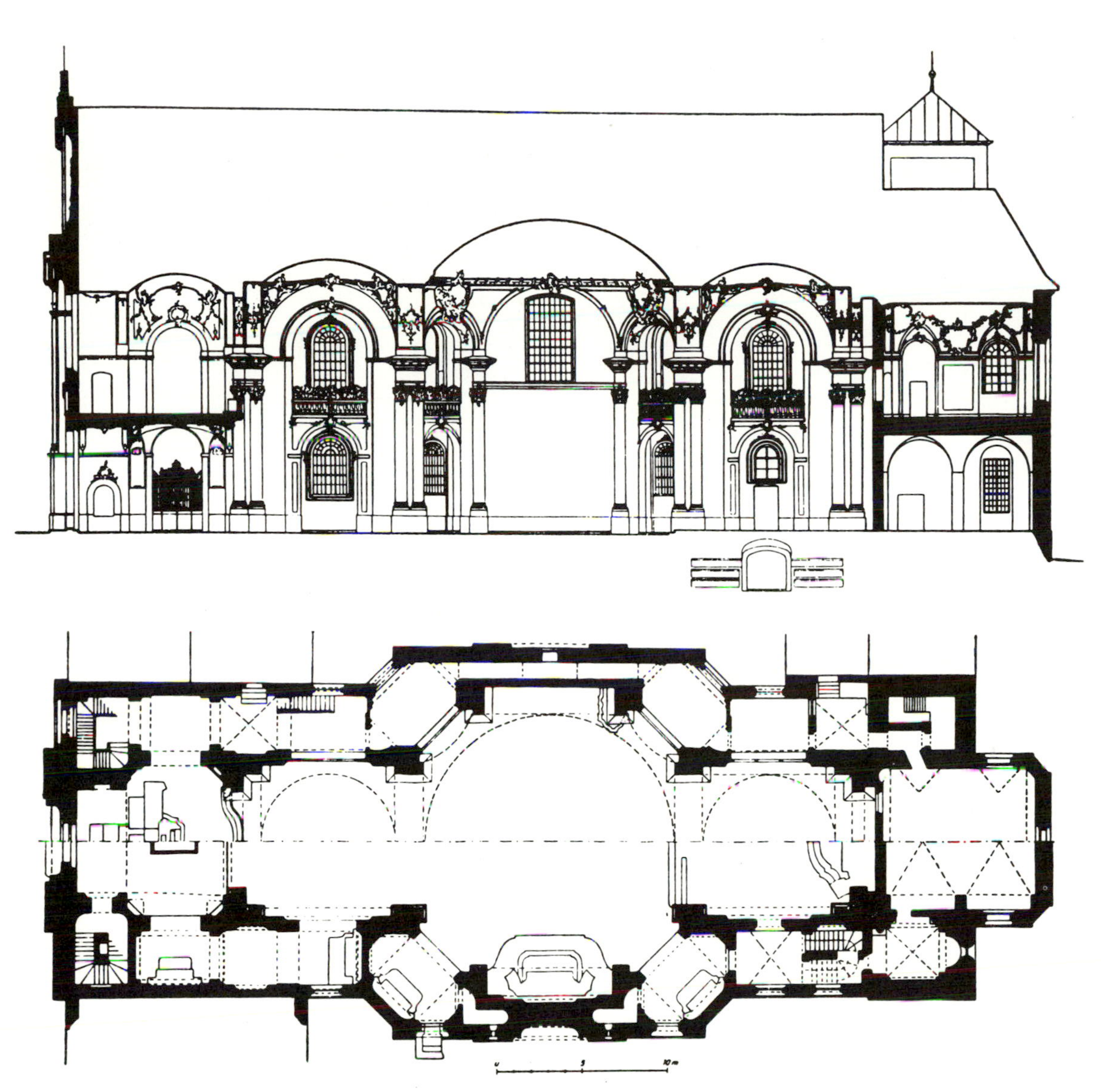

84. Rott am Inn, Benedictine abbey church, section and plan

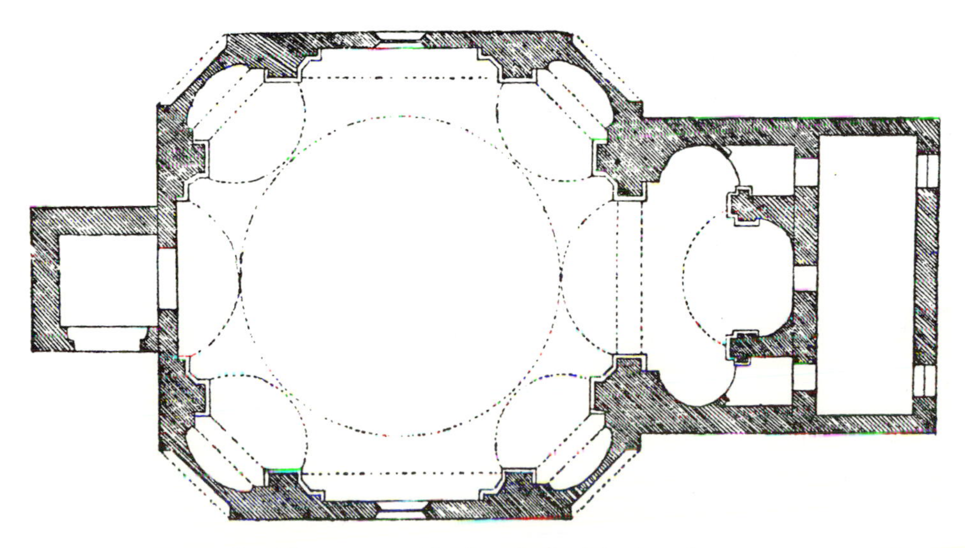

85. Unering, parish church St. Martin, plan

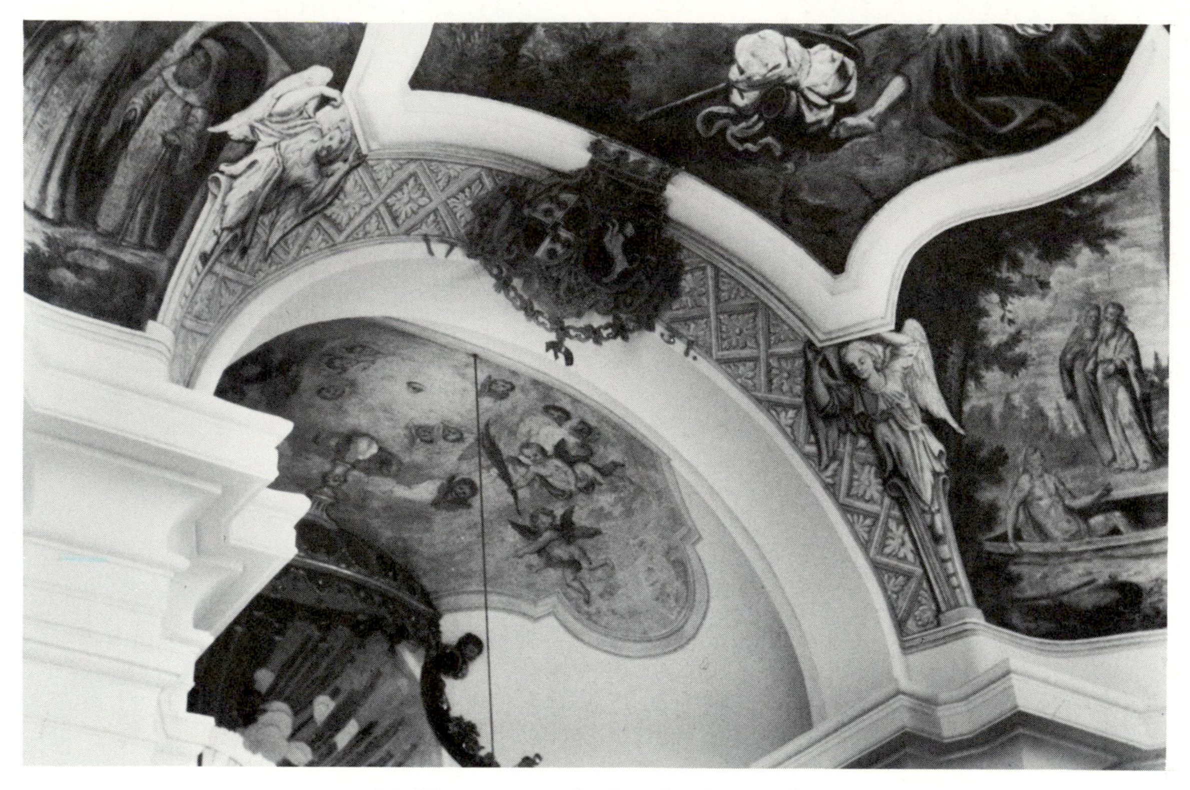

86. Unering, parish church, choir arch

at the plan shows the bipolarity of the church. The bay before the choir functions as a very weak transept, or rather as a prosceniumlike joint linking nave and choir. In the church Simon Frey built for the Augustinians of Suben (1766–70) Schäftlarn found a worthy successor.

Diaphanous Walls and Weightless Vaults

Hans Jantzen has spoken of the diaphanous structure of the Gothic cathedral. The term calls attention not only to the increased penetration of its nave walls, but to the ways piers and galleries, columns and arches form a seemingly weightless screen, a quasi-sculptural figure placed before a ground that may remain dark or appear as a foil of colored light.[39] The Bavarian rococo church invites a similar analysis: architectural, ornamental, and painted elements join in picturesque figures set off against a lucent, white ground; seemingly weightless pillars support tentlike vaults—an appearance heightened by the collusion of architect, decorator, and painter. As we have seen, a central space wrapped in a light-filled mantle provides a ready frame for such play.

But only churches of a certain size allow for the required complexity; the simple, more or less rectangular nave of the average village church rules out such solutions. Yet here, too, we find the same artistic intention at work. That the part of the architect would be much reduced, that of the decorator correspondingly greater, is to be expected: furnishings, ornament, and fresco join to place pictorial or ornamental figures before the paper white-

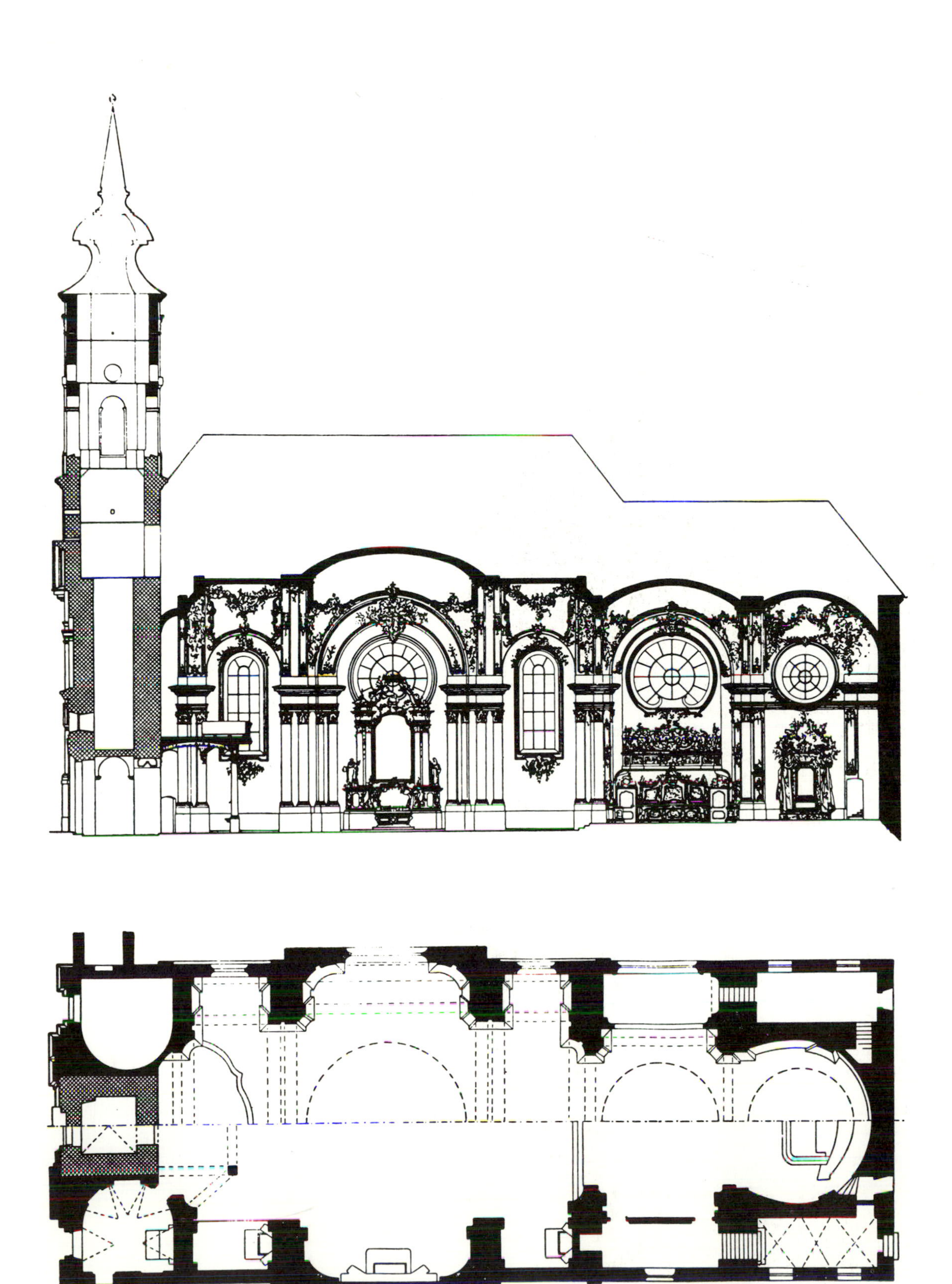

87. Schäftlarn, abbey church, section and plan

ness of the walls. More even than larger structures, these modest interiors show how important the plain white wall is to the Bavarian rococo church, or rather, how important it is to transform walls into an all-but-immaterial background, sensitive to every change of light outside. Everything is avoided that would lead us to experience the wall as solid boundary. The Bavarian rococo church thus resists articulation of the nave wall by pilasters and an entablature that would call attention to the wall as architecture. Where pilasters do appear they tend to play an ornamental part. Johann Michael Fischer's paired scagliola columns in Zwiefalten illustrate a common strategy to achieve such ornamentalization: pedestals and entablatures are kept simple and white; this isolates columns or pilasters—they begin to float, exchanging their tectonic for a more purely ornamental function (fig. 1).[40] Decisive is the contrast between marbled, usually red, scagliola and a white that lets us forget that the rococo church, too, is built with bricks and mortar; its walls are spiritualized as they appear to absorb the light pouring in. Is it too farfetched to link the rococo's intoxication with light to the old Christian interpretation of the cosmos as a veil diffused with divine light, and to interpret the gleaming white of its churches as a repetition and reflection of the light of heaven?[41]

The Bavarian rococo church demands many and large windows. Windows, however, tend to call attention to the walls into which they have been cut. This is less of a problem where it is possible to conceal windows by wrapping a central space in a mantle of light. But even when it is impossible to hide windows from view, their architectural reality can be obscured by treating them as if they were ornaments. Almost as much as the scalloped frame, the ornamental window is part of the vocabulary of the rococo church. Dominikus Zimmermann especially liked to give his windows ornamental shapes, most unforgettably in Die Wies: the windows grouped around the side altars form a figure of light, and the wall has little more substance than paper supporting an ornamental fantasy.[42]

Plate 6

It would be easy to continue. Especially Bavarian Swabia furnishes delightful examples: Franz Xaver Kleinhans's Liebfrauenkirche in Bobingen (1749–51) and Hans Adam Dossenberger's Theklakirche in Welden (1756–51) deserve to be singled out. Or consider the windows of St. Michael in Berg am Laim (1738–51). Compared with Zimmermann's extravagant window forms, Johann Michael Fischer's may at first seem rather sober and uninteresting. But this is a false impression. Faison calls our attention to the way "great lights are daringly cut right through the pendentive supports of the central space, and then by a stroke of genius contrasted with the smaller stucco reliefs of similar shape (representing the Church Fathers) in the lower choir space, which gets a strong side-lighting."[43] Both the daring and the parallel contrast serve to dematerialize the architecture, one by supporting the impression of almost weightless vaults, the other by inviting us to look at the large windows as if they were ornamental niches. The Bavarian rococo church depends on such metamorphic play that transforms architectural into ornamental or pictorial elements (fig. 88).

Schopenhauer insisted that

> it is absolutely necessary for an understanding and aesthetic enjoyment of a work of architecture to have direct knowledge through perception of its matter as regards its weight, rigidity, and cohesion. . . . If we were told clearly that the building, the sight of which pleases us, consisted of entirely different

88. Munich—Berg am Laim, St. Michael, interior

> materials of very unequal weight and consistency, but not distinguishable to the eye, the whole building would become as incapable of affording us pleasure as would a poem in an unknown language.[44]

The Bavarian rococo church is such a poem; its style is defined by the architectural lie. Consider its frescoed vaults: painting and decoration join to let us forget the materiality of the vaults and their supports. Particularly revealing is another Fischer church, the Premonstratensian abbey church of Osterhofen (1729–35). Once again the decoration is by the Asam brothers; as at Aldersbach, the middle three of the five bays of the nave of this wall-pillar church are united by one large fresco, here more rectangular and occupying an even larger part of the vault. But to speak of it simply as "more rectangular" misses the contribution made by the fresco's shape. To appreciate its originality a more detailed comparison with Aldersbach is instructive. In Aldersbach the first and the fifth bays have round, securely framed frescoes; clearly articulated rib-bands separate these bays off from the middle three and give them a certain unity of their own. In Osterhofen, too, we find such rib-bands, but now they no longer respect the architectural division of the nave into bays; they deviate from the positions that division would lead us to expect, pushing instead toward the center (fig. 89). This push seems to have "caused" the concave indentations of the main fresco, while the deflection of the rib-bands seems to have its "cause" in turn in an expansion of the smaller quadrilobed frescoes of the first and fifth bays, which have penetrated into the adjacent bays.

But to give such a description is to speak of the frescoes as if they were merely fields on the vault. The perspectival art of the painter does not let us see them as such. We experience the deflection not as horizontal, which of course it is, but as vertical; the space has begun to breathe, to lift itself; and since architecturally this lift makes no sense, we are left to feel that somehow the tectonic had here cast off its heaviness, as if the vault had become a sail lifted by some mysterious wind. I know few churches where fresco and stucco join so effectively to negate the heaviness of the vault.

In many later churches this look of weightlessness is enhanced by the widespread practice of constructing vaults not of stone, but of timber, lath, and plaster. In Bavaria the technique goes back at least to Johann Jakob Herkommer's St. Mang in Füssen (1710–17), but as Christian Otto remarks, "It was not until the 1730's that lath and plaster vaults came into their own. . . . The aesthetic consequence of this procedure can be demonstrated at Die Wies, where the Zimmermanns carved away and hollowed out the lower zone of the vaults to produce a hallucinatory effect in terms of stone technology (fig. 65)."[46] The architects of the Bavarian rococo like to do just what Schopenhauer would not have them do: presupposing expectations based on a much heavier and more difficult-to-use material, a church like Die Wies has to seem unnaturally light; its perforations and penetrations make for a magically diaphanous architecture that, while very sensuous, yet appears to have freed itself from the heaviness of matter (fig. 90). *Plate 7*

Pictorialization and Sacralization

Rupprecht rightly makes the pictorialization of the interior a defining characteristic of the Bavarian rococo church. The Bavarian rococo church is architecture that turns against architecture, that puts itself into question by becoming picture. But emphasis on its

89. Osterhofen, Premonstratensian abbey church, interior

pictorial character should not lead us to overlook its equally essential, if quite traditional, bipolarity. This bipolarity dictates that the degree of pictorialization not be the same throughout the church. Choir and nave should possess different degrees of reality: the pictorialization of the choir is more developed than that of the nave—raised to the second power, one might say.

In the Bavarian rococo church pictorialization is inseparable from sacralization; pictorial distance fuses with the distance that separates the sacred from the profane, a fusion that may let us wonder to what extent the Bavarian rococo church presupposes a willingness to sacrifice the sacred to the aesthetic. In this aestheticization of the sacred the death of an essentially sacred architecture begins to announce itself.

By itself the bipolarity of the church is hardly characteristic of the Bavarian rococo alone. As we have seen, it has a long prehistory, especially in Bavaria. Nor is the pictorial or theatrical treatment of the choir peculiar to the rococo. It is equally characteristic of the baroque and can be traced back to the late Gothic period. In this respect, too, the Bavarian rococo only takes up and develops a quite traditional theme, but the way in which it takes up and *plays* with this theme is peculiar to the time and to the region. To understand the Bavarian rococo church we have to understand the nature of this play.

90. Die Wies, pilgrimage church, southern gallery of the choir

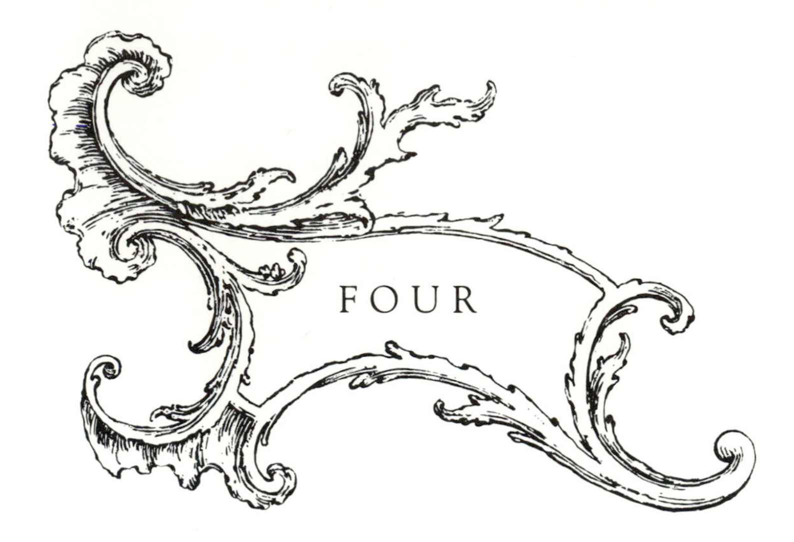

THEATRUM SACRUM

A Lesson of Two Tournaments

The use of ornament to create a mediating zone between fresco above and white architectural elements below helps to define the Bavarian rococo church. But why is such mediation demanded? Our analysis of the Bavarian rococo fresco provides at least a partial answer: unlike the illusionistic creations of a Pozzo, who uses his mastery of perspective to open the real space of the church to the glories of heaven above, the large frescoes of Bavarian rococo churches tend to raise a second earth, with its own heaven and its own horizon, above the earth to which we belong. To make this other earth seem real, the Bavarians adopted some of the devices of Italian illusionism, but such adoption had to remain incomplete. A consistent illusionism fuses pictorial and real space; the inconsistent illusionism of the Bavarians establishes a distance between the two and, in this respect, retains something of the character of panel painting. This marriage of illusionism and panel painting is never without tension. As the frescoes increase in size and the illusion becomes more convincing, it becomes more and more difficult to see them as panel paintings; and yet the appearance of a horizon on the frescoed vault makes it impossible to see the space of the painting as an illusionistic extension of the space in which we stand. As has been shown, this tension or ambiguity requires a new approach to the frame: illusionism demands that the frame be abolished, while panel painting invites it. The Bavarian rococo does neither. Instead it creates an ornamental framing zone that is weaker than the traditional frame in that it links the world of the fresco to the space in which we stand, but strong enough to create some distance between the two.

While this account answers some questions, it raises others. How are we to understand the ambiguity of this response to illusionism? It is almost as if artists like the Asam or the Zimmermann brothers could not take baroque illusionism quite seriously; so they began to play with it. This suggests that the rococo, at least in Bavaria, can be understood as a playful potentiation of the baroque that at the same time implies its negation. *In the rococo the baroque destroys itself.*

To give some plausibility to this thesis let us consider two examples that may at first seem far removed from the rococo church. Throughout the baroque and rococo period, tournaments continued to play an important part in the self-representation of the nobility and especially of the ruler, in spite of the fact that with the invention of gunpowder armor had become useless and tournaments an anachronism, "a romantic masquerade."[1] But precisely because the tournament had lost touch with everyday reality, it could acquire a more ideal significance. Instead of a sport that really tested the skill of the competitors, it became a ritual play in which the nobility presented to itself its own knightly ethos. As the play character was emphasized, increasing effort was spent on the theatrical frame that would help to establish the tournament's higher meaning, until finally this frame became more important than the tournament itself, which was now little more than an occasion for a theatrical transfiguration of the life of the court.

Munich witnessed such a tournament for the first time in 1654, two years after the marriage of the elector Ferdinand Maria to Adelaide of Savoy, who did so much to bring the high baroque to Bavaria.[2] The tournament was introduced by a dramatic presentation. Mercury and Mars claim special rights to the virtuous Elidauro, prince of Florida. To support his case Mercury points out that the prince had gained glory and honor by devoting himself diligently to the study of the arts and letters. Mars, he charges, is deflecting the prince from his path by tempting him with the promise of military glory and, even worse, by seducing him to the ways of love. Unmoved by these complaints, Mars exhorts the prince to battle in honor of love. Passionately enamored of Edilaleda, the *cavaliere di Marte* challenges Celidoro, the prince of Erida, known as a devotee of science and an enemy of love. The discord of Mercury and Mars offered thus the mythic background for the tournament, in which the elector himself took the part of Elidauro, leading a party showing the blue and white of Bavaria, while the part of Celidoro was taken by the elector's brother, Duke Max Philipp, whose followers sported the white and red of Savoy. The intent to glorify the elector is evident. The virtue and fame of this in fact rather boring ruler were shown to be such that they move even the gods to jealous squabbling. Not surprisingly, neither side gained a decisive victory. Sitting on the imperial eagle (it had been hoped that the emperor would attend the festivities) Jupiter bids Mercury and Mars, Elidauro and Celidoro, be friends. The harmonious ending shows how in the true ruler love, arms, and letters are inseparably joined.

The difference between baroque and rococo becomes tangible when we compare this tournament with another, held in 1723, eight years after Max Emanuel, his imperial dreams shattered, had returned to Munich from his French exile.[3] This time the frame was of a quite different sort: a carnival procession introduced the tournament, led by Count de Costa and Alois Fugger, dressed as Bacchus and Silenus. The tournament judges appeared as parliamentarians, while the two contesting parties were dressed, not as knights, but as hunters, peasants, moneylenders, Jews, old men on crutches, fools, and apothecaries. The procession included Scaramuccio and Brighella, Hanswurst, Pierrot and Harlequin.

A school class, complete with teacher, brought up the end. In keeping with the character of the event, the orchestra played on an odd mixture of toy and real instruments. Of course, we have to keep in mind the time of the year: It was carnival! But that was also true of the earlier tournament. Carnival had long offered a welcome occasion for the celebration of elaborate festivals. But only in the eighteenth century did the tournament turn into a playful parody. The theatrical performance with which the court had transported itself into a more ideal sphere and exhibited to itself its knightly ethos had ceased to convince. The rococo plays with the theatricality of the baroque which it can no longer take quite seriously. Theatre becomes meta-theatre.

That there are similarities between the Bavarian rococo's playful heightening and negation of baroque illusionism and this rococo tournament is too obvious to require discussion. Rococo religious art appears to have become an aesthetic game, suggesting that what had long been thought of utmost importance could no longer be taken seriously. How close the religious art of the rococo could come to parody is shown by an example to which Wilhelm Messerer calls attention: flanking the high altar of Berg am Laim we see the archangel Gabriel, his mouth opened to announce to the Virgin that she will bear the Son of God.[4] But the Virgin's place has been taken by a putto, who mimicks her traditional gesture, expressing humility and acceptance. In an open book we read *ECCE ANCILLA DOMINI*, "Behold the handmaid of God" (fig. 91).

Should we interpret the religious rococo of the Bavarians, too, as a playful parody of the sacred theatre of the baroque? I shall return to this question. But enough has been said already to show that the Bavarian rococo is not simply theatrical in the baroque sense, but plays with its theatricality. It is the nature of this play that must be understood if we are to understand the nature of the Bavarian rococo church.

Frescoes as Theatre

By now it has become a commonplace to speak of baroque and rococo art in terms of the theatre. And yet there is a sense that to do so is somehow to discredit that art. Wittkower, for example, after having demonstrated the proximity of the theatre to Bernini's Cornaro Chapel, a work that had a profound impact on the Bavarian rococo, feels that he has to defend Bernini against the charge of theatricality. "To be sure," he admits, "Bernini used effects first developed for the stage in works of a permanent character and in religious settings; the concealed light in the Cornaro Chapel or the carefully directed light in his churches may be recalled." But Wittkower denies that such devices suffice to support the widespread insistence that Bernini's art is theatrical in a deeper sense.

> What is, however, generally meant by referring in this context to the theatre is not that the experience gained in the one field was successfully applied to the other—a procedure well known to students of the Middle Ages and the Renaissance—but that, through the borrowing from the theatre, religious art itself became 'theatrical'; that in short the Baroque enthusiasm for the theatre infected even religious art.

Wittkower considers this conclusion "entirely fallacious; it was arrived at when people mistook emphatic gestures and emotional expression for the declamatory and oratorical

91. Munich—Berg am Laim, St. Michael, Gabriel and putto from the high altar

requisites of the stage. It denies to the Roman Full Baroque precisely those qualities of deep and sincere religious feeling, which are its most characteristic aspect."[5] Given such works as the Cornaro Chapel, I would not hesitate to say that here the theatre "infects" religious art (although "infects" is a rather unfortunate term, suggesting, as it does, disease). The Asam brothers brought Bernini's sacred theatre to Bavaria. Their work, in turn, helped to determine the undeniable theatricality of the Bavarian rococo church. But does theatricality deny "deep and sincere religious feeling"? Does rhetoric imply insincerity?

The Bavarian rococo church, at any rate, must be understood as an art that is self-consciously theatrical. That it was seen, and meant to be seen, in this manner is suggested by the language of a sermon on the occasion of the consecration of the just-completed Augustinian church at Baumburg on August 30, 1758. The Jesuit Ignatius Bonschab likens the vault, which Felix Anton Scheffler had decorated with scenes from the life of St. Augustine, to a stage, each fresco to an act.[6] This is indeed how we see the frescoes. We experience what we see not as simple representations of events drawn from the life of the saint, but as representations of a theatrical performance of scenes from that life. The frescoes represent a play glorifying St. Augustine and the Augustinians, a "theatrum honoris," not unlike the theatrical performances glorifying the rulers of the baroque.[7]

What kind of theatre are we dealing with? Johann Baptist Zimmermann's main fresco at Schäftlarn (1755) offers a quite characteristic example (fig. 92). As so often in Bavarian rococo churches, this fresco represents the founding (1140) of the church. At the same time it places this event in the context of the divine plan. Just as in the case of the tournament the action of the gods formed the theatrical background for a highly stylized representation of the actions of men, so here the heavenly assembly gathered around the Lamb of God provides the background for an idealized rendition of the story of the monastery's founding. Even the landscape indicates the nature of this idealization. There is no relationship between the landscape the visitor walking to this church has just experienced and what he now sees, not a real landscape, but a stage set.

Similarly, no attempt is made to portray the founders. Instead we see actors playing the parts of these founders. Someone familiar with the story of the monastery's founding will recognize in the splendidly attired bishop Otto of Freising, who here hands a document to the monastery's first prior, Engelbert. Behind the bishop his brother, Duke Leopold, strikes an elegantly theatrical posture. But no attempt is made to render historic personages; we see actors in rococo dress.

The Isar has turned into a theatrical river. A ship carries a Premonstratensian. The frailty of that ship is answered by the strong vertical of the tower that supports a rococo St. Norbert, the founder of the Premonstratensian order, whom we see raising the Holy Sacrament, blessing the landscape spread out beneath him. The beaconlike tower is the strongest link between the oval of the landscape below and the oval of heavenly clouds that support angels and the patron saints of the church, Dionysius and Juliana. This link is reinforced by the light of the Sacrament, a feeble echo of the burst of light emanating from the sacred emblem of the Heavenly Lamb, which occupies the center of the fresco. Only this heavenly theatre, which furnishes the events on earth with a divine background, recalls the glory compositions of the baroque. And even here there is a striking difference: the composition of the heavenly assembly has become much airier and lighter. The fresco's blue is not so much the color of heaven as the color of the familiar sky. This atmospheric blue makes it difficult for us to think that we are allowed a glimpse of heaven itself. What we see is a theatrical representation of an Arcadian landscape, spanned by a blue sky and the arclike zodiac. In this sky what remains of baroque glory compositions seems quite out of place, a strange appearance that reminds one of the machine theatre of the baroque. This theatre in the sky seems to have been staged not so much for us, nor for the founders of the church, nor for the Premonstratensian in his frail boat. We and they seem to belong to a different sphere. Only St. Norbert belongs to both spheres, and thus links heaven and earth. The theatre in the sky is his vision. The fresco thus proclaims that it is through St. Norbert, and through the order he founded and that built this church, that we, who are standing in it, are linked to heaven.[8]

If the glory compositions of the baroque let the heavenly realm break into the church,

92. Schäftlarn, abbey church, fresco *(The Founding of the Abbey)*

if an artist like Pozzo wants to overwhelm us with the verisimilitude of his painting, blurring the boundary that separates reality and theatre, the Bavarian rococo no longer aims at such fusion. It does not let us forget that what the painter furnishes is no more than theatre. To make this reminder explicit and to exhibit the theatricality of their art, the painters of the Bavarian rococo liked to introduce curtains into their already theatrical compositions. Divine transcendence becomes manifest only as a play within a play.

Good examples are found in Steingaden, another Premonstratensian church, whose vaults were frescoed only a few years before Schäftlarn by Johann Georg Bergmüller. Here two frescoes tell the story of the founding of the church. In the eastern fresco we see an angel who presents the plan of the monastery of Steingaden to St. Norbert. Another angel has already begun to dig the foundations. The real architects and builders of the monastery are the angels. Like Schäftlarn, Steingaden is another Bethel, a place where the earth is joined to heaven. And as in Schäftlarn it is the vision of St. Norbert that establishes the ladder linking heaven and earth. An angel lifts a curtain and lets us (or rather St. Norbert) see a crucifix, bathed in light, descending to earth. St. Norbert's vision is represented as an angelic theatre, set within a theatrical fresco (fig. 93).[9]

The device of the curtain appears again in the fresco above the organ. Here, however, the curtain is pushed to the upper left in such a way that, given Bergmüller's perspective, it seems to belong to a plane lying before both the scene showing the actual founding of the church by Duke Welf VI and the visionary appearance above it. Instead of presenting itself to us as part of the fresco, establishing a theatre within the fresco's theatre, here it helps to establish the theatricality of the fresco in its entirety.

Plate 2

93. Steingaden, Premonstratensian abbey church, fresco (*A Vision of St. Norbert. An Angel Shows the Plan of the Monastery*)

Altar and Stage

The theatrical quality of the rococo church is most readily apparent in its altar compositions.[10] Once again the Asam brothers pointed the way with the high altars at Rohr and Weltenburg (1721–24). Both are witness to the debt the Bavarian rococo owes the Roman baroque: Bernini and, even more, Pozzo provide obvious antecedents—one senses the importance which the latter's decoration of the Jesuit church in Vienna (1703–05) had for all of Southern Germany.

Already in Munich's Theatinerkirche the mensa of the high altar had been detached from and placed before the altar's column architecture. No longer a piece of furniture, the altar had become architectural. But in the Theatinerkirche the theatrical potential of such integration is not yet exploited. Given the altar's lack of depth, its paired columns continue to function rather like a picture frame. In Rohr this frame becomes a stage architecture, complete with a blue drapery that shows the Bavarian coat of arms and functions as a backdrop (fig. 94). The altar's scagliola columns seem to have the same kind of reality as the columns of the crossing; similarly, the entablature continues that of the nave. Only its darker tonality resists complete integration and establishes some distance, reinforced by the dark choir stalls encircling the mensa, which help to give the altar the look of a raised stage and separate it from the tabernacle (see fig. 100). Enacted on that stage is the Assumption of the Virgin. In some ways Egid Quirin Asam remains closer to Titian than

94. Rohr, Augustinian priory church, choir and high altar

to Rubens or to Peter Candid[11] or even to Pozzo's dramatic high altar painting in the Jesuit church in Vienna. Like Titian, Egid Quirin organizes his drama in three zones. Gathered around the empty sarcophagus we see apostles, their dramatic gestures expressing bewilderment and astonishment at what is happening (fig. 95). Above them the Virgin floats upward, supported by two large angels, toward the heavenly realm that fills the altar's broken pediment with its gold and light. Like the dove of the Holy Spirit above, she seems suspended in midair. Her ascent recalls the fantastic flights that the baroque theatre liked to conjure, often with incredibly elaborate machinery. Here it is only a carefully concealed rod (fig. 96).

Especially theatrical is the use of light. Frontal illumination is provided by the large window broken into the façade. Windows in the apse, concealed from our view, light the composition from the sides, a theatrical effect the younger Asam had learned from Bernini. The large oculus above the altar provides a very visible third source of light. This time, however, light is not used to illuminate the drama, but is itself part of it. To represent the heavenly realm the sculptor fuses stuccoed clouds and a burst of golden rays with the warm light entering through yellow panes. Real light and the golden rays representing light are made part of one pictorial whole. Once again the boundary between art and reality is obscured, or rather becomes the object of artistic play. In this respect Rohr points both forward to the rococo to come and back to the high baroque of Bernini, particularly to the Cathedra Petri.[12]

Even if the high altar at Rohr is obviously "infected" by the theatre, it is impossible to speak here of illusionism. As Hitchcock remarks, the altar "preserves aesthetic distance, despite all the realism of the astonished apostles' poses and their existence, life-size, in our own space, by the abstract whiteness of the figures, as in the present-day work of George Segal."[13] This whiteness recalls the marble whiteness of Bernini's sculptures, although here the material is not marble, but stucco; in this respect the decoration of the Theatinerkirche and the work of the Wessobrunners provide more obvious antecedents. This whiteness, which was to become characteristic of subsequent rococo sculpture, plays an important part in the play with illusionism that provides one of the keys to the Bavarian rococo.

Even more theatrical is Weltenburg. In his *Perspectiva pictorum et architectorum* Pozzo had recommended opening the apse to a light-filled stage (fig. 97). Cosmas Damian Asam follows that recommendation and extends it to the nave vault, into which an oval has, quite literally, been cut that allows us to see the heavenly theatre painted on the flat ceiling above (figs. 98 and 99). The nave's darkness contrasts with the light that floods the two "stages" of the main fresco and the high altar from concealed windows. The altar's Bernini columns provide less a stage architecture than a proscenium arch. Similarly the gilded statues of St. Martinus and St. Maurus, which flank the polychromed central group, are not actors in a play, but part of the frame, although they are also speakers, mediating between us and the sacred spectacle. St. Maurus on the right is also a portrait of Maurus Bächl, the abbot who had called the brothers Asam to Weltenburg and to whom we therefore owe this heavenly theatre.

Plate 9

Cosmas Damian's fresco of the Immaculata furnishes a bright backdrop; the concealed

95. Rohr, priory church, high altar

97. Andrea Pozzo, altar design from the *Perspectiva pictorum et architectorum*

windows, their light intensified by a hidden reflecting mirror, let us experience this image not so much as lit as itself a source of light. Silhouetted against this light, St. George on his charger possesses all the fragile elegance of a rococo knight. The glittering dragon and the elegant princess hint at fairy tales—magical, but not quite to be taken seriously. Once again it is impossible to speak of illusionism. Aesthetic distance is established by the pedestal that makes this St. George a *representation of a statue*, recalling a host of such statues, including representations of heroic emperors and kings and of even more heroic Christian saints. A strange kind of play: the princess and the dragon threatening her are separated by a statue that does not possess their kind of reality; their colors contrast with his gold and silver, their engagement, underscored with parallel S-curves, with his seeming disregard of her plight and even of the devilish beast, which is pierced by his flaming sword. This is a remote St. George, in a trance rather than heroic. And indeed, the strength that slays the dragon is not his; the real victory belongs to her whose light illuminates him (fig. 100).[14]

Dominikus Zimmermann's Johanneskirche in Landsberg (1750–54) offers a high rococo counterpart to the theatre the Asam brothers had staged at Weltenburg. Once again the darker nave contrasts with a bright choir, illuminated by hidden windows, although in the Landsberg church everything has become lighter. White and pastels dominate. As at Weltenburg, a figural group, here representing Christ's Baptism, is placed before a painted

Plate 10

96. Rohr, priory church, *The Virgin Ascending*

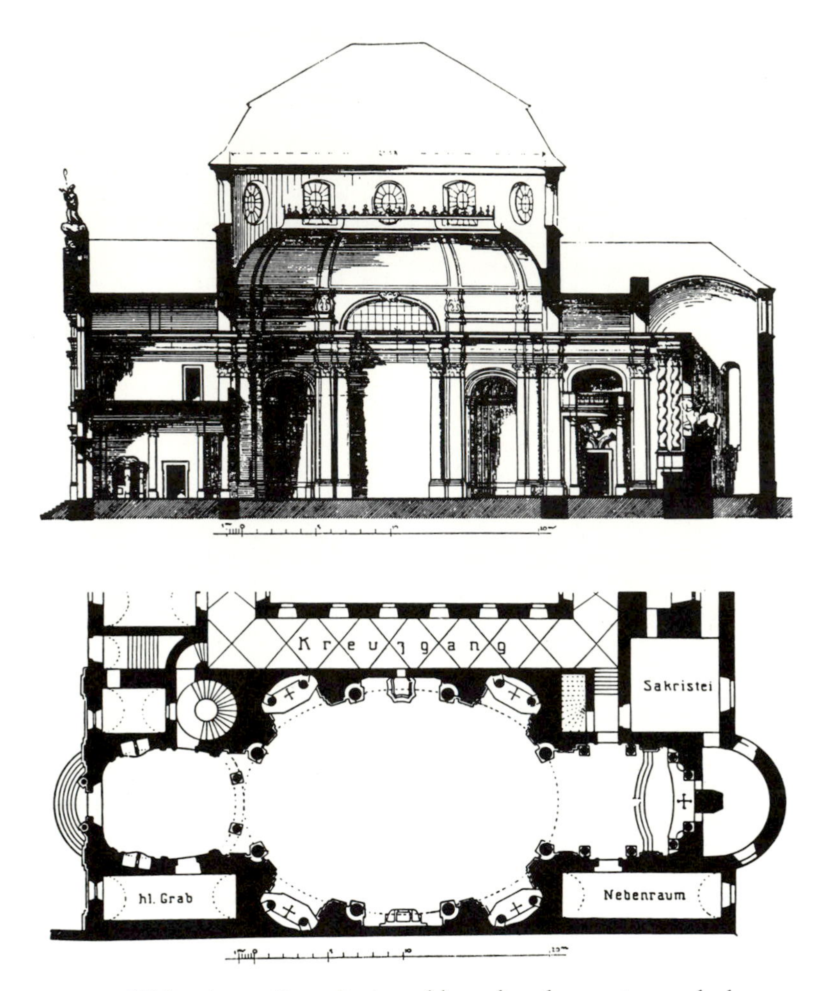

98. Weltenburg, Benedictine abbey church, section and plan

backdrop. Figures and the landscape background both are the rather uninspired work of local artists. Far more interesting is Zimmermann's curious rocaille architecture. Very much like rocaille ornament in contemporary Augsburg engravings, it simultaneously provides a frame for Johann Luidl's figures and functions as a scenic object. Once again we meet with the ambivalence of the frame so characteristic of the Bavarian rococo.[15]

At Diessen, the integration of altar and architecture is carried even further than at Rohr. As at Weltenburg, the columns of this altar function not as a stage architecture, but as a framing proscenium arch (fig. 101). Joachim Dietrich's large, somewhat academic statues of the church fathers are part of this frame. This suggests that the real theatre is provided by Balthasar August Albrecht's painting of the Assumption of the Virgin (1738). Missing in the painting, however, is a representation of the realm of heaven. The painted drama is incomplete. It demands the sculptural group of the Trinity, which here, as at Rohr, is placed above the altar's cornice. But if dramatically these sculptures belong with the painting, aesthetically they are part of the frame and belong with the church fathers below. This play with the frame, which is also a play with aesthetic distance, is analogous to the play that the ornamental framing zones of rococo frescoes help to inaugurate.

99. Weltenburg, abbey church, interior

100. Weltenburg, abbey church, high altar

101. Diessen, priory church, choir and high altar

In one respect Diessen goes beyond what was attempted at Weltenburg: the high altar painting can be lowered to reveal what is now quite literally a narrow stage, complete with movable sets that allow for representations of the Nativity, the Crucifixion, the Entombment, and the Resurrection, depending on what high holiday is being celebrated. Faison calls attention to the "little concealed staircase (for trumpeters?) leading to a platform behind the top of the altar. Here indeed is a Theatrum Sacrum!"[16]

Wherever we find a rococo altarpiece the theatre is not too far away. The high altar at Rottenbuch, the work of the Weilheim sculptor Franz Xaver Schmädl, furnishes a good example.[17] Although unusually elaborate, in keeping with the importance of the Augustinian Rottenbuch, it may stand for countless other altars that show the influence of Bernini as mediated by the brothers Asam (fig. 102).

Plate 13

Behind the freestanding mensa with the tabernacle, flanked by gilded statues of Peter and Paul, rises a typical column architecture, supported by a massive pedestal and crowned by a broken pediment. Characteristic, too, is the horde of putti who frolic in this altar, as they do throughout the church. The theatre is suggested not only by the dramatic placement of the main figures and by the way the altar's columns provide a stage architecture, but by the curtain motif, which appears here not once, but twice, suggesting once again theatre within theatre. Putti draw these curtains, or rather play with them. Their playfulness makes it difficult to take the theatre which they present, and over which they seem to preside, too seriously. In the gable we see God the Father, surrounded by more putti, bathed in that golden Bernini light the Asam brothers brought to Bavaria. His right hand raised in blessing, He looks down from His height. Below, before a small, empty bed that forms the painted backdrop, Joachim and Anna, their heads and hands raised in humble expectation, await the imminent birth of the Virgin. The central part of the altar attempts to unveil the mystery of that birth. Above the bed the Virgin as child descends on a cloud, enveloped in gleaming rays. In this child divine grace and human expectation meet; heaven and earth are gathered together. Putti carry the familiar symbols of the antiphon: "Who is this that looks forth like the dawn, fair as the moon, bright as the sun, terrible as an army with banners?" Another putto points to a pearl in an open shell, the traditional symbol of miraculous conception. The birth of the Virgin is the dawn that announces the coming of the sun, of Jesus Christ. The mensa below reminds us of His redeeming sacrifice.

The curtain of this play within a play is supported by a large half-shell, a familiar Marian symbol, which at the same time functions as God's throne. The Virgin, who bears Him Who bears all things, is the throne of God.[18] A second half-shell in the gable forms a sheltering baldachin. Together these two half-shells enclose the Deity.

> Thy Makers maker, and thy Fathers mother;
> Thou' hast light in darke; and shutst in little roome,
> *Immensity cloysterd in thy deare wombe.*[19]

The child we see below is the mother of Him Who sent her forth.

To this paradox the theatre cannot do justice. The sculptor's scenic approach has to break down before the central mystery of the Virgin's birth. Just as the fresco painters of the rococo were often content to express the central mystery of their faith with the

102. Rottenbuch, Augustinian priory church, high altar

geometric symbol of the Trinity, so in the very center of the altar we see no longer theatre, but the monogram of the Virgin, its crown signifying that she, who is both child and mother of God, is also His bride and queen of heaven.

Fascinated as they were by the theatre, those who were responsible for this altar were aware of the inadequacy of all theatrical representations of the mysteries of faith. Despite their fondness for rhetoric, for grand gestures, they remained aware of the superficiality of their art, of their inability to carry us to the core of what matters. *In this diffidence born of faith* the play with the theatre has its foundation. Emphasis on the theatre's theatricality is a device to prevent us from taking it too seriously. That device is raised to a higher power when the more profound mysteries of faith are presented as theatre within theatre. And further, this second theatre, pushing closer to the central mystery, has to become emblematic and less scenic. The image of the child is thus joined to the symbol of the shell. Together, they point to the mystery that finds expression in the name Maria.

Stages Within Stages

Likening wall-pillars to the wings of a theatrical set is more than a simile. To enter a Bavarian rococo church is to step onto a splendid stage, although, as we take our place in the nave, this stage is transformed into the orchestra; the stuccoed curtain that so often decorates the choir arch and loges that establish the antechoir as a proscenium transform the altar room into a stage. Upon that stage the high altar appears as yet another stage: a stage within a stage within a stage.[20]

Playing with the theatre, the Bavarian rococo church forces us to acknowledge its theatricality. In this respect it may seem to differ from the baroque. Is not baroque illusionism supposed to make us forget that what we are seeing is just theatre? But who was ever convinced by an illusionistic fresco that the heavenly scenes above him were reality? The illusionism of a Pozzo does not so much lead us to mistake illusion for reality as it makes us wonder where one leaves off and the other begins: what is three-dimensional architecture and what two-dimensional painting? The painted ceilings of the baroque do not lead us to mistake theatre for reality; instead, they make us wonder whether reality is more than theatre, more than a dream surrounded by silence. The theatricality of the baroque church is symbol of the theatricality of the world.[21]

In this respect the rococo church remains very much part of the baroque. Its play with the theatre, the delight it takes in theatres within theatres, is familiar from Shakespeare and Calderón. The rococo church can indeed be interpreted as a more effective realization of baroque theatricality than the illusionism of a Pozzo. That illusionism is limited by the necessity of assigning the spectator a specific point of view. Only for a moment do we wonder where reality ends and deception begins. A few steps and the illusion collapses; the quite different realities of architecture and fresco reassert themselves. Pozzo's illusionism owes both its power and its limitations to perspectival painting, which here threatens to triumph over the baroque theatre. The consistent employment of one-point perspective establishes a distance between spectator and painting. Illusionism invites us to forget this distance, which is yet preserved and remains unchanged. So is the boundary separating reality from illusion. Theatre that subordinates itself to the logic of perspective may let us forget ourselves and our reality, but it is unable to put that reality into question. Such questioning, however, is inseparable from the baroque sense of theatre. It demands theatre that plays with aesthetic distance, theatre that is also about theatre. Pozzo's illusionism fails as theatre precisely because it succeeds so well as perspectival painting. Such painting can transform the worshiper into a spectator of a sacred play, but it does not assign him a part in that play. Just this is the goal of the Bavarian rococo church. *Its play with the theatre and with perspective denies us a firm point of view that would leave us outside the play that delights us.* The baroque view of the theatricality of the world finds here a last effective expression.

Consider Johann Baptist Zimmermann's Judgment fresco in Die Wies (1753–54). As in any successful rococo church, the fresco lacks the kind of integrity and unity that would make it into a self-sufficient whole; it is essentially incomplete. To do justice to it one has to consider the contribution it makes to the architectural whole, the greatest achievement of the painter's brother Dominikus (fig. 105). The church fuses successfully the hall church scheme with an oval design, a fusion that has its precursor in Dominikus's earlier Steinhausen (fig. 103). As in Steinhausen, this fusion is motivated at least in part by the special requirements of a pilgrimage church. A space had to be created that would allow the pilgrims to walk around the sacred image. Zimmermann solves the problem by enveloping both the oval central space and the roughly rectangular choir with an aisle or mantle, which not only functions as an ambulatory, leading the pilgrims around nave and choir, past the miraculous image of Christ in the high altar, without disturbing those praying, but also obscures the boundaries of the church. Here, too, ornament both separates and mediates between pictorial and architectural reality, furnishing a frame that negates itself (figs. 65, 90, and 104). Thus, the rainbow that spans the frescoed ceiling has to be seen together with the piers below and the stuccoed ornament that provides the connecting link. The large cartouches and the stuccoed balconies above provide transitions that let us see this ensemble of painting, ornament, and architecture as a portal or triumphal arch. The fantastic throne that rises in the fresco just above the choir is the keystone of a second arch set inside the first. Painted blue drapery heightens the theatrical quality of the throne; at the same time it connects it with the stuccoed vases and cartouches, which in turn are seen as extensions of the piers that support pulpit and abbot's loge. Inside this arch the columns of the high altar help to define yet a third arch. Its keystone is the apocalyptic Lamb with the Seven Seals. Again blue drapery, now stuccoed rather than painted, mediates between it and the altar's red columns. To appreciate this theatrical arrangement of arches within arches—and it would be easy to pursue this theme much further—we have to stand near the entrance. Yet that point of view cannot be said to do justice to the church, not even to the main fresco. Its perspective demands that we walk around it. Die Wies is theatre that demands not passive spectators, but active participants. Changes in point of view enable us to make new discoveries. Die Wies is full of surprises—here I only want to call attention to the curious openings in the upper ambulatory, which reappear, fantastically transformed, below the choir vault, providing shifting frames for the ambulatory's small frescoes (figs. 90 and 104).

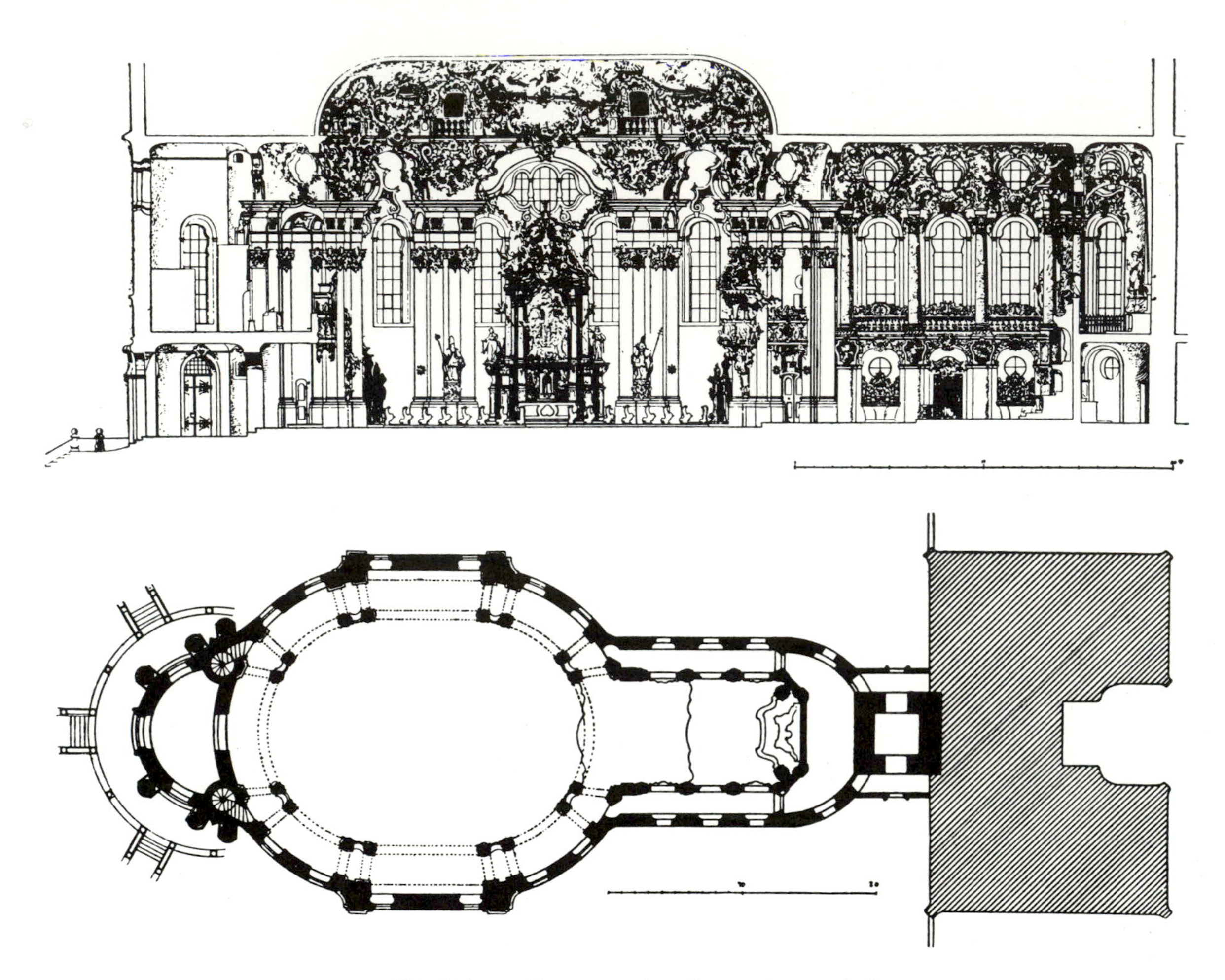

103. Die Wies, pilgrimage church, section and plan

Looked at as self-sufficient works of art, most of the frescoes of the Bavarian rococo are disappointing. They demand the interplay with architecture. As the arch motif in Die Wies illustrates, the rococo fresco helps to pictorialize architectural space, but as we move through this space, we reassert the primacy of architecture and reduce the fresco to an ornamental accessory—which yet refuses such subservient status, reasserts itself, and pictorializes the architecture. Ornament is the medium of this unending play or strife. The iconography of the main fresco of Die Wies gives it a deeper meaning (fig. 105). Two angels with open books and the trumpet-carrying angels below the ends of the rainbow tell us that the throne rising above the choir arch is the throne of the Last Judgment. But not yet has the judge descended from his rainbow. Its colored arc is still the reassuring sign of God's continuing covenant with the earth: there still is time, although the portal that looms up over us in the fresco as we prepare to leave the church bears the warning inscription: *Tempus non erit amplius* (Ap. 10, 6), "There should be time no longer." The emblem of the snake biting its own tail makes this the gate of eternity. Chronos has fallen to the ground; the hourglass has dropped from his hands. What lies beyond time lies hidden behind the gate's closed doors (fig. 106).

Representations of the Last Judgment tend to oppose the Glory of Heaven to the

104. Die Wies, pilgrimage church, southern ambulatory

105. Die Wies, pilgrimage church, main fresco

torments of the damned. The absence of the latter in Die Wies is surprising. Color and composition make this a joyous painting. But how, given its theme, can this joy be justified? Where are the damned? To be sure, the judgment has not yet been made; there still is time. But where are those to be judged? The answer is obvious enough: *we ourselves*, standing in the church, are necessary to complete the picture.[22]

At Birnau this attempt to make the spectator part of the picture led Gottfried Bernhard Goez to introduce a real mirror into the fresco. Given the correct point of view, we can see ourselves literally in the fresco.[23] Here the device is too obvious, the integration of the spectator into the fresco too artificial. The Zimmermann brothers play a more subtle game. Of course we know that what we see above us is just a picture. We are real in a quite different sense; we belong to the three-dimensional space that shelters us. And yet, that space proves elusive and transforms itself into picture. We cannot keep our distance from the theatre that is being performed for us; we are drawn into it. Inseparable from that interplay between picture and architecture that helps to define the Bavarian rococo church is the interplay between actor and spectator. The irreality of the fresco affects us: "We are such stuff as dreams are made on."

Aesthetic and Religious Play

Ever since the eighteenth century rococo art has been criticized for its lack of seriousness, for its frivolity. The obvious playfulness of this art makes it difficult to simply reject that charge. Consider again the rococo parody of the baroque tournament. Such parodies do indeed suggest some recognition of what Hauser terms "the unreality of court life, which is nothing but a party game, a brilliantly staged theatrical show."[24] Hauser interprets this sense of unreality as a function of social changes that had robbed the nobility of its former significance. The baroque embraced the theatre with such enthusiasm to cover up these changes. Medieval themes return; there is

> a new aristocratization of society and a fresh renaissance of the old chivalrous-romantic concepts of morality. The real nobleman is now the "*honnête homme*" who belongs to the birthright nobility and acknowledges the ideals of chivalry. Heroism and fidelity, moderation and self-control, generosity and politeness are the virtues of which he must be master. They are all part of the semblance of the beautiful, harmonious world, clothed in which the king and his entourage present themselves to the public. They pretend that these virtues really matter and, deceiving even themselves at times, they pretend that they are the knights of a new Round Table.[25]

The rococo is no longer able to take this theatre seriously. It knows that reality lies elsewhere—thus, while the masquerade of the baroque tournament conjured up an idealized world of gods and knights, the rococo parody borrows its masks from the peasantry and the middle class. But such borrowing is tied to a deep-rooted conservatism. Even as the nobility discovers the bourgeois values of privacy and artless sincerity, even as it learns to prefer the intimacy of small rooms and gets bored by etiquette and ceremonial, recognizing the artificiality of its own life and ideals, it refuses to relinquish them. Unable to embrace inherited conventions, it is yet unable to break with them and to adopt the ethos of the rising middle class. Instead it exploits the tension by making it the subject of its own

106. Die Wies, pilgrimage church, interior to the west

aesthetic games. The rococo's play with the theatre of the baroque betrays an aestheticism that is inseparable from the decay of the old order.

It is possible to offer a similar analysis of the religious rococo. If one can speak of an anachronistic return of knightly ideals in the baroque period, can one not also speak of an anachronistic return of essentially medieval patterns in the religious life, and especially in the religious art of the Counter Reformation? What necessity still links spiritual content and artistic expression? Immediacy of experience seems to have given way to rhetoric, what once was genuine to theatre. The playful theatre of the rococo betrays a recognition of the hollowness of the baroque theatre, but such recognition does not lead to revolution, to an overthrow of what has been inherited. On this view the religious art of the rococo has to be seen as an essentially aesthetic play with the inherited religious tradition and its images.

In spite of the undeniable suggestiveness of such an interpretation, we should not be too quick to apply an analysis based on the aristocratic rococo, especially of France, to the Bavarian rococo church. Almost any village church built in the seventeen-forties or fifties should make us wonder. Or take the curious, almost disturbingly organic ornament in the choir of Die Wies. Is this the product of a tired aestheticism? It may be possible to analyze the French rococo in terms of the tensions between a tired aristocracy and the rising bourgeoisie, and such an approach retains its suggestiveness when applied to the rococo at the court of Max Emanuel and Karl Albrecht; but it fails to do justice to the Bavarian rococo church. In spite of all its sophistication, the Bavarian rococo church retains its foundation in what remains a peasant culture. Its creators lived in a world that had changed little since the Middle Ages. In that world miracles still happened and were taken for granted.

Plate 7

In this context it is well to consider the events that led to the building of Die Wies.[26] In 1730 Hyacinth Gassner, the abbot of Steingaden, had introduced the Good Friday procession into the area; for it he needed an image of the flagellated Christ. In an attic filled with paraphernalia a head was found, then a chest, arms, and feet. The parts did not quite fit together but they would do: rags were used as stuffing and the whole was covered with canvas and painted. For three years this simple image was carried in the procession, until something better was demanded and the statue was stored away, together with other props that might find use in future theatrical productions. Finally it was given to a local innkeeper, who had taken a liking to it. His cousin, a peasant woman who lived an hour's distance from Steingaden, "in der Wies," in the meadow, begged him to let her have the statue. A month later she found tears on its face. When the miracle recurred, the terrified woman called her husband. A simple chapel was built and soon there were miraculous cures.

The monastery appears to have been not at all pleased with what was happening out "in the meadow"—was it not the eighteenth century? The monasteries were in the forefront of a rather modest Bavarian enlightenment. So the peasant woman, Maria Lori, and her husband, Martin, were questioned and publicity discouraged. But the number of people who made the pilgrimage to the humble statue increased rapidly. Soon the provisional church that had been built proved insufficient. There were days on which several thousand pilgrims arrived from as far away as Bohemia, the Rhineland, and Switzerland. Given such success, which translated into funds, and given increasing complaints about the inadequacy of the existing shelter, the abbot decided to build a large and costly church. The peasants to whom the church owes its origin contributed their labor.

It was the piety of the people, a piety that centered more on pilgrimages than on the liturgy, that gave rise to many of the best rococo churches, and the piety extended to the builders of these churches. When his wife died Dominikus Zimmermann asked to be allowed to spend the rest of his life in the Premonstratensian monastery Schussenried, where one of his sons was a monk; a daughter was abbess in the nearby Gutenzell. His request was refused, in part because the monastery could not quite forgive him how much more than expected Steinhausen, Zimmermann's other great pilgrimage church, had cost it, but also to avoid difficulty with its own architect. So he built himself a house right next to Die Wies, where another son, Franz Dominikus, who had assisted his father, had married the widowed Maria Lori.

Plate 14

The life of the Asam brothers was similarly linked to religion. Two of Cosmas Damian's daughters entered convents. Next to his house in Thalkirchen he built himself a chapel. Religion played an even greater role in the life of the unmarried Egid Quirin. St. Johann Nepomuk in Munich, the Asamkirche, has its origin in his resolve to build a church in honor of the newly elevated saint. How many other architects sacrificed their wealth to build a church?

The more one learns of religious life in eighteenth-century Bavaria the more difficult it becomes to accept an interpretation that would have us understand the rococo church as no more than an aesthetic play with a religious past that could no longer be taken seriously. At the same time we cannot deny that the rococo of the court and the rococo of the church belong together. Not only does the latter draw much of its language from the former, but more significant, both have to be understood as responses to the preceding baroque and both betray an inability to take the illusionistic theatre of the baroque quite seriously. But what accounts for this inability on the part of the church? Could it be that the rococo plays with the sacred theatre of the baroque as it does precisely because it takes the theatre so seriously?

The Insufficiency of Perspective

Defending Bernini against the charge of theatricality, Wittkower contrasts the theatre with an art that expresses "deep and sincere religious feeling." The expressiveness of his art is supposed to have saved Bernini from the theatre. Presupposed is the familiar stance that the theatre deals with surface appearance: the actor is not himself; and art that is theatrical pretends to be something that it is not. Similar presuppositons let Jacques Maritain claim that all postmedieval art places us "on the floor of a theatre," that "with the sixteenth century the lie installed itself in painting, which began to love science for its own sake, endeavoring to give the *illusion* of nature and to make us believe that in the presence of a painting we are in the presence of the same as the subject painted, not in the presence of the painting."[27]

In spite of its exaggeration and oversimplification—Maritain is quick to admit that great artists, artists like Raphael and Greco, Zurbarán and Watteau, or even Bernini, "purified art of this lie"—the passage yet points to a condition with which the visual arts have been struggling ever since the Renaissance: the triumph of perspective. For although Maritain speaks of the theatre, it isn't the theatre as such that is at the heart of the problem. There is, after all, a ready answer for those who would criticize the art of the Counter Reformation for its theatricality. Is the liturgy not in its very essence dramatic action? At a very early date that action was elaborated to include dramatic presentations, particularly at Christmas and Easter. Processions offered further occasions for theatrical productions. With their turn to the theatre baroque and rococo develop and continue practices that go back at least to the early Middle Ages and that may well be inseparable from religious life.

But when Maritain speaks of the theatre he is not thinking of medieval mystery plays; nor does he want to condemn the theatricality of baroque oratorios. Indeed, he is thinking not so much of dramatic actions as of pictorial illusions that invite us to mistake them for reality, letting us forget their merely artificial being. This presupposes that the art of faithfully representing appearance has been mastered. The lie that is said to have "installed itself in painting" is inseparable from mastery of perspective; instead of signifying a higher reality art now presented a second reality. When Alberti likens the artist to another God this is more than a rhetorical flourish:[28] the artist's work is to possess the same kind of unity and integrity that tradition attributes to God's creation. With the turn to perspective painting enters a development that will lead it to art for art's sake.

Medieval art possesses a twofold inadequacy. First of all it is inadequate to the appearance of our world. From that appearance it draws abstract "images" of a transcendent reality. But these "images" may not be considered more or less literal representations of that reality. It is this second inadequacy that lets them function as signs that preserve the transcendence of the divine. Perspective, having its measure in the beholder, cannot be separated from a secularization of the visible. Thus, it proves an obstacle to attempts to use the visual arts to point to transcendence. This is the condition faced by the religious art of the Counter Reformation: Shut off from transcendence by its subservience to perspective, it still seeks to use the magic of perspective to incarnate transcendence. But is the power of such incarnation given to the artist? Can such attempts result in more than an illusionistic theatre?

Such considerations led Plato to condemn all mimetic art as an imitation of mere appearances, thrice removed from reality. To the extent that the artist accepts the rule of perspective, he surrenders all claim to serve the truth. In his ability to create a second world the artist may well seem like a godlike magician; yet the power of his magic depends on the infirmity of our senses. To us, as Plato points out,

> the same object appears straight when looked at out of the water, and crooked when in the water; and the concave becomes convex, owing to the illusions about colours to which the sight is liable. Thus every sort of confusion is revealed within us; and this is that weakness of the human mind on which the art of conjuring and of deceiving by light and shadow and other ingenious devices imposes, having an effect on us like magic.[29]

Similarly, the Renaissance saw the artist as brother to the magician, art as akin to thaumaturgy, which John Dee defined as "that art Mathematicall, which giueth certaine order to make strange workes of the sense to be perceiued, and of men greatly to be wondered at."[30] When Brunelleschi demonstrated the power of his system of perspective to make the spectator, seeing a painted panel, feel that he was actually looking at the exterior of San Giovanni in Florence, he established himself as such a magician. And the same is true of the great stage designers of the baroque, of a Torelli da Fano or an Andrea Pozzo. But although one has to grant the delight that Pozzo claims is furnished by such deceptions, what place do they have in a church? Is not Maritain right to mourn the turn of Renaissance and post-Renaissance art to the magic of illusion? The development of perspective has given special weight to Plato's attack on imitative art. How, if art is ruled by perspective, can we take seriously the claims of art to serve reality? And more generally, if the visible as such is subjected to that rule, must not all art be just "a kind of play or sport," the artist a follower of Daedalus, who created marvelous statues that with their motions imitated the appearance of living things? Like Daedalus, he can create another labyrinth, but can he help us find the way out of the labyrinth of the world? How can such games have a religious significance?

A hint of the answer is provided by an art form that, while it never had more than peripheral importance, yet made perspective and the problems connected with it thematic: anamorphic composition. Seen in a normal way such compositions show one thing; given a second, quite different point of view, they reveal another, hidden meaning. An early example, and perhaps the most famous, is Holbein's *Ambassadors*, where a shift in point of view transforms the curious shape in the lower half of the painting into a skull. A change of place lets the splendid appearance of the ambassadors give way to the power of death. Such optical tricks were especially popular in the first half of the seventeenth century. And, somewhat surprisingly, it was a religious order, the Minims, that pursued these experiments with particular enthusiasm.[31] Large anamorphic frescoes were painted, of which only one has survived, Emmanuel Maignan's *St. Francis di Paola* in the cloister of the Minim monastery in Rome.[32] Why should such perspectival games be given space and time by a religious establishment? How are we to understand this interest in anamorphosis? Simply as a playful concern with perspective, devoid of deeper significance?

Facing such paintings one sees little more than arabesques suggesting a landscape, but not coherent enough to be seen convincingly as such—riddles in search of an answer. That answer is given when the normal point of view is given up; a different point of view lets us recognize the painting's real significance. Anamorphosis would thus seem to function first of all as a metaphor for the fact that the world presents itself to us in labyrinthine confusion. Only a change in point of view reveals its deeper meaning. But another point must be made: the very fact that such compositions call attention to the power of perspective prevents us from taking the second point of view too seriously. By playing one point of view off against another, anamorphic composition is perspectival art that proclaims the insufficiency of such art. In this respect it resembles a theatrical performance, where the illusion is broken by someone reminding us that what we are watching is only theatre, as Egid Quirin Asam does when he places his brother's portrait before the fresco at Weltenburg (fig. 107).[33] And yet this play with perspective, which is at the same time a play with aesthetic distance, is itself part of a theatrical performance. Anamorphic painting should not be taken too seriously. It is born of a love of tricks and games. But it is precisely this lightness that gives it a particular adequacy in an age that had despaired of the adequacy of the visible to the divine.

Like the rapidly changing images of the machine theatre of the baroque, anamorphosis is an emblem of the illusoriness and the unreliability of the world. Here we have a key to the theatricality of the baroque. The baroque theatre is itself an emblem of the finitude of human existence, caught in changing perspectives.[34] Far from simply placing the power of perspective at the service of dramatic presentations, the baroque theatre uses a multiplicity of perspectives to put the rule of perspective into question.

I would suggest that this is how we have to understand the theatricality of the Bavarian rococo church as well. Its play with perspective is more than an aesthetic game; it is part of a last successful attempt to create a genuinely religious art in an age that knows about the insufficiency not only of art, but of the visible. The Bavarian rococo's unwillingness to simply adopt the illusionism of a Pozzo does not stem from an inability to take the theatre seriously. Quite the contrary. Because the Bavarian rococo continues to take the

107. Weltenburg, abbey church, the shell of the nave vault (detail with bust of Cosmas Damian Asam)

theatre so seriously, because it is unwilling to subject it to the rule of perspective, it cannot accept that pictorialization of the theatre which fascinated a Pozzo or a Gaulli.

Theatre and Reality

Dramatic action and pictorial spectacle place quite different demands on the theatre. It is not necessary to think of theatrical performances as moving pictures; and yet, when thinking about the theatre, we take the primacy of the eye for granted. Thus "in producing a play, we begin by extinguishing the house lights, so that the only visible part of the theatre is the stage; we assume that the primary way to control the audiences's attention is through its eyes. And, a logical corollary, we always say that we are going to *see* a play, never to hear it."[35] This darkening of the house seems so natural to us that it is surprising to learn that only Gustav Mahler, following the example of Richard Wagner, dared to do this at the conservative Vienna Hofoper, where baroque traditions were stronger than elsewhere and one went to the theatre not only to see the theatre on the stage, but also and more important the theatre of the world in which one was oneself one of the actors. We are reminded that at least in certain respects we have carried that pictorialization of the stage, which had begun in the Renaissance with Serlio and Peruzzi and been perfected in the baroque, even further.

The extent to which the theatrical tradition of the baroque continues to live is shown by our understanding of the opera as a building type. We still expect a pictorial stage, opposed to an auditorium with galleries, often divided into boxes. The pictorial quality of the operatic spectacle is underscored by a framelike proscenium arch that separates the spectators and the reality to which they belong from the artificial world of the stage. Raised stage and orchestra pit strengthen that separation.[36]

Although we owe this building type to the baroque, we should keep in mind that the baroque knew many other forms of theatre. Thus, like their medieval precursors, the sacred plays that were put on as part of the great religious festivals did not require a special stage: the church, a square in front of it, or a marketplace would do. The nobility found convenient theatres in its arcaded courtyards. Often one had to be content with a large room: a few boards would represent the world, a curtain behind which the actors could change and from which they could emerge would be the backdrop.

Only in the late Renaissance do we meet with attempts to apply the mastery of perspective to the theatre. At first the scene that was to be represented on stage was actually reconstructed with canvas-covered frames. Lope de Vega mourns that the carpenter is becoming more important than the poet, that the theatre is becoming a matter of rag-covered frames.[37] Such frames had the disadvantage of making changes of scenery very difficult. They were therefore better suited to the French drama, which retained them long after the Italians had turned to more flexible staging. In Italy the unity of the theatrical performance had been progressively weakened. Just as the tournament became an occasion for theatrical elaboration, so the play became an occasion for intermezzi that eventually developed into full-fledged opera. The demand for more rapid changes was met by the introduction of *periacti*, three-sided prisms covered with canvas, which could be rotated to effect a change of scenery. It was on such a stage that the first opera, Peri's *Dafne*, was performed in Florence in 1594. By the time Inigo Jones introduced this new form of stage design into England Giovanni Battista Aleotti had already replaced the *periacti* with movable wings. His theatre in the Accademia degli Intrepidi in Ferrara established the form of the baroque theatre: a deep stage with movable wings and an auditorium with galleries and boxes.[38]

It is impossible to interpret this development simply as an increased pictorialization of the stage. What motivated it was rather the demand for rapid changes of scenery. The interest was not so much in pictures as in their change. Delight in the evanescence of beauty—fireworks were an essential part of the festal culture of the baroque—mingled with the dread of time's passing. The point was not so much to make pictorial illusion more convincing as to underscore its ephemeral and dreamlike quality. In the flow of images the transitoriness of life finds symbolic expression. Given the intimate connection between the evolution of stage design and the rise of opera, it is not surprising that Paris never rivaled Florence, Venice, or Bologna as a center of innovative stage design. From Venice the new art spread to Vienna and to Munich, where in 1654 Francesco Santurini built a theatre in the new style, the first building in Germany to function purely as a theatre.

A new step, heralding the rococo, was taken by Ferdinando Galli-Bibiena. Bibiena abandoned the symmetrical designs of the high baroque with their central vanishing point, shifting it instead to the side of the stage. In 1703 the *scena per angolo* is used for the first time in the Accademia del Pesto in Bologna, which by then had become the center of theorizing about perspective (fig. 108). Ferdinando's son Giuseppe lets the stage appear as only an accidental part of a much larger space into which we are allowed to peek from without (fig. 109). In keeping with the intention of illusionism, baroque stage design sought to join the pictorial space created by the stage designer to the real space of the auditorium by giving the former the axis of the latter. The distance that separates pictorial from architectural reality is thereby blurred. The *scena per angolo* asserts that distance; theatrical and real space are divorced.

Rupprecht links this shift from high baroque theatre design, which like illusionistic fresco painting had culminated in the work of Pozzo, to the *scena per angolo* and the shift from the baroque to the rococo church. Cosmas Damian Asam, familiar with the revolution in stage design, is said to have based his own approach to fresco painting on it.[39] Its first mature expression is the fresco at Aldersbach (fig. 39). Here, too, the fresco space is no longer experienced as a mere extension of the real space. The two spaces possess a very different reality. The means by which this is accomplished and the significance of Cosmas Damian's work for the subsequent development of fresco painting in Bavaria have already been discussed. Asam's interest in the theatre is obvious enough. In 1711 Ferdinando Galli-Bibiena had presented his innovations to the public in his *L'architettura civile*. Filippo Juvarra, another important figure in the evolution of the new approach, had been a teacher at the Accademia di San Luca when Asam studied there. That there were other factors that tended to lead him in the same direction has been shown. Rupprecht is right to emphasize the relationship between Bavarian fresco painting of the rococo and the new fashion in stage design. Both imply a rejection of baroque illusionism.

108. Ferdinando Galli-Bibiena, perspectival stage design

Illusionism rests on the primacy of the eye. As we have seen, a certain distance from life is implicit in this primacy. Paradoxical as this may sound, for the sake of the eye baroque illusionism surrenders the integration of theatre and reality that characterized the ritualized theatrical spectacles that played such an important part in the religious life of the period. For while illusionism may succeed in fusing pictorial and real space for the person occupying the right place, the illusion has to collapse when that place is left. If it is to succeed the spectator must remain in his place, passive, a mere eye. The further pictorialization of the stage achieved by the *scena per angolo* only makes the loss of reality inseparable from the reduction of the spectator into an eye more pronounced. The other side of this loss is a heightening of the purely aesthetic character of the events on stage.

Changes in the theatre architecture of the eighteenth century correspond to this change. Characteristic of the high baroque is the participation of ruler and nobility in theatrical performances, in tournaments, masques, and ballets, which generally concluded when the aristocratic performers left the stage to rejoin the court and to lead it in a grand ball.[40] To this fluid boundary between actor and spectator corresponds the fluid boundary between stage and auditorium. Toward the end of the seventeenth century these boundaries tend to become more rigid. The introduction of the court box, placed in the back of the auditorium, which not only gave the ruler a much better view of the events on stage but also removed him from the burghers who had come to furnish an ever-increasing part of the audience, is a significant symptom. It makes an early appearance in the Dresden opera

109. Giuseppe Galli-Bibiena, design from *Architetture e prospettive*, 1740

house (1664).[41] The ruler's place had been in the center of the auditorium, in the midst of the aristocracy. As the ruler withdraws into his box he is no longer there to represent himself to the nobility; he becomes part of the audience. Implicit is a growing conviction that the theatre is just theatre, just art. It had been much more than that.

To be sure, the baroque's attitude to the theatre had always been ambivalent. It knew about the connection between the theatre and the lie and recognized that to play his part well the actor had to deny himself. Thus, the professional actor, successor to the traveling minstrels, jugglers, acrobats, and magicians of the Middle Ages, was denied a place in society. His, and especially her, immorality was almost taken for granted.[42]

At the same time, the theatre was valued for its educational potential. It was the Jesuits who first made Munich a center of the baroque theatre. They emphasized the educational value of acting as well as of watching an edifying play. The young noblemen entrusted to the care of the Jesuits were asked to act, because by so doing they would learn how to behave, how to speak, how to move.[43] Playing the part of a nobleman, a student prepared himself for the part he would have to play in life. Taking the parts of heroes and demigods, aristocrats raised themselves to an "ideal realm between heaven and earth, a realm of high humanity and of heroic virtue."[44] Orgel contrasts the aristocratic masquer with the professional actor thus:

Masquers are not actors; a lady or gentleman participating in a masque remains a lady or gentleman,

> and is not released from the obligation of observing all the complex rules of behavior at court. The king and queen dance in masques because dancing is a perquisite of every lady and gentleman. But playing a part, becoming an actor or an actress, constitutes an impersonation, a lie, a denial of the true self.[45]

And yet, as Jakob Bidermann's *Cenodoxus* shows, the distance between the aristocratic masquer who plays his part well and the professional actor who in acting betrays his true self is not so easily maintained. *Cenodoxus* is the play of a Faust-like Parisian doctor whom everyone admires and considers a saint and who is yet damned. He has played the part the world assigns to man all too well; the part assigned by God he has betrayed. We get a sense of the effectiveness of Jesuit theatre from the fact that after one performance of *Cenodoxus* fourteen Bavarian noblemen, crushed by what they had seen, asked the Jesuits to permit them to join them in their exercises.[46] An echo of the play's impact is preserved in the Asam brothers' St.Johann Nepomuk. Above a confessional we see the unfortunate dissembler, reminding us of the deceptiveness of outer appearance and of the necessity of death, recalling us to our true selves.

To play the part demanded of us by society do we have to betray the part we have been assigned by God? It is a question that suggested itself especially to the aristocracy, which, as Hauser points out, had come to at least half-recognize the artificiality and hollowness of the order that defined its ethos. But how was one to escape from this artificiality? By recovering within oneself that natural man of whom philosophers were speaking? Did reason point the way out of the baroque *theatrum mundi*? The theatrical culture of the baroque loses its foundation when man begins to believe that he is able to seize reality, as it is, without divine grace.

As this sense is lost—as reality is freed from the theatre— the theatre is freed from reality; it becomes mere theatre, mere art. The aesthetic sphere begins to emancipate itself—and we should keep in mind that such emancipation marks the birth of aesthetics in the eighteenth century. Rupprecht's discovery of the connection between the *scena per angolo* and the development of the rococo fresco points in the direction of such emancipation, as does Bauer's interpretation of rocaille. Rococo ornament, too, retreats to the merely aesthetic. (Chapter 1 has shown the strength of this suggestion.)

We must agree with Rupprecht and Bauer: the rococo no longer takes seriously that fusion of reality and theatre aimed at by baroque illusionism. And yet, illusionism is not simply rejected; the rococo preserves it by playing with it, and this play still has such power that we easily forget that it is just play. But how are we to understand this play? Bauer's interpretation of the rococo would place it on the threshold of a quite modern aestheticism. The Bavarian rococo church invites, yet resists, such interpretation. If the Bavarian rococo church cannot accept the illusionistic theatre of the baroque, this is not because it wants to carry the pictorialization and hence the aestheticization of that theatre still further, but because baroque illusionism has gone too far in this direction already, and threatens to deny the worshiper the role of an actor.

In this connection it is important to keep in mind that the Bavarian rococo church almost never has only one fresco. Besides a large fresco spanning the nave, there is at least one other over the choir. In larger churches, especially in medieval churches redecorated in the eighteenth century, this number is greatly multiplied. Thus, while it is true that the rococo church places special emphasis on a point of view near the entrance (rightly one of Rupprecht's key characteristics), it is equally true that this point of view is usually unable to do justice even to the main fresco, let alone to the fresco scheme as a whole. That discloses itself only to someone who is willing to change his point of view, to walk through the church. Think of the small frescoes that in so many churches accompany us as we circle the nave. The multiple perspective of the large frescoes of Bavarian rococo churches similarly presupposes a moving spectator. The popularity of processions must be remembered. We can do justice to a church like Die Wies only if we keep in mind how it functions as a pilgrimage church. Processions and pilgrimages make those who join them both actors and spectators. The same is true of the mass. It is this very traditional theatricality of religious life that denies not only a sharp boundary between spectator and spectacle, between audience and actor, but also that illusion of a fusion of picture and reality accomplished by illusionism. The frescoes of the Bavarian rococo church embody this twofold denial.

The obvious connections between the rococo of the court and the rococo church should not lead us to overlook dissimilarities that betray their very different foundations. For the rococo of the court Hauser's analysis may well be right: its play with the theatre suggests a merely aesthetic playing, the tired art of a class that had already lost much of its leadership to the bourgeoisie. But that analysis does not ring true when applied to the rococo church. Churches like Steinhausen and Die Wies, let alone countless small village churches that were built or redecorated in the fourth and fifth decades of the eighteenth century, demand a very different interpretation, which locates this art not only between the baroque and the Enlightenment, but also between the baroque and the Middle Ages. The Bavarian church rococo is the art of a society that remained in important ways closer to what had existed in Bavaria before the Reformation than to what went on in Paris or London. This helps to account for the deep affinity between rococo and late Gothic art.

TIME, HISTORY, AND ETERNITY: THE TEMPORAL DIMENSIONS OF THE ROCOCO CHURCH

The Church and Religious Action

Before its rediscovery in the late nineteenth century the Bavarian rococo had long been considered a sad aberration in the history of art. Given what aestheticians have demanded of art, it is indeed difficult to justify this architecture. In a successful work of art nothing is supposed to be superfluous, while it should be impossible to add anything without weakening or destroying the aesthetic whole. Excess is to be avoided. "Less is more." This leaves little room for a style as intoxicated with ornament as the rococo.

Not only the rococo church, but all religious art has to reject the ideal of aesthetic self-sufficiency. As Louis Dupré points out, religion "cannot survive as a *particular* aspect of life."[1] Religious art dies when art claims autonomy. It is impossible to reconcile religious art with modernity, at least if modernity is understood to imply the splintering of a once coherent value system that finds expression in such slogans as "war is war," "business is business," "art for art's sake." Religion and art for art's sake have to be enemies. All genuinely religious art has to be aesthetically incomplete in order to remain open both to life and to the higher dimension which it serves. What makes the Bavarian rococo church unique is therefore not that it is incomplete and preserves openness, but the way in which it plays with the aestheticism implicit in the progressive pictorialization of the visual arts ever since the Renaissance, and playing with it, puts this aestheticism in its place.

The aesthetic approach also cannot do justice to architecture. The architect has to take into account the uses to which his work is to be put; and those using it cannot keep aesthetic distance from it. As long as we measure buildings by the aesthetician's conception of what constitutes a complete work of art, architecture has to appear, as Kant considered it, deficient and impure, a not-quite-respectable art. To succeed as architecture, a building must be aesthetically incomplete.[2] To do justice to successful architecture we have to refer it to the actions that alone can complete it; to do justice to a church we have to keep in mind the function that it serves.

A church is a house in which the congregation joins the priest in holy celebration: the mass is more than a drama of sacrifice and thanksgiving enacted before the faithful in grateful commemoration of the passion. Christ's sacrifice must also be the sacrifice of His people, who in this drama are both spectators and actors. A church may be no more than a structure hallowed by the action it serves. But often it will be more than a perhaps-decorated shelter, providing a stage for the sacrifice of the mass. Especially the church of the Counter Reformation seeks to prepare the individual for this sacrifice. Such preparation takes time; it implies a movement out of the secular and everyday into a sacred and festal dimension. This movement is first of all a movement of the body. The worshiper approaches the church, enters it, sits down, rises, steps forward. To understand a baroque or rococo church we have to understand how it links this movement of the body to a movement of the spirit. Our progress through the church prepares us for the mystery of communion.

Every church approaches this task in its own way, and yet there is general pattern. To point to that pattern I shall first sketch the movement suggested by St. Michael in Munich, the church that more than any other determined the course of Bavarian church architecture in the ensuing two centuries. This sketch will be followed by an examination of Johann Michael Fischer's Augustinian priory church in Diessen, which will enable us to appreciate not only the extent to which the rococo church is just a variation on a baroque theme, but also what separates it from the baroque.

The Triumph of St. Michael

Even though it is the precursor of countless churches, St. Michael remains unique.[3] In part this uniqueness is explained by the extraordinary contribution made by its builder, Duke Wilhelm V, to the Catholic cause. The complicated program governing the façade still speaks of the duke's aspirations (fig. 45). Especially the statues tell a story that joins secular and sacred history and helps to prepare us for what awaits us within. With its rows of rulers this façade has no immediate precursors, just as it found no successors.[4] One has to go back to French cathedrals with their galleries of kings, which similarly merged theological and dynastic considerations.[5] The key to this merger lies in the politics of the time, which placed the dukes of Bavaria in the forefront of the increasingly militant Counter Reformation in Germany. The role played by Wilhelm V, by Albrecht V, his father, and by Maximilian, his son, in preventing the total victory of the Protestant Reformation in Germany cannot be overemphasized. In the Bavarian dukes the Jesuits found their most valuable German allies.

The façade's program goes back to Wilhelm V himself. Three rows of rulers were framed, above, by the statue of Christ holding a golden globe that once occupied the niche just beneath the golden cross that still crowns the entire façade, and below, between the two portals, by Hubert Gerhard's statue of St. Michael defeating the devil. The duke's confident self-assertion expresses itself in his decision to place three early rulers of Bavaria, associated with the Christianization of the land, in the top row, above Charlemagne and other emperors. One senses Wilhelm's refusal to yield first place to the emperor in Vienna. We see the duke himself, holding a model of the church he founded, in the center of the second story, next to his father, Albrecht V.

If the political statement made by the façade cannot be misread, it is more difficult to understand its justification: why should rulers appear on the façade of a church? The question was both asked and answered by the *Trophaea Bavarica*, a learned commentary on the church published at the time of its consecration,[6] which tells us that these rulers are St. Michael's fellow fighters, protecting the church against its enemies. We are reminded of the military iconography of early Romanesque churches, which often found its focus in the western part of the church, which was conceived as a bulwark against the onrushing hordes of the devil, defended by St. Michael leading the angelic host.[7] But here the angels have become Christian rulers. In their forefront we see the founder of the church, whose actions are placed by the façade in the context of a history understood as the ongoing struggle against evil.

The special significance of St. Michael for Bavaria—and for her duke, who had been born on the archangel's feast day—is hinted at by the Golden Fleece, which we see below the statue of the angel. St. Michael and the Golden Fleece are linked in a story told by the Byzantine historian Nicephorus, which provided the authors of the *Trophaea Bavarica* with an introduction. At a place near Constantinople called Sosthenium the Argonauts had once been put to flight by Amycus, when a man with eagle's wings appeared to them, renewed their courage, and foretold victory. In thanksgiving the Argonauts erected a shrine with a statue of their unknown helper. Centuries later Emperor Constantine visited the old sanctuary. After that visit St. Michael appeared to the emperor and revealed that he had been the unknown helper of the Argonauts. Just as he had come to their assistance, he now would help the emperor in his first fight against godless tyrants. Repeating the action of the Argonauts, Constantine too built a sanctuary, the Michaelium. Wilhelm V repeats this action for a second time. St. Michael in Munich is the new Michaelium, the duke the new Constantine. But he also belongs with the Argonauts, who, braving danger, had succeeded in rescuing the Golden Fleece from the dragon. Wilhelm V had in fact just been decorated with the Golden Fleece, the highest order of the House of Hapsburg, for his help against the Turks and his effort in the victorious struggle against the former archbishop of Cologne, who had turned Protestant and had sought to transform his diocese into a worldly principality. For the duke it was a happy intervention. Religious and political interests coincided: for the next two hundred years the archbishops of Cologne were to be members of his family, the House of Wittelsbach.

The façade glorifies these deeds by presenting them as a reenactment of a mythical archetype. The present is given deeper significance by being placed in the context of sacred history; at the same time it gains mythical significance. Time is transformed into a mythical present. Characteristic of the Bavarian baroque and rococo is both this transformation and the way it depends on words, on interpretations that open up dimensions at which what we see barely hints. Like all emblems, these churches remain fragments unless this verbal dimension is taken into account. The façade invites us to liken the ruler both to Christ and to St. Michael. But the ruler also exemplifies the human condition. We all have been created in the image of God and are all called to battle; and like the duke we can count on the assistance of "the unknown helper" of the Argonauts.

The interior of the church surprises with its monumental spaciousness. The light choir, dominated by the three-storied high altar, draws us forward and upward to the altar's apex marked by the golden disc of the sun with the initials IHS. Much more decisive than on the façade is the victory of the vertical over the horizontal, prefigured by the more difficult victory of the nave's rising wall-pillars over the horizontals of the entablature, and interpreted by Christoph Schwarz's painting of St. Michael's victory over the devil (fig. 110). The battle theme of the façade is thus carried into the church, but it now sounds a different, more psychological note.

If in the high altar and the architecture the vertical appears to triumph, the earthbound horizontal dimension is given special emphasis by our own progress through the church. We belong to the horizontal, to time, not to the triumphant verticals, which lack the

110. Munich, St. Michael, interior before World War II

power to cancel the burden-character of our own existence. The images that accompany our progress recall us to the battle within our own selves. More dangerous than infidels or apostates, more serious than the enemies without, are the enemies that dwell within us, threatening a worse kind of death than weapons can inflict. St. Magdalen and St. Ursula, to whom the first two chapels were once consecrated, demand repentance and purity.[8] As we move on, St. Andrew and St. Sebastian call on us to follow Christ even unto martyrdom and death. Of death speak the relics of saints and martyrs that accompany our progress. *Tota domus tumba est, superis commune sepulchrum.*[9] The whole church is a tomb, a sepulchre. The *Trophaea Bavarica* speaks with special pride of the relics: the complete bodies of eight saints, relics of almost all the apostles, a relic even of the Virgin. That our progress through the nave is a journey unto death, and in this respect an image of human life, was made still clearer when the beginning of this journey was marked by the Christ Child at the portal and its end by the altar of the cross, whose base was meant to represent Golgotha, and by Giovanni da Bologna's crucifix rising behind it, which together dominated the crossing. It was here that Duke Wilhelm V asked to be buried.[10] The church is not only the tomb of saints; it is his tomb as well. In the contrast between the founder's proud image on the façade and the grave monument in the crossing (never completed), the triumph of death would have found another striking expression.

But the triumph of death is only one theme. Just as verticals triumph over horizontals, eternity triumphs over time. The scepter of death is broken by Christ's free submission to it, repeated by the martyrs' imitation of his example. The instruments of the passion, the *arma Christi* carried by the large angels that occupy the niches of the wall-pillars and accompany our progress through the nave, are the only weapons that can defeat death. Sacrifice turns death into triumph. The theme of sacrifice, stated in the nave, becomes explicit in the paintings Antonio Viviani created for the two side altars of the crossing, reminding us of the sacrifice of the old and new covenants, of Abraham's sacrifice of Isaac and of God's sacrifice of His Son. The choir arch, which once framed Giovanni da Bologna's large cross, now in the eastern arm of the transept, proclaims the transformation of death into victory.

Choir and nave belong to different domains. The nave is to be walked through, but our progress leads only to the crossing, only to the cross, to death, not through the triumphal arch into the light choir, from which we are separated by seven steps. With its ascending rows of apostles, saints, and angels, the choir represents the Glory of Heaven. The nave belongs to time, the choir to eternity. The crossing joins the two, just as the cross joins vertical and horizontal, heaven and earth.

Journey to a Bavarian Heaven

The tensions between vertical and horizontal that give St. Michael a heroic cast seem resolved in the deceptively simple façade Johann Michael Fischer designed for the Augustinian priory church (1732) at Diessen (fig. 111).[11] Geometric order based on the equilateral triangle helps to account for its balanced harmony. Its gentle undulations, which shift from concave to convex and back, recall, if only from a distance, work by Borromini

111. Diessen, priory church, façade. The tower was built 1846–48.

and Guarini. More immediate antecedents are provided by the churches Christoph Dientzenhofer built in Bohemia.[12] But none of them show the effortless ease of this façade. Not that tension is altogether absent. Fischer, too, plays off verticals against horizontals. The vertical impulse is strongest at the façade's center, where the force generated by the dark portal extends beyond the small oval niche that holds a bust of the Virgin to bend upward the center of the windowsill above. Reinforced by the masterly grouping of the windows, this force proves strong enough to dent the horizontal of the entablature's architrave; in the large rococo cartouche that bears the priory's coat of arms it floods into the broken pediment; continuing into the gable, it bends and breaks through a second cornice with the large niche that holds a statue of St. Augustine, only to come to rest in the semicircular arcs at the peak of the gable.

But is it quite right to speak here of "rest"? Like an Italian fountain, Fischer's façade generates its own downward movement. From the eye of God, which crowns the gable, it flows down the terminal cornice and comes to a preliminary rest in the two vases that mark its endpoints; from there it descends through small volutes to the broken cornice, follows it a brief distance, cascades down concave arcs to the two large vases that frame the attic, to return to the earth in the outer pair of pilasters. This circular motion of ascent and descent gives the façade an unending life.

The dark low space beneath the organ tribune that first receives the entering visitor is not part of the picture that presents itself to him (fig. 112). Like a darkened auditorium it only lets him focus his attention on the bright, stagelike interior, from which he is separated by an iron grille. Hitchcock has criticized this interior for its uneasy marriage of tectonic baroque and decorative rococo elements. Especially the architecture he considers baroque: "Fluted pilasters and tall entablature blocks give strong tectonic character to the wall-pillars, and this tectonic emphasis is even stronger at the choir arch, which is narrower than the nave, and either side of the choir, where pairs of engaged columns reinforce the piers." Diessen does indeed have its place in that tradition of wall-pillar halls inaugurated by Munich's St. Michael and developed by the architects from the Austrian Vorarlberg, although the omission of tribunes over the side chapels owes more to that Gothic variation of the wall-pillar scheme renewed by Hans Alberthal with the Jesuit church in Dillingen; an omission that, according to Hitchcock, "strongly emphasizes . . . the wall-pillars as important structural elements (fig. 113).[13] Their "unmistakable structural significance" is said to make them the interior's "most conspicuous inherited Baroque elements" and to stand in the way of the homogeneity desired by the rococo and of its "emphasis on continuous surface framed by decoration." This "stylistic ambiguity," Hitchcock claims, "definitely lessens the value of the whole as a consistent aesthetic, or even religious experience."[14]

But is this really how we experience this interior? Bergmüller's frescoes, which cover most of the vault, prevent us from seeing that vault as a firmly established architectural boundary, let alone as a mass requiring massive supports. The impression they give of billowing sails is heightened by the arrises formed by the intersections of the transverse vaults of the side chapels and the main vault; in Bohemian fashion they sway inward in three-dimensional arcs. Together the frescoes form a unified zone of color, interrupted

112. Diessen, priory church, interior

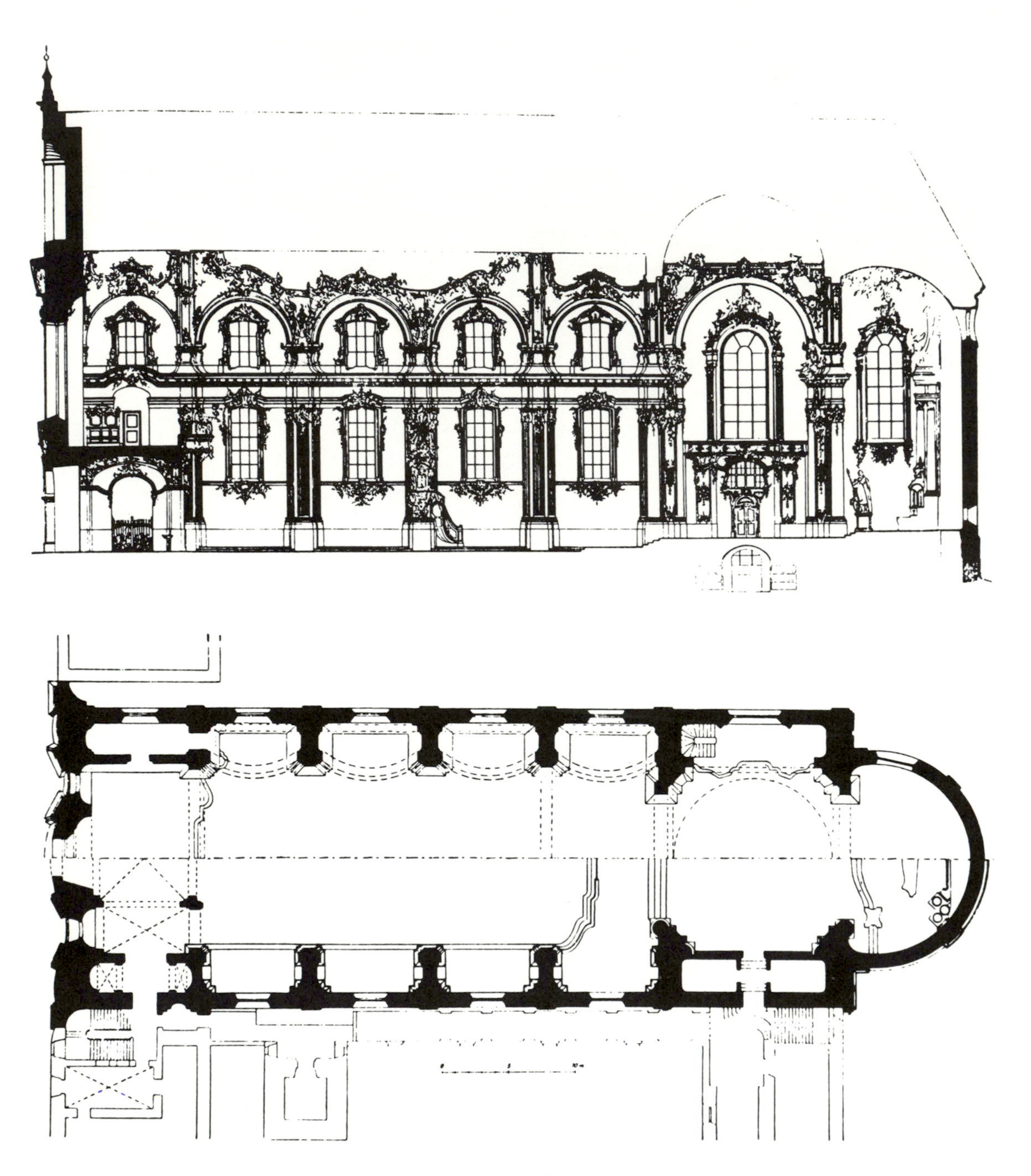

113. Diessen, priory church, section and plan

only by the choir arch and the rib-band separating the large fresco covering the three central bays of the nave from the smaller fresco beyond. A second such zone is formed by the altars of the church. The brown, yellow, and gold of their architecture dominates over the colors of the altar paintings; white sculptures provide accents and at the same time establish a link to the white ground provided by the architect. The unity of this zone is enhanced by the careful pairing of the altars, each pair the work of a different sculptor-decorator. The lightest and most elegant of these is the second, the work of Johann Baptist Straub, distinguished not only by paintings by the Venetians Pittoni and Tiepolo, but by the altars' elegant asymmetry, which invites us more insistently to see the pair as a single whole. The altars' asymmetry lets them become brackets that help to give unity to the interior. This device, often particularly effective in such small village churches as Hörgersdorf or Eschlbach (fig. 152), is one of the most characteristic and revealing features of the rococo church.

From this point on the paired altars increase in size and complexity. Architectural elements become more important. The columns of the paired altars flanking the choir arch reappear in more monumental form in the high altar. This shift to columns parallels the already-mentioned shift from the fluted pilasters of the nave to the columns of the choir and of the triumphal arch that is its gate. In both cases columns are used not because of their tectonic significance, but because of their festive appearance, appropriate to the sacred character of this part of the church. They have a symbolic and pictorial rather than an architectural function.

The altar zone below is quite as pictorial in its way as the fresco zone above. Characteristic of the rococo church is the *separation* of these two zones, each of which possesses a certain integrity of its own. At Diessen their separation is emphasized not only by the strong cornice with its modillions, but also by the way the foot of the tall attic, reminiscent of both St. Michael and Fürstenfeld, curves outward, mirroring the cornice's own outward turn. The only place where this separation breaks down is in the high altar, which thus links the two zones.

The pictorial quality of this space makes us pause but does not discourage us from entering it, as it would if the picture were a more complete whole. But here too much, including the main fresco and the fresco above the choir, has remained half or completely hidden. As we enter and walk through the church its pictorial quality, so strong as long as we remain near the entrance, begins to disintegrate; the architecture begins to speak more strongly as architecture. Only now do we see the large windows that were first hidden by the wall-pillars, and experience the walls that bound this space. There is indeed tension between pictorial unity and Fischer's architecture. But in assessing that tension we have to keep in mind that the point of view near the entrance cannot be given too much emphasis if the church is to function as a church. That point of view can only be a beginning, the experience that it grants can only be an overture that demands further development, demands that we move through the space that has presented itself to us as a picture. It is not simply the pictorialization of architecture that is characteristic of the Bavarian rococo church, but the unending play between pictorial and architectural reality that it establishes.

If a standpoint in the west, near the entrance, lets us see the interior as a picture having its center in the high altar, walking through the church we become more conscious of the difference between nave and choir; the latter remains inaccessible and pictorial. In the preceding chapter I called attention to the way the choir arch, with its stuccoed curtain, helps to transform the choir into a second stage. The inaccessibility of the altar room, which goes along with its pictorial quality, is underscored by two steps and a marble balustrade that bar us from entering the fifth bay. Separated from the altar room by three more steps, this bay becomes a transitional zone, very much like a proscenium.

As in St. Michael, our progress through the nave is accompanied by reminders of our mortality (fig. 114). Of death and hell speak the paintings of the first pair of altars, representing the death of Joseph on the right, the fall of Lucifer on the left. The second pair, including Tiepolo's *Death of St. Sebastian* and Pittoni's *Death of St. Stephen*, links death to martyrdom. And yet that linkage also ties death to that ecstasy that allowed St. Stephen to say: "Behold I see the heavens opened, and the Son of man standing at the right hand of God" (Acts 7:56). The third pair opposes St. Augustine in ecstasy to the repentant Mary Magdalen. The last two altars, with paintings of *Christ on the Cross* and *St. Catherine and St. Dominic Receiving the Rosary from the Virgin*, represent a climax to this series, and yet, as the balustrade that separates us from them makes clear, they belong already to that more sacred space that finds its culmination in the high altar.

Time, in the clock (now broken) above the choir arch, presides quite literally over our progress through the nave.[15] A stone in the pavement below calls our attention to the vault beneath the choir in which the founders of the church lie buried. Like St. Michael, this church does not let us forget that it is the grave of saints. Just before the balustrade stops us, this sepulchral character of the church asserts itself most forcefully: in glass shrines we see the bones of St. Rathard, an ancestor of Count Berthold I who founded the priory in 1132, and of the count's daughter, St. Mechthild.

In one rococo church after another such bones fascinate and disturb the modern visitor. What is their place amidst all this elegance and beauty? But like the clock above the choir arch, they state a theme that is to prevent us from losing ourselves in the merely aesthetic: *Memento mori*! Gravestones similarly not only commemorate, but have a symbolic significance, especially when they recall the death of someone as powerful as Count Berthold I. Again and again this church calls our attention to the House of Diessen and Andechs, before its tragic end one of the leading families of the Middle Ages, and more important, a family that could boast of twenty-eight blessed and holy men and women, among them St. Hedwig, the patron of Silesia, and St. Elizabeth of Hungary. The names and relics of members of this family, once so powerful, speak of the triumph of time, but also of a saintliness that triumphs over time. Although dead, they live, and live in this church. The building attests to that continuing life.

If the authors of the *Trophaea Bavarica* could call St. Michael *imago coeli*, and defend this claim by pointing to the relics that had been assembled and let the apostles be present in the church, Diessen deserves to be called the image of a quite *Bavarian* heaven. The saints who are present in this church are, first of all, Bavarian saints. The history that culminated in the present building could be cited as proof that theirs is a living presence. This emphasis on a church's unique history inseparable from the *genius loci* is a characteristic feature of the Bavarian rococo. The historical dimension, which in St. Michael was relegated to the façade, is now brought right into the church. Most often frescoes spell out this history, as they do in Diessen.

In the eastern part of the main fresco we see the founding of the priory and its confirmation by Pope Innocent II (fig. 22). Interesting is a small detail: the founder points

114. Diessen, priory church, St. Jerome from the high altar

to a design showing Fischer's rococo church, an anachronism that seems to say that the six-hundred years that have elapsed since the priory's founding did not matter. The rebuilding of the church is *deliberately confused* with its first building.[16] The past is appropriated in a way that lets it be present. Once again we encounter an attempt to heighten the significance of present events not simply by placing them into the context of history, but by annulling that history. The priory's founding and the life of its founders are not events that we are now done with. They are still happening. This appeal to the past, which at the same time conflates past and present, echoes the temporality of the mass, which not only commemorates a sacrifice that took place long ago, but brings it into the present. Similarly the fresco invites us to consider temporal events *sub specie aeternitatis*. Time and eternity are reconciled.

Plate 1 The western part of the fresco shows St. Mechthild as a young girl entering the convent of St. Stephen. The frescoes of the adjoining bays add scenes to this historical play: the smaller fresco over the choir arch represents the founding of the Augustinian priory's predecessor in 815 by St. Rathard (fig. 115), while the fresco over the organ gallery tells of the discovery of the bones of St. Rathard in 1013. As so often in the churches of the Bavarian rococo, all these events are presided over by the Virgin, whom we see in the center of the main fresco as queen of heaven, surrounded by the patrons of Diessen. This central group possesses a different degree of reality than the rest of the fresco. Once again one is tempted to speak of theatre within theatre. Significant is the way this representation of the Virgin differs from that of the high altar. There we see the Virgin ascending; here she seems to come down. Again the circle of descent and ascent: heaven comes down to earth so that we may participate in the ascent from earth to heaven. In this Virgin the nave possesses its real center. She is the real theme of the events portrayed.

Especially the large fresco, spanning as it does the three central bays of the nave, helps to counteract the primacy of a point of view near the entrance and the orientation toward the east, toward the high altar, that it entails. To be sure, those parts of the fresco showing the priory's founding and the Virgin in heavenly glory demand a point of view in the west, as does the smaller fresco showing the founding of the priory's predecessor. But the scenes along the main fresco's long sides are best seen when we stand right beneath it, while the Mechthild scene and the fresco above the organ demand that we turn around and face west. This use of multiple perspectives helps to give the nave a certain autonomy. Johann Baptist Straub's splendid pulpit, while it does not compete with the high altar, nevertheless provides the nave with a secondary focus.

The nave *invites* movement; the choir *discourages* it. Not only do steps and balustrade inhibit us from going further; a certain distance is established by Fischer's choice of a vocabulary that helps to mark the choir as a more sacred zone. The curtain of the choir arch and the shift from pilasters to columns deserve to be singled out, but we should also note the way the semiellipses of the arcs spanning the nave give way in the choir to more festive semicircles: the almost organic movement of the arrises in the nave is stilled, and instead of the scalloped frames of the nave we have now a ringlike circle, which functions less like a frame than it suggests a hole cut into the vault, placing the painted heaven behind or above it. The bipolarity of the church interior finds here a particularly convincing articulation (fig. 115).

115. Diessen, priory church, decoration of the vault

The large inscription circling the dome of the choir recalls St. Peter and other Roman churches. But these Roman reminiscences are given a local significance. As the inscription tells us, what the fresco represents is not simply the glory of heaven, but "the glory of the saints and blessed of Diessen and Andechs." The same saints whose bones have found a resting place in and beneath the church, whose activities on earth are celebrated by the frescoes of the nave, are now seen gathered in heaven with Christ. This representation of heaven gains special significance when we remember that it rises right above the founders' burial vault. Visually and symbolically the fresco thus helps to establish a vertical axis that transforms death into triumph. This transformation, however, is only theatre. Moreover, the strength of the fresco's circular frame and the painting's darkness prevent us from taking this illusion of heaven too seriously. We are given no more than a prelude for the mediation which only the high altar can provide. Only here at the place of the divine sacrifice are heaven and earth truly united. Only in the representation of the Assumption of the Virgin, to which the church is consecrated, are the two zones, which have been kept more or less separate up to this point, really brought together. The interplay of ascent and descent that governs the façade reveals here its deepest significance.

At the time of its consecration the church at Diessen was being celebrated as "a new heaven"; as "an incomparably holy new Jerusalem." In support of this interpretation of the church as an image of heaven one could point to the horde of angels and putti, 397 in all, that are found in this church. But no more than St. Michael can this church be understood as a more or less literal representation of heaven. Rather it points to and means heaven, and it does so in different ways.

In the nave heaven and its queen appear as a force presiding over time and transforming what would otherwise be meaningless events into sacred history. Special emphasis is placed on the part played by Diessen and its founders in that history. To stage this play—a play written by his employer—the painter had to raise a second earth above and paralleling our own, distinguished by its peculiarly ideal and dreamlike sense of place and time, which blurs here and there, past and present.

The fresco of the choir bay presents us with an illusion of heaven. That Bergmüller here retains the illusionistic approach is no peculiarity on his part. We find the same difference between nave and choir frescoes in countless other rococo churches. The reason for this is obvious enough: the choir should appear closer to heaven than the nave. But it should not only appear so. We must keep in mind that our progress toward the choir is a figure of man's progress toward death. The power of death makes it difficult to take this theatrical presentation of heaven too seriously. Only the divine sacrifice promises to defeat that power.

Even Kings Must Die

Just after entering St. Johann Nepomuk in Munich, in the place usually given to an image (say a St. Magdalen) admonishing us to repent, we see on top of the confessional a sculptural group showing a corpse, entwined by snakes, one arm raised in anger, the mouth opened in a scream. Towering over the restless corpse a man, perhaps a monk, raises his right arm in a gesture that does not so much extend help as establish distance. This gesture is echoed by the putto below, who uses one of his wings to shield his eyes from the disturbing vision. MORS PECCATORUM PESSIMA, proclaims the inscription above: "The death of sinners is the worst."

Egid Quirin Asam's contemporaries would have had no difficulty recognizing in this group a representation of the last scene of Jakob Bidermann's *Cenodoxus*.[17] The play closes in heaven. After a very sudden death, the doctor of Paris, who with Faust-like pride had sought to raise himself beyond the human condition, is called before God's judgment throne and condemned to eternal suffering. Meanwhile, on earth, those mourning the death of this honored man are frightened by the corpse's refusal to lie still. Three times it raises itself and speaks, the first two times to report on the trial taking place in heaven, the third time to tell of the judgment and to curse both the mother who bore him and himself. One of those watching this terrifying spectacle, a certain Bruno, recognizing the vanity of what the world thinks important, leaves society and becomes a hermit. Friends follow his example (Bruno is the founder of the Carthusian order); their example in turn was followed by members of the audience. The theatrical performance spilled over into life.

It is a typically baroque conclusion. The obsession with time and death, the emphasis on pride that refuses to acknowledge man's mortality, are thoroughly Christian, and especially baroque. And yet, as the doctor's sudden and unexpected end dramatizes, death is the reef on which all pride must suffer shipwreck. Vain are all our attempts to secure our existence, to hold onto things, to hold onto our own life. In his sand-clock poem Góngora reflects upon the futile attempt to build time prisons of glass that would allow us to hold it in our hands, and thus to master it. Even the most powerful are not masters of their lives. Life is like smoke, pulled apart by a strong wind; or like a carnival play, or like a firework that, hardly begun, is already over. In poem after poem, play after play, we hear the same refrain: *Vita enim hominum,/Nil est, nisi somnium*, as Bidermann's *Chorus mortualis* sings. "We are such stuff as dreams are made on." For Descartes, who in this respect belongs very much to his age, the deepest root of the suspicion that life may be nothing more than a dream, of our inability to seize reality as it really is, is our subjection to time. Man cannot escape its tyrannical rule. Even kings must die.

But death is not only frightening, it also possesses healing power. Otherwise death could not be considered the just and fitting punishment for original sin. It is fitting because to open oneself to the unavoidability of death is also to recognize that the snake's promise, "You will be like God," is vain. In his pride Cenodoxus suppressed such recognition, thus doing violence to man's essentially finite being. The doctor's damnation is inseparable from his refusal to acknowledge his own mortality. The *memento mori* that his unhappy end shouts at us calls on us to repent and to tame our pride. Thus it calls us back to our true selves, and, by forcing us to acknowledge our impotence, prepares us to receive the divine sacrifice.

Egid Quirin Asam's representation of the end of Cenodoxus is only a particularly striking example of the countless ways in which the rococo church restates the baroque theme of mortality and repentance. In church after church clocks sound the same call. Large and small, we find them most often above the choir arch, but also above the organ, in the high altar, or even in the fresco. Their *memento mori* is repeated by altars, by grave monuments, and, most disturbingly perhaps, by the jewel-bedecked bones of martyrs and saints. They are the trophies of time.

And yet, the seriousness with which the old Egid Quirin Asam makes Bidermann's theme his own seems to belong to the seventeenth century more than to the eighteenth. For even if the rococo church does not let us forget tyrannical time, its celebration of color and form, of the mysteries of changing light, its joyful acceptance of the visible in all its evanescent beauty, prevent us from taking this *memento mori* too much to heart. In these interiors death seems to lose its sting. The rule of time is recognized, but has lost its terror. It is perhaps in this respect that the rococo church may most truly be called *imago coeli*. In this world it lets us glimpse something of a world that is not subject to aging and death. Not that the Bavarian rococo experienced the world as paradise. But better than most periods—better certainly than the baroque, which placed so much emphasis on the gap between heaven and earth, on the irreality of this life and the necessity of preparing for the next, on the struggle against death and devil—the Bavarian rococo knows that all has not been lost with Adam's fall. Within itself our world carries a piece of paradise. Here we have a key to the presence of countless putti in these churches. The play of these "children without age" points to an existence that does not suffer from the burden of time and does not know the rift between time and eternity.[18]

The Bavarian rococo church presupposes the ability to accept human temporality. The sacrifice of Christ appears not so much to open a gate to a reality beyond time, and thus life, as to redeem them. It is this accepting attitude toward time, so much more difficult for us to understand than the baroque's dread of it, that triumphs over every *memento mori*.

Herein lies the profound difference between the Bavarian rococo church and those artificial ruins that began to be built at about the same time all over Europe. To be sure, as Hermann Bauer has insisted, rococo and ruin architecture are closely related phenomena.[19] How closely is suggested by the first artificial ruin in Bavaria, the Magdalenenklause (1725–28), which Joseph Effner built for Max Emanuel in the park of Nymphenburg. Here the aging elector, who had known both pride and the vicissitudes of fortune better than most, may have found comfort and edification meditating on St. Magdalen (fig. 116).

The Magdalenenklause is not without predecessors. Hermitages, places that invite meditation on the vanity of life, had long played a part in the life of the baroque court. The inconspicuous location of the building, tucked away in a corner of the park, the rustic simplicity of the interior, and the rock and shell work that transform its chapel into an artificial grotto had become standard elements of such buildings.[20] What is new and forward looking, however, is that the building is now given the look of a ruin: in places plaster seems to have fallen off; the walls are furrowed by very visible cracks. At first there may seem nothing very surprising in all of this. Ruins had long been experienced as "the trophies of time" and as signs of the limits placed on man and his work.[21] In his *Tower of Babel* Bruegel had contrasted the huge tower that tries to reach heaven, and precisely

116. Munich, Nymphenburg, Magdalenenkapelle

because of the enormity of the undertaking must remain a ruined fragment, with small houses that surround it; some of these cling, like swallows' nests, to the tower, which even as work continues on it seems to revert to nature. These houses suggest a very different conception of building and dwelling, a more intimate, less prideful, and more trusting relationship to time.[22] But if the ruin had long been a motif in literature and painting, it did not occur to Brueghel's contemporaries to actually build ruins, to anticipate the ravages of time in this way. This became popular only in the eighteenth century.

The built ruin is architecture that turns against architecture, and it does so in a number of different ways. First of all, it subjects architecture to the logic of painting. Architecture becomes a picturesque motif. As Bauer has emphasized, the aesthetic approach that betrays itself in this pictorialization of architecture also marks rococo architecture.[23] The ruin also challenges architecture by its incompleteness. Time and nature appear to have triumphed over man. And yet this appearance is itself managed by man. In this ruin architecture man is to experience his own impotence. But far from feeling depressed by this, he enjoys it, for he senses that it is in this more natural environment rather than in the artificial realm of the court, with its rulebound behavior, its rulebound architecture and gardens, that man is truly at home. The ruin beckons the aristocrat who has grown tired of his aristocratic existence to a more natural life. Thus from the very beginning the Magdalenenklause was placed in a "jardin sauvage," which avoided the geometry of the French park and offered the delights of serpentine paths and the natural look that were to become characteristic of the English park.[24]

We should, however, bear in mind that this attack on artifice is itself highly artificial and betrays distance from rather than proximity to nature. The trophies of time have become human creations. How much more natural is a church like Die Wies, lying in its meadow before the Alps, belonging to this landscape. Even more than the miraculous statue which a contemporary pamphlet calls *flos campi*, flower of the meadow, the church invites such metaphors suggested by the Song of Songs (fig. 117). The Bavarian rococo church does not owe its origin to that nostalgic distance from nature that gave rise to ruin architecture. It knows little of the tension between artifice and nature so characteristic of the rococo of the court.

We should also keep in mind that the Magdalenenklause in its artificially natural setting remained, spiritually and literally, on the periphery of courtly life. Members of the court, and especially the tired elector, enjoyed playing here the part of hermits, as elsewhere they enjoyed playing the part of peasants. In such games, too, a contradictory attitude to the artificiality and ceremonial of court life finds expression. The Magdalenenklause certainly cannot be interpreted as a serious attack on it. It is itself artifice, a game that hints at the possibility of a more natural mode of existence—that may even, if we look far enough ahead, hint at the revolution that was to overthrow the old order—but it does no more than that. There is a deep connection between the parody of the baroque tournament, discussed in the preceding chapter, and this architecture. Just as the tournament of 1723 distances itself from the baroque tournament, becoming an ironic play with its conventions, so the ruin distances itself from past architecture, even as it plays with it. In this connection the historicism of the Magdalenenklause must be mentioned. Not only the Italian baroque, but Moorish and Romanesque motifs are quoted. This play with the architecture of the past presupposes that architecture is beginning to lose its place in the architectural tradition. This loss of place betrays itself at about the same time in Fischer von Erlach's *Entwurff einer historischen Architectur* (1721), the first history of architecture, and in his attempt to create a "historical" architecture, most convincingly realized in the Karlskirche in Vienna (1715–25). Different as they are, the Karlskirche, built less in honor of St. Charles Borromeo than as a monument to Emperor Charles VI, and the Magdalenenklause both give a weight to the historical dimension that points forward to the historicist architecture to come and to that loss of style inseparable from it.

But do the baroque and rococo church not also insist on the importance of the historical dimension? In this respect one can liken the Karlskirche to St. Michael, the Magdalenenklause to Diessen. The comparison, however, hides more than it illuminates: St. Michael and Diessen invoke history only to idealize and transfigure it. Historical time is transformed into a repetition of events that possess a significance transcending time.

117. Die Wies, pilgrimage church, exterior, looking south

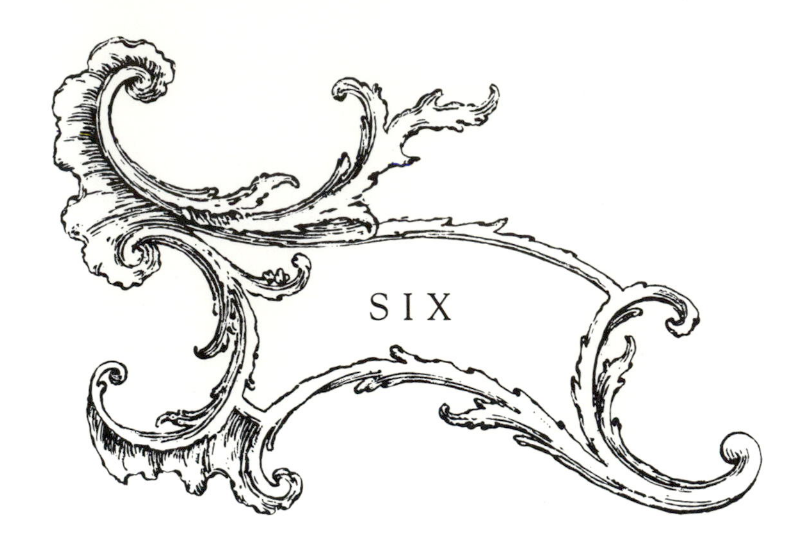

ECCLESIA AND MARIA

The Church as Symbol of the Church

In a side chapel of Munich's Frauenkirche is the gravestone of Johann Michael Fischer. Its inscription tells something of the ethos that governed his work. It deserves to be quoted in full.

> Here rests an artful, industrious, honest, and upright man (Job 1:1), *Johann Michael Fischer*, proven architect of three most excellent princes, also municipal master mason in Munich; who never rested, building with his artful and tireless hand 32 churches, 23 monasteries, besides very many other palaces, but edifying many hundreds with his old German and honest uprightness, until finally, on May 6, 1766, in his 75th year, he put down for a foundation stone of the last building of the house of eternity (Eccles. 12:5) that stone which is the firm cornerstone of the church (Eph. 2:30)

The references to the Old and New Testament call our attention to what we might otherwise overlook: the significance of Fischer's life is assured by its scriptural background. His life is prefigured by that of Job, while the churches he built prefigure that house of eternity which is man's true home. Characteristically baroque is the wordplay on "building." Fischer is presented as a builder in three quite different senses; he built (*erbauete*) churches, monasteries, and palaces; he also edified (*erbauete*) many hundreds by his character; and finally he laid the foundation stone of the house of eternity. We are likely to see in such wordplay little more than equivocation. For us to build is no longer to edify, nor are we likely to see a strong connection between the many churches the architect built and the house of eternity. But in the eighteenth century—at least in Catholic Bavaria—architecture still helped to articulate man's place in a larger order, his ethos. It still possessed that ethical or moral function hinted at by our use of the word "edify."

In the preceding chapter I tried to exhibit the moral or tropological meaning of the rococo church. A church like Diessen speaks to us of who we are, how we are to live, what we are to heed. In this chapter I want to examine the allegorical significance of the rococo church as a figure of the Church and, intertwined with it, its anagogical significance as a figure of "the house of eternity." Like its precursors, the Bavarian rococo church continues to be understood as a figure of that spiritual community which St. Paul describes with an architectural metaphor in the passage to which the inscription of Fischer's gravestone refers us at the very end:

> So then you are no longer strangers and sojourners, but you are fellow citizens with the saints and members of the household of God, built upon the foundation of the apostles and the prophets, Christ Jesus himself being the main cornerstone, in whom the whole structure is joined together and grows into a holy temple of the Lord; in whom you are also built into it for a dwelling place of God in the Spirit [Eph. 2:19–22]

The church building is understood as a figure of the community of saints. Thomas Aquinas gives succinct expression to this understanding: *Domus, in qua sacramentum celebratur, ecclesiam significat et ecclesia nominatur.* [1] The house in which the sacrament is celebrated is not just called "church," but signifies the Church. To build a church is thus not simply to erect a structure that serves certain functions. What the Thomistic definition demands is not satisfied by a functionalist approach that insists only that the church building provide a suitable frame for the liturgical action. A church must be more than what has been called a prayer-barn, a serviceable shed to which decorations may have been added. The church must present itself to us as a *symbol of the Church.*

Hieroglyphic Signs

How can this signification become visible? Perhaps the most common response has been to exploit the conception of the faithful as members of the City of God.[2] Just as the Church in history, this "pilgrim city," as St. Augustine calls it, points toward the eternal glory of heaven, so the churches man has built are figures of the city that is described in Revelations as a new Jerusalem, "coming down out of heaven from God, prepared as a bride adorned for her husband" (Rev. 21:2). Built as a perfect square of pure gold, this city is not in need of sun or lamp. Lit up by the Glory of God, "its radiance is like a most rare jewel, like a jasper, clear as crystal" (Rev. 21:11). At least since Clement of Alexandria the church has thus been understood anagogically as a representation of the Heavenly City. The traditional language of the dedication ritual makes this understanding explicit and authoritative. It governs the Bavarian rococo church quite as much as the medieval cathedral.

But if the church is "mystically and liturgically an image of heaven,"[3] this still does not say how this image character is to be understood. The key passage from Revelations speaks of a splendid city; but how literally is this to be taken? Does the spirituality of the conception not render all attempts to build its earthly image inappropriate? In this connection it is important to keep in mind that as the figure or image of the Heavenly Jerusalem the church is itself prefigured by other historical places and structures. To understand the Christian church we have to understand it as pointing not only forward to what is to come, but also backward to what has been, especially to that place where in a dream Jacob saw heaven open and linked to the earth by a ladder. A new Bethel, the church, too, is "none other than the house of God" and "gate of heaven" (Gen. 28:17). Similarly, it is prefigured by such divinely inspired structures as Noah's ark, Moses' tabernacle in the desert, and, most significant perhaps, the temple Solomon built in Jerusalem.[4] As sermons and treatises demonstrate, well into the eighteenth century the authority of these paradigmatic buildings, to which one can add such visionary structures as the temple of Ezekiel, is taken for granted.[5] These biblical paradigms are supplemented with Christian structures. St. Michael thus invokes Constantine's Michaelium, Diessen St. Peter in Rome.[6]

But even when spelled out in this way, the definition of the church as signifying the Church provides no more than hints that invite imaginative elaboration and widely different responses. The early Christian basilica which, according to one interpretation, imitates a Roman city, complete with entering gate and arcaded streets, represents one such response; its golden or starred ceiling functions as a metaphorical device, designed to show that what is being imitated is not simply a city, but the City of God, ruled over by Christ as king.[7] The church architecture of the early Middle Ages rests on very different presuppositions. Here the idea of a city seems to have suggested a place of peace, a refuge, offering protection from the evil and insecurity reigning in the world. The outside of the church now gains often a fortresslike appearance, while the inside with its mosaics and murals "is to make us forget that we find ourselves in a building of stone and mortar, since inwardly we have entered the heavenly sanctuary."[8]

Similarly, Hans Sedlmayr has interpreted the Gothic cathedral as an illusionistic image of the light-filled Heavenly City.[9] Challenging that interpretation, Otto von Simson has shown that the sense in which the cathedral is an image of the Heavenly City must be given a less literal interpretation. Responding to the qualities of light and order associated with the City in Heaven, the architect could try to create an analogous work here on earth. Such a response is reinforced by the traditional association of the abode of the saints with the superlunar world and its unchanging harmony and order. Simson's discussion of a passage by Abelard helps to make clearer some of the presuppositions that guided Gothic architecture and remained active throughout the Renaissance.

> After identifying the Platonic world soul with world harmony, he first interprets the ancient notion of a music of the spheres as referring to the "heavenly habitations" where angels and saints in ineffable sweetness of harmonic modulation render eternal praise to God. Then, however, Abelard transposes the musical image into an architectural one; he relates the Celestial Jerusalem to the terrestrial one, more specifically to the Temple built by Solomon as God's "regal palace." No medieval reader could have failed to notice with what emphasis every Biblical description of a sacred edifice, particularly those of Solomon's Temple, of the Heavenly Jerusalem, and of the vision of Ezekiel, dwells on the measurements of these buildings. To these measures Abelard gives a truly Platonic significance. Solomon's Temple, he remarks, was pervaded by a divine harmony as were the celestial spheres.[10]

Abelard's discussion points to the "dual symbolism of the cathedral, which is at once a 'model' of the cosmos and an image of the Celestial City."[11] Since the order of the visible world, especially that of the heavens, is itself supposed to be analogous to that of the City of God, this dual reference is to be expected, although emphasis on this duality should not let us overlook that the divine order which informs the cosmos as well as the Heavenly Jerusalem also speaks to us in the archetypal structures of the Old Testament as it does in the body of man, the microcosm, especially in the body of the perfect man, Christ, which also means the Church.

That this understanding of the signification of the church building survives well into the eighteenth century is shown by the countless sermons and treatises that were published to help celebrate the consecration of the more important churches. As Bernhard Rupprecht points out, in Bavaria at least the rococo church continued to be understood as a sign of Jerusalem, heaven, the City of God, and the cosmos.[12] But if the basic meanings that helped to shape church architecture from the early Christian basilica through the Middle Ages remained thus very much alive, this leaves open the question of how this understanding of the signifying function of the church now translates into architectural terms. Can the rococo church still be understood as the image of heaven? Are we to think of the Heavenly City, which needs neither sun nor lamp because lit by the Glory of God, when we respond to the magic of the indirect light that spiritualizes the architecture of the rococo church? Does the profusion of gold represent the City in Heaven, which was built "as a square of pure gold"? Such associations were no doubt present to those who built these churches and those who worshiped in them. But what was said above about the rise of perspective and the resultant secularization of the visible[13] makes it difficult to take such associations very seriously.

The gap that has opened up between the visible and the spiritual, between picture and reality, makes it impossible for the church of the Counter Reformation to simply return to the medieval understanding of the church as a more or less literal representation of the divinely established order of the Heavenly City or the cosmos. I fail to be convinced by Gisela Deppen's suggestion that, like the Gothic cathedral, St. Michael is a representation of both heaven and the cosmos: the light-filled nave represents the sun, the darker and smaller side chapels the six planets. The interpretation seems farfetched. Citing and endorsing it, Herbert Schade points to the text of the *Trophaea Bavarica*, which does speak of the church as a *coelum creatum*, a created heaven, as *imago coeli*, an image of heaven.[14] But what are we to make of such supporting evidence? To what extent did such conceptions, while undoubtedly very much in the mind of the learned authors of the *Trophaea Bavarica*, actually shape the architecture? Do we *see* the church as an image of heaven? To be sure, the angels that are found in such great numbers in this church have a more than merely ornamental function; they signify heaven. And so do the sun discs with the monogram IHS and the rose of angels that before World War II took the place of the missing dome above the crossing, an ornament which to Schade recalls Dante's image in the *Paradiso* (fig. 110). But such intimations of significance cannot establish the architecture of St. Michael as an image of heaven in the sense in which Simson, let alone Sedlmayr, interprets the medieval cathedral as an image of the Heavenly City.

When the *Trophaea Bavarica* calls the church an image of heaven it does not speak of how the church looks, but of the numerous relics that have been assembled there. These relics, which, the *Trophaea Bavarica* asserts, let the chorus of the apostles become a present reality, make the church an image of heaven. We may well wonder what this has to do with the appearance of this particular church. Pamphlets like the *Trophaea Bavarica* force us to ask to what extent the traditional meanings of the church, while undoubtedly still very much in everyone's mind, still helped to shape and are realized by the architecture. In this connection we should note the importance of the commentary. Not only does it explain in what sense the church is to be understood as an image of heaven, but it plays a significant part in establishing these meanings. The interpreting word gains this importance precisely because the church no longer provides an illusionistic or even analogous image of the City of God or of heaven. The signifying function of the church has become hieroglyphic. The church still signifies the Church, but the mode of signification has changed.

In an early baroque church like St. Michael ornament plays an important part in establishing this hieroglyphic character. In the rococo church this part is taken first of all by frescoes. But in both cases what is seen is incomplete without the interpreting word. This need for interpretation is of course not peculiar to the Counter Reformation church. Suger's *De consecratione ecclesiae sancti Dionysii* shows that treatises like the *Trophaea Bavarica* have their place in a long tradition. But I doubt whether any earlier period was equally insistent on accompanying architecture with explanatory texts. Not that the interpretation furnished by interpreting sermons or tracts is simply an ingenious ex post facto construction: if the church seems incomplete without the interpreting word it is because it presents itself to us as possessing meanings demanding interpretation. We sense that the building and decoration of the church attempt to translate a text into visible terms. This translation depends on images that, like hieroglyphs, are signs rather than pictorial representations. A baroque or rococo church presents itself to us as an emblem awaiting interpretation.

Emblematic Play

Andreas Alciatus's *Emblematum liber*, first published in Augsburg in 1531, established the emblem as an art form that joins *pictura* and *scriptura*, image and text. Alciatus's emblems are first of all pictures whose hieroglyphic character lets us see them as signs. This sign character is further emphasized by the motto that heads each emblem and helps to establish it as a sign calling for interpretation. This signification is spelled out by the explanatory text that follows the picture. This triple structure of *inscriptio*, pictorial *res significans*, and explanatory *subscriptio* defines the emblem.

The emblem presupposes a still medieval understanding of the things of nature and of historical events as signs or figures. Alan of Lille summed up this view of things in the often-repeated lines:

Omnis mundi creatura
Quasi liber et pictura
Nobis est et speculum;
Nostrae vitae, nostrae mortis,
Nostri status,

Nostrae sortis
Fidele signaculum

All the world's creatures are like a book, a picture, and a mirror to us, the truthful sign of our life, death, condition, and destiny.[15] Bestiaries, herbaries, and lapidaries are the dictionaries that help us to read these signs, which have their foundation not in human invention, but in God's two books, Scripture and Nature.

The art of the baroque and rococo remains indebted to this tradition, but the insistence on enigmatic images and ingenious interpretation suggests a changed attitude. It has become much more difficult to decide where discovery becomes free invention. Hovering between the two, emblematic art and its interpretation are necessarily playful. This is so because God's two books are thought to have been written in a language man does not fully understand. The signs given us by God have become hieroglyphics. Here it is of more than historical interest that the emblematic tradition, while it presupposes the medieval view of the spiritual significance of things, has another and more immediate root in the Renaissance preoccupation with Egyptian hieroglyphics.[16]

Why such interest at that time? I have suggested earlier that the new subjectivism and rationalism has to lead to a secularization of the visible. This has to call into question the understanding of nature as a text addressed to man. The visible threatens to lose its spiritual meaning. By insisting on the sharp distinction between *res cogitans* and *res extensa* Descartes accepts this loss: if things have hidden significations it is not given to man to decipher them. This understanding of the being of nature is incompatible with the art of the emblem, which refuses the Cartesian separation. To understand the importance of the emblem for the arts of the seventeenth and eighteenth centuries one has to keep in mind that the emblem expresses an understanding of reality that has its place between the figural understanding characteristic of the Middle Ages and the literalism of the moderns. In this respect the emblem belongs together with the baroque theatre. Like the emblem, the theatre joins picture and text, the art of the painter with that of the poet. This led to arguments for the superiority of the drama as a living and speaking picture over either painting or poetry.[17] Important is the emphasis on image and text. To be genuinely emblematic the drama must do full justice to the rights of the eye. It must understand itself as *Schauspiel*, where the spoken words help to interpret the emblematic character of the images, just as words, not only sermons and pamphlets, but much more important the words of the mass, interpret the meaning of a baroque and rococo church. It is this play that links the eye and the ear, image and text, which has to be recovered if full justice is to be done to such a church.

The modern visitor, no longer at home with the tradition in which these churches have their roots, will find it difficult to respond to such play. In a rococo church we find ourselves somewhat in the position of someone who hears a poem in a language of which he understands only a few words. Given this difficulty we are likely to respond in the way which is most readily available to us: we experience the church as an aesthetic phenomenon. The spiritual dimension is neglected. But just as we cannot appreciate an emblem by responding only to its picture part, ignoring the motto and interpreting text, so we cannot appreciate a baroque or rococo church without an understanding of its motto and without a recovery of the interpreting text.

Marian Piety

Nowhere is the emblematic character of the baroque church more apparent than in the Hofkapelle of the Residenz in Munich (1601–30).[18] Here the threefold structure of the emblem—picture, motto, explanatory text—governs the decorative scheme. Stucco reliefs provide images that are traditional figures of the Virgin, many of them taken from the Song of Songs. Each is accompanied by an inscription. Together they constitute a litany to the Virgin (figs. 118 and 119). The two foci of this decoration are provided by the monogram MRA, at the center of the nave vault, and the monogram IHS at the center of the choir vault: *Per Mariam ad Jesum*, through Mary to Christ. The monogram of the Virgin is bracketed by verses that interpret the whole scheme for us: the plants, heavenly bodies, temples, and houses that we see above are signs given to us by the prophets, icons of the hidden nature of the Virgin to which the monogram points.

The architectural images deserve special attention. Many of them—the City of God, Solomon's temple, the Gate of Heaven, for example—we have already encountered as figures of the Church. Their presence here should not surprise us. The Virgin herself is a figure of the Church. This allows us to say that the Hofkapelle, too, not only is a church, but signifies the Church. It does so, however, not as a quite direct representation of heaven or of the City of God, but by presenting emblems of the Virgin.

We can assume that the program of the Hofkapelle was not the work of the artist responsible for this decoration, Hans Krumpper, but was handed to him by his noble patron, Elector Maximilian, who relied presumably on his Jesuit advisers. Following the Council of Trent the veneration of the Virgin had become a central theme of Counter Reformation piety. Even Descartes made a pilgrimage to the Virgin of Loreto, in thanksgiving and to reassure himself of the legitimacy of the method that had come to him. Nowhere was the power of this Marian piety more visible than in Bavaria, whose ruler consecrated his chapel

Virgini et mundi monarchae
Salutis aurorae

"to the Virgin and queen of the world, dawn of salvation." To her he pledged his life and to her he entrusted his country.[19] We still see the *Patrona Boiariae*, the work of Hans Krumpper, on the façade of Maximilian's Residenz under the inscription:

Sub tuum praesidium confugimus
Sub quo secure laetique degimus

"We seek refuge under your protection, under which we live secure and happy." Similar madonnas appeared on the houses of the burghers.

Yet these were not happy times. In the name of the Virgin Maximilian gained victory in the Battle of the White Mountain, which fueled the Thirty Years War.[20] Not to own a rosary became a crime. But it would be a mistake to overemphasize the extent to which the veneration of the Virgin was imposed by Maximilian and such post-Tridentine orders as the Jesuits and the Capuchins on a population that had almost been lost to Catholicism. The vigor and spontaneity of the popular response argues differently. A population

118. Munich, Residenz, Hofkapelle, decoration of nave vault

119. Munich, Residenz, Hofkapelle, decoration of choir vault

suffering from war, disease, and hunger, inclined to interpret these as signs of God's anger, turned to the Virgin as a child seeks refuge under her mother's coat. This was the theme of the rapidly growing cult of the Maria Auxiliatrix Christianorum, focused on the copy of a Cranach painting that had been placed in a chapel above Passau in 1622. To her, who was thought to have been the real victor over the Turks in the Battle of Lepanto, one turned for deliverance from the Swedes and, later in the century, from the Turks.[21] In the happier eighteenth century this cult has its counterpart in that of the Schöne Maria, the Fair Mary of Wessobrunn. Their juxtaposition reveals something of the difference between baroque and rococo.[22] That this Marian piety is as much a renewal of medieval attitudes as a product of the Counter Reformation is shown by the many medieval, usually late Gothic, images of the Virgin that still form the venerated center of otherwise baroque or rococo altars and churches, as in Steinhausen and Andechs.

Given this Marian piety, which even contemporaries found particularly characteristic of the Bavarians,[23] it is not surprising that the model provided by the Hofkapelle, so unlike anything Bavaria had seen up to this time, was soon imitated. The decorations of the Hofkirche in Neuburg (1616–19) and of the Stiftskirche in Hall in the Tirol (1629–30) offer good examples, as do such smaller churches as Aufkirchen (1626), Feldkirchen (ca. 1630), and Essenbach (ca. 1670).[24] Such Marian programs become particularly popular in the eighteenth century, and it is no accident that the church that, as we have seen, for the first time exhibits all the essential characteristics of the Bavarian rococo church, the Zimmermann brothers' Steinhausen, is a pilgrimage church consecrated to the Virgin. Marian piety is a presupposition of the Bavarian rococo church.

The Church as Symbol of the Virgin

Comparing the decoration of the Hofkapelle with the way Steinhausen realizes a very similar Marian program, one is struck first of all by the part the rococo church assigns to the painter. In a manner that recalls devotional pictures of the baroque (fig. 120) Johann Baptist Zimmermann's main fresco gathers familiar Marian symbols to form a coherent composition (fig. 121). As in the Hofkapelle or in Neuburg, in Steinhausen, too, the program derives at least in part from the Lauretanian Litany. Following its invocations the fresco shows Mary as queen of heaven, standing on the crescent moon, circled by angels carrying lily and rose, olive and palm branch, attended by patriarchs and prophets, apostles and martyrs, confessors and virgins. All the world, here represented by the four continents, praises her. Without antecedents in Southern Germany and of decisive importance for subsequent developments is the way the fresco joins traditional Marian symbols in an Arcadian landscape that recalls the Venetian rococo.[25] This striking appearance of landscape and the airier and looser composition that distinguish Zimmermann's frescoes from the work of Cosmas Damian Asam, in comparison still baroque, are motivated by the intent to establish the church, especially its nave, as a figure of the Virgin. We should recall here that the Book of Revelation likens the New Jerusalem to a bride. The simile points back to the bride of the Song of Songs, which is read as a figure of both the Church and the Virgin. The Song of Songs is the sacred text that legitimates the fresco's

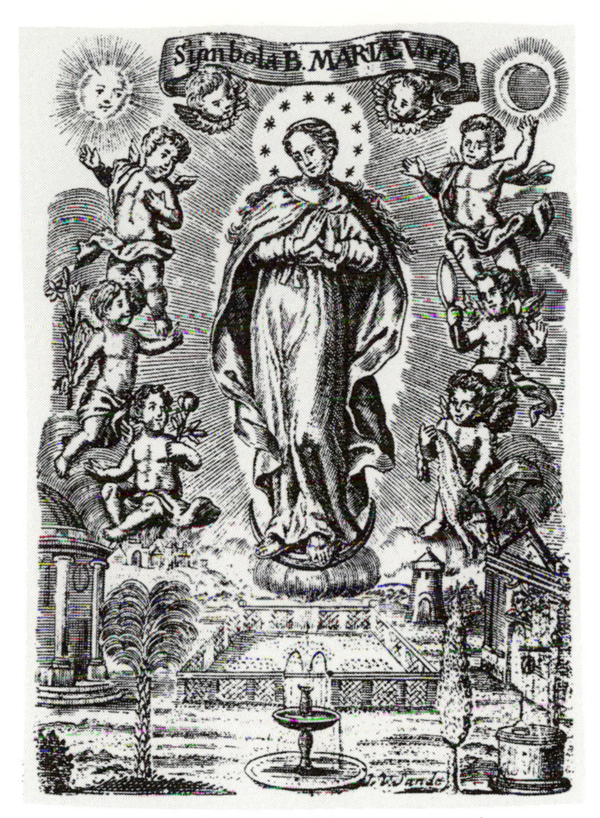

120. Devotional picture of the seventeenth century

garden imagery. Like the motto of an emblem, the inscription of the cartouche above the choir arch expresses this intent in unmistakable fashion:

HORTUS CONCLUSUS
ES DEI GENITRIX
FONS SIGNATUS

Above the inscription we see a fountain in a garden that recalls contemporary parks. In this park grow cypress and cedar, they too signs of the Virgin.

The meaning of these signs is enriched by the juxtaposition of this garden with another at the opposite, western end of the fresco, less tidy, a bit more like an English garden. Adam and Eve, whom we see beneath the tree at its center, make this the terrestrial paradise, suggesting that the garden above the choir arch is the paradise to come. Not only in this case do juxtapositions within the fresco encourage interpretation. The correspondences established by the painter engage us in a hermeneutic game.[26] Rupprecht's interpretation of the fresco and its function in the church traces some of the relations:

> Because the symbol *hortus*-garden has been taken literally and made into a concrete object, it can be placed into a readily seen relationship to the historic garden of paradise. In this juxtaposition the visible fountain oscillates between being object and symbol. It is a garden fountain and yet it is juxtaposed with the forbidden fruit and Eve. The tree thus becomes a symbol. As the source of evil it stands opposite the *fons signatus* = Mary. Eve, however, standing opposite the fountain, lets us personify it. Mary = fountain as the second Eve.[27]

Not only in this fresco do we find that oscillation between literal and symbolic meanings that lets Rupprecht speak of a "rococo of hermeneutics." It is inseparable from the way the rococo church signifies the church by signifying the Virgin. Consider, to give just one other example, the fresco that Zimmermann's student Martin Heigl painted for another pilgrimage church, Marienberg near Burghausen (fig. 122). Here we see above the chronogram *Deo aC VIrgIneae CoeLItVM RegInae*—"to God and to the virginal Queen of Heaven"—a large ship. Pope, cardinal, and bishop make this the ship of the Church. Cistercians invite us to board it. Its blue-and-white pennant beneath a star inscribed with the name of the Virgin points to the close relationship between her and the Church. We see her, close to the mast, providing a link between the ship and God at the fresco's center. This ship is juxtaposed with a path decorated with roses on which we see the blessed journeying toward the Gate to Heaven. Another chronogram interprets this part of the fresco: *MarIa DeIpara seCVra CoeLI IanVa*—"Mary, mother of God, secure Gate of Heaven." A much more involved interpretation would be required to even begin to do justice to the many traditional symbols of the Virgin found in this fresco, including garden and fountain, cedar and rose, the Tower of David and the ark. But enough has been said to point to the central constellation: entrusted to and protected by the Virgin, the ship (*navis* = nave) of the Church is at the same time a figure of her who is the Gate of Heaven and the garden of the Song of Songs. Church = ship = garden = Virgin.

122. Marienberg, pilgrimage church, main fresco

121. Steinhausen, pilgrimage church, main fresco

Given the purpose of this chapter, one aspect of this equation deserves to be singled out: the ship, that is, the nave of the church, is a figure of the Virgin. We get here a hint of the foundation of that analogy that has suggested itself a number of times: *Mary is to Christ, as nave is to choir.*[28]

Like much baroque poetry, the frescoes of Steinhausen and Marienberg presuppose a then-well-known vocabulary of symbolic images. What makes the frescoes of the Bavarian rococo distinctive is not the presence of such images, but the way in which they become the material of a play that lets the painted objects hover between their literal and their symbolic significance, where the latter tends to proliferate into a multiplicity of significations established by the many relations in which any part of the fresco stands to others. Consider again the ship in the fresco of Marienberg; all the other images may be taken to unfold its significance. Often the motto or inscription of such a fresco is provided by one or more large cartouches. Sermons or treatises furnished the interpretation that made the emblem complete.

Many such sermons have survived. As Rupprecht points out, like the frescoes of the Bavarian rococo, they delight in a logic that to us may seem exasperating and surreal. To give just one example: trying to establish the identity of the Bavarian Gotteszell with Shiloh, mentioned in the Old Testament as a sacred place of peace and rest, prefiguring the peace that shall reign in heaven, a sermon appeals to the commentator Cornelius à Lapide, according to whom Shiloh was that mountain on which the ark found its resting place. He refers to it as *tabernaculum Dei*. But translated into German this becomes *Gotteszell*: and the Cistercian convent in Bavaria and the Old Testament mountain are thus shown to be one and the same place. The sermon is not content to claim that the latter prefigures the former; it insists on identity.[29] We noted a similar confusion of the now and then, the here and there in the main fresco of Diessen.[30] Such confusions are indeed inseparable from that sacralization of space and time attempted by the rococo church in which, as in any church, events that took place long ago in a faraway place are to become present reality. We may find it difficult to take seriously the rococo frescoes' playful combinations, the sermons' obvious delight in ingenious and fantastic argumentation. How are we to reconcile them with our understanding of religion as something sublime and very serious? But has it not become playful precisely because art is here still taken to have its center in mysteries that we cannot seize without destroying?

Marian Naturalism

Given Thomas Aquinas's definition of the church building as signifying the Church, how does the rococo church establish this signification? The preceding discussion of the main frescoes of Steinhausen and Marienberg suggests the answer: The Bavarian rococo church signifies the Church by signifying the Virgin. Often it is the fresco over the nave that helps to establish this signification.

Our discussion has centered on two churches consecrated to the Virgin. Can we generalize and claim that the Bavarian rococo church, especially its nave, is to be interpreted as a figure of the Virgin? This much at least must be granted: The main fresco of Steinhausen inaugurated a type of fresco that helps to define the Bavarian rococo church. Crucial is the introduction of landscape elements that suggest a garden in late spring. In Steinhausen these have to be understood as figures of the Virgin. I would suggest that this remains true even when a fresco is not obviously governed by a Marian program. Consider the landscape elements in the main fresco at Schäftlarn. As we saw in chapter 4, it represents the monastery's founding (fig. 92). After Steinhausen it is difficult not to see the theatrically idealized Isar landscape as an emblem of the Virgin. Whenever the frescoes of the Bavarian rococo suggest a garden in late spring we should think of the Song of Songs. Representing a garden the fresco means both the Virgin and the Church.

This is not the only, nor even the most obvious, way in which the rococo fresco signifies the Church: at the center of nearly every main fresco we find a glory composition with angels and saints. In this respect, too, Steinhausen is quite characteristic. Zimmermann here returns to a by-then-quite-traditional representation of the Church. But compared with earlier glory compositions—and one does not have to go back to the ecstatic visions of Correggio or Lanfranco or Pietro da Cortona, but only to the glory compositions of Cosmas Damian Asam—Zimmermann presents us with little more than a theatre in the clouds. In good part this is a function of the way we read the blue rising above the garden landscape as a quite earthly sky. This threatens to reduce the clouds of the glory composition, in spite of the yellow and golden hues that have not quite lost the metaphoric force of the gold backgrounds of medieval paintings, to merely atmospheric phenomena. What we see is a strange apparition in the sky, possessing a very different and more remote degree of reality from that of the garden below. If the fresco as a whole has its center in the Virgin, this heavenly theatre has its center in the luminous Name of God. The fresco may thus be said to have two centers: the Virgin and God. The same is true of the church as a whole. As pointed out before, choir and nave possess different degrees of reality. In keeping with that difference the choir fresco is free of all landscape elements. While the main fresco, with its impossible perspective, raises a second, idealized earth above our heads, the choir fresco, more faithful to Italian illusionism, offers us a spectacle set in heaven: ranged around God the Father and the Holy Spirit, an angelic orchestra is awaiting the Son. While the spiritual center of this fresco is the absent Christ, the main fresco has its spiritual center in the Virgin. The bipolarity here reveals its significance: nave is to choir as the transfigured earth is to heaven, as the Virgin is to Christ. Joining the two, the church hints at the wedding of the Song of Songs, which is both, the wedding of Mother and Son and of the Church and Christ. Another symbol of this wedding is the Assumption of the Virgin. Small wonder that so many of these churches are consecrated to it.

There is nothing surprising about the Marian character of the main fresco of Steinhausen. Unusual, however, is the elimination of the traditional architectural symbols taken from the Song of Songs. In the fresco we see neither the Tower of David nor the Temple of Solomon, neither the Gate of Heaven nor the City of God. Symbols that belong to the sphere of the garden are singled out for special emphasis. This allows the painter to create a symbolic landscape that betrays its origin in the secular rococo.

It is an origin that Zimmermann's art and, beyond that, the art of the Bavarian rococo never quite cast off. Hans Sedlmayr has suggested that in the *régence* period all the arts gravitate toward the realm of Pan. In the work of Watteau this world "with its dryads and oreads, its copses and hills, nymphs and shepherds, merges with an idealized state of social being and with elements from the dream-world of the theatre, until nature, art, and love combine to form a mystical paradise on earth in which eternal youth, brightness, beauty and transfigured sensuousness deny age, infirmity, sin, and death."[31] Much of this can also be said of the work of Zimmermann. How small the step is from sacred to secular art is shown by the large fresco Zimmermann painted twenty years after Steinhausen for the elector Max III Joseph in the Great Hall of Nymphenburg (fig. 123). How important is it that this fresco celebrates, not the Virgin, but the Olympian gods? Zimmermann's art threatens to blur the world of Pan with the garden of the Song of Songs. The distance that should separate Christ and the Virgin from pagan deities does not manifest itself. This returns us to the suspicion that the Bavarian church rococo, too, unable to take inherited meanings seriously, uses them as material for a charming but only aesthetic play.

Are we to conclude, then, that such blurring of the sacred and the profane, the Christian and the pagan, betrays a superficiality possible only when religion is no longer being taken very seriously? Are we to say, disregarding the considerations advanced in chapter 4, that such confusions are just another expression of rococo decadence?

123. Munich, Nymphenburg Castle, fresco of the great hall

But such confusions are by no means confined to the rococo. In this respect, too, the Bavarian rococo only takes up and develops a baroque theme. Perhaps the most moving evidence is provided by the Latin odes of the Jesuit Jakob Balde, in which he celebrated the Marian pilgrimage churches of the region, about a hundred years before Steinhausen was built.[32] Reluctant to use the name Maria, Balde does not hesitate to describe the Virgin in figures borrowed from antiquity. Descriptions of nymphs and nereids are now applied to her: associated with the moon she is Diana; juxtaposed with Venus, the destructive *mater saeva cupidinum*, she is the *mater blanda cupidinum*.[33] There is something highly artificial about such neo-Latin poetry that celebrates the Virgin in Horatian measures, always playing with the model provided by the Roman precursor, trying to pour Christian wine into a pagan vessel. But this artificiality not only lets us become aware of the inadequacy of the words the poet has inherited to say what he has to say, but this very inadequacy lets us recover the experience to which this poetry is a response. Still capable of moving the modern reader are those poems in which Balde ties the Virgin's presence to a particular place as its *genius loci*. Three stanzas from his ode to Maria Waldrast (Forest Rest), a pilgrimage church almost lost in the forests and mountains of the Tirol, can stand for others.[34]

Spirat ex antris pietas et horror
Conscius Nymphae. Locus ipse gratum
Terrect ac mulcet Superique per prae-
cordia fusi.

Sive nimbosas quatit Auster alas
Sive brumali Boreas minatur
Ninguidus cornu, niveae tenemus
Virginis aulam

. . . .

O Quies semper memoranda Silvae,
O tuum vere meritura nomen,
Da frui fessis aliquando vera,
Silva quiete.

Grace and awe breathe down from the grottoes.
The nymph nearby. The place
Frightens and soothes the welcome visitor and gods
Move through the heart.

Let the west beat its cloudy wings,
Let the north threaten us winter
With its horn full of snow, we hold fast to the court
Of the snow-white Virgin

. . . .

Forest rest, ever memorable
Truly will you deserve your name,
Let the weary some day enjoy true,
Forest, Rest.

A particular landscape is experienced as a numinous maternal presence. Inseparable from the Marian piety of the Bavarian baroque and rococo is a sense of still being at home in nature. It is this that lets nature become a figure of the Virgin and of paradise, of the paradise that was and of the paradise to come. This Marian naturalism helps to explain the anticlassical, even antiarchitectural cast of the Bavarian rococo church. More is at stake here than simply an aesthetic preference for organic forms. If the church means heaven, heaven is now thought of not as a city in heaven nor as a cloudy realm but in the image of the terrestrial paradise, that is to say, as a garden. There is little place for architecture in that garden. Adam did not need a house in paradise. And just as paradise is not sought beyond the earth, so it is not sought beyond time. The turn to nature goes along with an acceptance of time. There may be something pagan about a naturalism that recognizes the power of death and yet refuses to take seriously the fall that has set spirit against nature and alienated man from the earth. But faith in the Virgin's immaculate conception and assumption implies faith that such alienation does not have the last word. It should not surprise us that in the beauties of nature the Bavarian experiences the proximity of the Virgin.

Plate 15

It is this Marian naturalism that has to be kept in mind if we are to understand a church like Steinhausen. It justifies the importation of the Arcadian sphere into Johann Baptist Zimmermann's fresco. With much greater immediacy it expresses itself in the architecture of his brother Dominikus, in the pillars that have been likened to rising tree trunks, in their sheltering oval, and in the stuccoes. Here we are no longer dealing with an idealized landscape. Fox and squirrel, beetles and bees, birds and flowers are taken directly from the landscape outside. The spring of the Song of Songs has become a German spring.

The Wedding of Sky and Water

Hans Sedlmayr has suggested that if *régence* art revolves around the world of Pan, the central figure of the *style rocaille* is Venus as Boucher painted her.

> Her attributes—rock and conch, coral and reed, water, wave, and foam—constitute the treasury of rocaille ornamentation. Her element, water, determines the fluidity of forms. Its movement, the wave, suggests the pattern of surging and plunging; its colors, the deep cool blue of the sea and the white of the glistening spray, together with the roseate hue of the conch and the iridescence of mother of pearl, produce a typically rococo color harmony.[35]

Sedlmayr is of course thinking here first of all of the French secular rococo. But the Bavarian rococo church also comes to mind. Consider the consonance of blue and white in Die Wies; or the pulpit in the church in Oppolding, which, no longer ornamented, has itself become an ornament, surging upward, dissolving, scattering spray (fig. 124), or the doorframe in Maria Medingen, which I used in the first chapter to illustrate the revolt of rococo ornament against its merely ornamental status (fig. 7). It would be difficult to deny that rocaille here remains faithful to its origin in the realm of Venus.

Again the question: What place does this realm have in sacred architecture? Does not Venus stand for that eternal power of the sensuous that Eve's transgression has made into a threat? But here we should not forget that Mary is the antitype of Eve. As the vesper hymn *Ave maris stella* suggests, accepting Gabriel's *Ave*, the Virgin overcame sin and

124. Oppolding, St. Johann Baptist, pulpit

turned around the name of *Eva*. With this reversal the sensuous and feminine is redeemed. There is no longer a reason to radically dissociate the figures of Venus and of the Virgin.

Indeed, the seashell is associated with the Virgin quite as much as it is with Venus. This association has one source in the old myth of the origin of the pearl in the wedding of sky (of dew or lightning) and water that takes place inside a shell.[36] The myth can become a figure for the immaculate conception as well as for the incarnation. Accordingly, the pearl can stand either for the Virgin or for Christ. It is the latter interpretation that makes the shell a figure of the Virgin. As the learned Jesuit Théophile Raynaud, who compiled one of those typically baroque dictionaries of Marian metaphors, argues: just as the pearl forms inside a lowly mollusk's shell without any outside influence, so Christ developed within the Virgin without a created father (fig. 125).

125. Weyarn, Augustinian priory church, *Annunciation*, by Ignaz Günther, 1764

This interpretation is brought to mind by the large stuccoed shells that so often cover the apse vault of Bavarian baroque churches, sheltering the altar beneath. We find them in Steingaden and Maria Birnbaum, in Obermarchthal and Unter-Windach, in the cathedral of Freising and Schliersee. The decoration of the apses in Murnau and Weyarn translates this shell motif into a delicate rococo ornament. To be sure, there is a more obvious interpretation of its significance. Originally a symbol of the life-giving womb, the shell signifies birth and rebirth. Granting life after death, the shell became a symbol of heaven. Shells have long appeared above apses and niches, exalting, like a baldachin, what they shelter.[37] One can also point to the way these shells mediate between what they shelter and the architecture, helping to bind the two together. In this respect they have somewhat the same function as rococo ornament. But these interpretations do not preclude the interpretation of the shell as a figure of the Virgin bearing Christ within her womb. Alive in that figure is the older meaning of the shell as a sign of the victory of life over death, of deathless life.

Perhaps this gives us another reason for the Bavarians' enthusiastic appropriation of rocaille. Inseparable from this ornament's origin in the shell is its ambiguous evocation of both Venus and the Virgin. Earlier I argued that the Bavarian rococo church requires an ornament that can mediate between the heaven opened up by the fresco and an earthbound architecture; its protean nature, which allows it to become either picture or architecture, predestines rocaille for this mediating role. But this mediating function can itself be taken as a figure of the Virgin, who is *scala coeli*, the ladder of Jacob's dream joining heaven and earth, *stella maris*, star of the sea, and the shell, the miraculous site of the wedding of sky and water.

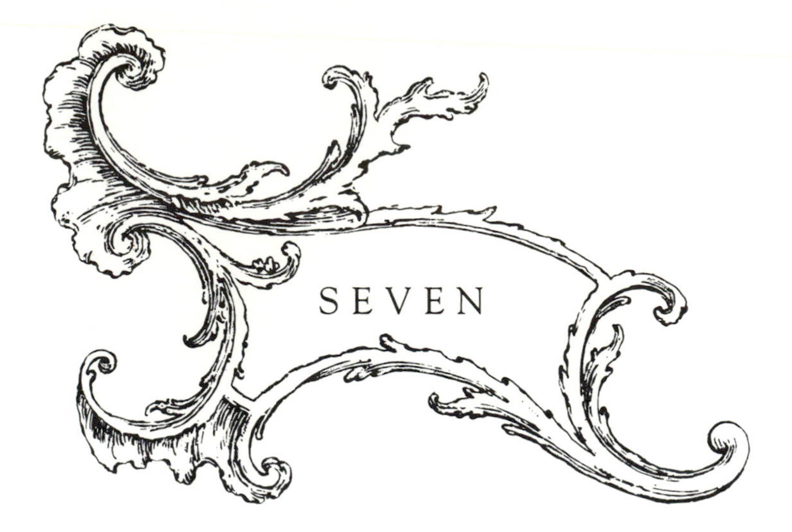

ROCOCO CHURCH AND ENLIGHTENMENT

An Ominous Mandate

In 1770 Elector Max III Joseph issued the following general mandate:

> In order to prevent all exaggeration when a new country church needs to be built, and so as not to leave the planning of the church to the self-centered whim of some priest or official, but rather to assure that a thoroughgoing uniformity in church architecture be observed as much as possible, following the example of Italy, we shall let experienced and skilled architects provide different model floor plans and elevations, depending on the number of parishioners, together with an estimate of the total cost, as accurately as this can be done, so that in this way a pure and regular architecture may be preserved, eliminating all superfluous stucco-work and other often nonsensical and ridiculous ornaments and showing in altars, pulpits, and statues a noble simplicity appropriate to the veneration of the sanctuary.[1]

This is not the only such document that has come down to us. Similar orders were issued at about the same time in Hungary and Silesia. They show something of the impact of neoclassicist aesthetics; more important, they betray the uneasiness with which the rococo church, with its extravagant decoration, filled an enlightened intelligentsia. How could such extravagance be justified? In the name of reason the Enlightenment challenged the culture of the rococo. The rococo church could not meet that challenge.

The elector, passionately devoted only to the pleasures of music and the hunt but filled with good intentions, had some right to consider himself an enlightened ruler. His paternal care for his subjects, which brought him the honorific epithet of *der Vielgeliebte*, the much loved, expressed itself in his attempt to popularize the potato as much as in his emphasis on education as the means of leading his subjects into a brighter and better age. One of his teachers had been the once-famous Johann Anton Ickstatt, a student of the rationalist philosopher Christian Wolff and one of those who worked tirelessly to bring the Enlightenment to the Bavarians.[2]

It was no easy matter. The same conditions that allowed the eye-intoxicated theatrical culture of the rococo to thrive here as in no other part of Germany made Bavaria inhospitable to the Enlightenment, with its reverence for the clear and distinct and the solid letter. There was no vigorous middle class. To be sure, there were cities, but for the most part they had remained small. Even the free imperial city of Augsburg, whose art academy, painters, and engravers had made it a center of the Bavarian rococo, had long since lost that European importance that belonged to it in the sixteenth century, when a Fugger financed the emperor. The centers of a middle-class culture that in Germany, too, had begun to assert itself were not Vienna, Munich, or Augsburg, but Zürich, Hamburg, and Leipzig. For its models it looked less to Italy than to France and, increasingly, to England. The literary culture that was to destroy the world of the Bavarian rococo was supported by a bourgeoisie that had found its *Weltanschauung* in the work of Wolff and Gottsched.[3]

Bavaria had remained a land of peasants. A Protestant visiting Bavaria in 1785 felt, not altogether unjustly, that the clock had been turned back one hundred and fifty years.[4] The Church, especially the large monasteries, still dominated the economic and cultural life of the country. More than half of the land was in its possession. At the same time the Church had retained or regained its popular base. Most of the parish priests and quite a few of the monks were of peasant stock. A career in the Church offered a son of a peasant a chance to break out of an otherwise rigid class structure and to meet aristocrats as an equal.[5]

This helps to explain why the Bavarian rococo church never lost its popular base. Churches like Steinhausen or Die Wies, Rottenbuch or Ettal are the work of local craftsmen who remained very much part of a peasant society. The phenomenon of Wessobrunn is instructive. From before 1600 this village of scattered farms sent its masons and plasterers throughout Germany and far beyond.[6] We know of well over six-hundred artists. Names like Zimmermann and Schmuzer, Feichtmayr and Üblhör hint at their importance: Wessobrunners were involved in the creation of almost all the masterpieces of the German rococo, usually in leading positions. Artist-craftsmen from Wessobrunn made a decisive contribution not only to Die Wies, Ottobeuren, and Vierzehnheiligen, but to such masterpieces of the courtly rococo as Karl Albrecht's Amalienburg or Frederick the Great's Sanssouci. This astonishing success would not have been possible without the Benedictine monastery in whose shadow many of these artists were raised. Faced with a scarcity of land to feed its subjects, the monastery encouraged them to become masons and stuccoers, employed them, and helped to secure commissions. At the same time it helped to educate them and saw to it that they knew about the latest developments in Italy or France. If the Bavarian rococo church ignores the split between high and popular art, if it ranks with the best art of the eighteenth century and yet in a profound sense remains folk art, it owes this to the integrative power of the Church.[7]

The elector's mandate heralds the coming change. A small literate elite now insists on norms that have no popular foundation. A new spirituality and a new aesthetic were to triumph over the rococo, which continued a modest life among the peasants. The delightful painted houses of Mittenwald, Oberammergau, and the Leizach valley, dating from the seventies and eighties, illustrate this transformation of the rococo into mere folk art.[8]

Bavarian Enlightenment

Not surprisingly, given the way Bavaria's intellectual culture had its centers in the monasteries, it was here that the Enlightenment made its first appearance. In 1722 (when Amigoni and Zimmermann were working in Schleissheim) three Augustinian monks, Eusebius Amort, Agnellus Kandler, and Gelasius Hieber, founded the journal *Parnassus Boicus* in the hope of fostering the growth of the arts and sciences in Bavaria.[9] Supported by such monasteries as Polling or St. Emmeram in Regensburg, this first and very modest Enlightenment was not at all anticlerical, but sought to clarify and reconcile the claims of religion with the new philosophy of Descartes, Leibniz, and Wolff: Its partisans were interested in history and natural science and became concerned about the lack of spirituality in popular religion, which seemed to content itself with spectacle and to make no distinction between superstition and genuine faith. This concern developed into law in the decree of 1746, renewing traditional condemnations of superstition, magic, witchcraft, and other devilish doings.[10] But it was reform rather than revolution that was desired by this monastic Enlightenment, and among the motives for such reform was the conservative fear that without it religion itself would collide with the new spirit.

The absolutist regime of the elector not only recognized the usefulness of these efforts, but provided them with a focus. With the foundation of the Bavarian Academy of Sciences in 1759 the Enlightenment became the servant of the state. Members of the academy were to be among the main supporters of efforts to subordinate the church to the state, an effort of particular urgency in Bavaria where the holdings of the Church made it difficult to dismiss characterizations of the Church as a state within the state. The attempt to establish the absolute rule of the elector seemed an essential step toward dissolving a still-medieval status-oriented society.

As elsewhere, the Bavarian Enlightenment saw its task as pedagogic above all. A good part of the work of the academy was focused on education, which was seen as the most effective way of breaking the hold of traditions that were obstacles to economic and spiritual progress. The attack on the culture of the Counter Reformation reached a first climax with the dissolution of the Jesuit Order in 1773, which had controlled most of higher education. Its assets were to be used to educate and better the lot of the elector's "children." A period of reaction in the eighties was followed by a more vigorous affirmation of the ideas of the Enlightenment by the administration of Count Montgelas, minister of state to another Max Joseph, who was to become the first Bavarian king. The secularization of 1803 brought the expropriation and destruction of all the old monastic communities. Many churches were now declared useless. Some were actually torn down; to salvage at least a fraction of the wealth that had built and furnished them, their inventory was auctioned off. The Benedictine abbey church of Wessobrunn was lost at that time, although the intense resistance which such destruction met from the part of the local

9. Weltenburg, Benedictine abbey church, high altar by Cosmas Damian and Egid Quirin Asam (1721–24)

10. Landsberg am Lech, St. Johannes, high altar by Dominikus Zimmermann (1752)

11. Oppolding, St. Johann Baptist, high altar by Matthias Fackler (1764). The marbling of the altar with its representations is the work of Georg Andrä and his son Franz Xaver Zellner.

12. Niederding, parish church St. Martin, right side altar, detail with St. Florian by Christian Jorhan the Elder (1762)

13. Altenerding, parish church Mariae Verkündigung. A work of the Erding architect Anton Kogler (1724), the church was decorated in the 1760s. Ship pulpit and right side altar by Matthias Fackler, figures by Christian Jorhan the Elder

15. Pilgrimage church Maria Gern before the Untersberg (1709, tower 1724)

14. Andechs, the "Holy Mountain," a center of the religious culture of the Bavarian baroque and rococo

16. Dickelschwaig in the Graswang valley, with its chapel St. Gertraud, built in 1694; inside, a charming fresco by Johann Jakob Zeiller (1765)

population (it is to this resistance that we owe the survival of Die Wies) shows what these churches continued to mean to the people.

Compared with these later developments, the elector's mandate of 1770 seems to have but little significance. Part of a flood of paper decrees, it does not seem to have been taken very seriously. But as a symptom it deserves consideration.

A Waste of Time?

Max III Joseph's mandate links pragmatic, aesthetic, and spiritual considerations. The economic argument against the extravagance, not only of the rococo church but of the culture that supported it, is especially a recurrent theme of the Bavarian Enlightenment. And indeed, how could one justify the enormous expenditures required by rococo architecture, expenditures that were often out of all proportion to the available resources? Zimmermann's two masterpieces, Steinhausen and Die Wies, offer perhaps the best-known examples. In Steinhausen the costs, which rose from an initial estimate of 9000 guilders to over 40,000, forced Didacus Ströbele, abbot of the Premonstratensian Schussenried, which was sponsoring the project, out of office.[11] Die Wies cost the staggering sum of 180,000 guilders, and in spite of generous gifts from the many pilgrims the monastery of Steingaden, which after initial doubts had supported the undertaking, was left with a huge debt.[12] In other monasteries, such as Rott am Inn, the situation was similar. Cost overruns were the rule rather than the exception. And even where the available resources or a more modest building project allowed a monastery to avoid debt, the strain placed on its economy was almost always severe. It would be interesting to know what percentage of the gross national product of Bavaria was spent at this time on religious spectacles, such as processions, theatrical performances, vestments, and the like, to say nothing of churches.

Even more revealing and more directly the target of the electoral mandate was the situation in the villages. Just two examples: 12,000 guilders were spent for Johann Schmuzer's impressive church in Garmisch. To be sure, Garmisch was a comparatively large village and the population growth in this part of the Alps had made the existing church too small. But did the populace really need this ornate a church? And we know that the local priest, Marquard Schmid, had hoped for something even more splendid. As often in such circumstances, higher authorities did not give permission to go ahead. Here it was the bishop of Freising who refused to approve a plan for a church with two towers, with the remark that an out-of-the-way place like Garmisch did not need a cathedral.[13]

The case of Bertoldshofen is similar. Here, too, it was the local priest, Johann Ulrich Julius, who pointed to the popular fraternity of St. Anthony that had been established in the village in 1685, to demand a church on the model of San Antonio in Padua with its five domes. With remarkable perseverance, begging for building materials and for funds, refusing to yield to the misgivings of higher authorities, he had his way. Even with generous donations of time and materials Johann Georg Fischer's church cost 14,000 guilders.[14]

It was the same story everywhere: priests and abbots, bishops and princes had been possessed by the *Bauwurm*, by an irrational desire to build, as Johann Philipp von Schönborn, prince bishop of Würzburg, said of himself. Very much tied to a desire, essentially still baroque, for public spectacles, for visual representation and dramatization, the *Bauwurm* cannot be reconciled with the rationality of the Enlightenment, which found its proper architectural expression in intimate interiors and in an often sober and functional public architecture.

It is symptomatic that in the sixties and seventies no really significant building projects were initiated by the Bavarian court. Cuvilliés's delightful theatre in the elector's Residenz (1751–53) and Johann Baptist Zimmermann's Great Hall in the palace of Nymphenburg (1755–57) were the last major creations of the courtly rococo in Bavaria. The fact that both served the elector's passionate interest in music is telling. In Bavaria, too, architecture was about to yield its place as queen of the arts to music and literature. The ear was becoming more important than the eye. This shift also had social significance. Even in Bavaria cultural leadership was soon to pass to the middle class, as it already had in the Protestant part of Germany, not to speak of other parts of Europe.

Yet just in the fifties building activity in the Bavarian countryside reached an absolute peak. These were the years of Die Wies, Andechs, and Schäftlarn. Just as, a generation earlier, Max Emmanuel had competed with the emperor in Vienna and the king of France in representing his own majesty to the world, so villages now competed with one another, to be sure *ad maiorem Dei gloriam*, although it is never easy to separate religion from all-too-human motives. Are this sensuousness and theatricality really compatible with the inwardness and spirituality demanded by the Christian faith? Was the elector's mandate not right to insist that sober simplicity is more appropriate to the House of God than theatrical ostentation? Especially so in the hunger years 1770 to 1773, when in some communities the infant mortality rate rose to over 80 percent.[15]

The gay splendor of the rococo has cast a light over this period that too easily lets us forget its misery. The reformers in Munich saw things differently. In all this splendor they saw mostly waste, a waste of funds and a waste of time. Would it not have been better to grow potatoes? Indeed, a key objection to popular religion was that it kept people from more productive activity. The reformers were concerned about the fact that half of the year was taken up by religious holidays. In one area of Lower Bavaria there were no fewer than 204 days on which work was forbidden.[16] The attempt to reduce their number goes back to the Middle Ages, but it was pressed with increased vigor by the Enlightenment. Austria led the way: in 1771, acceding to the wishes of Empress Maria Theresia, Pope Clement reduced the number of religious holidays to fifteen, not counting Sundays. A year later Elector Max III Joseph succeeded in having the reduction extended to Bavaria.

Such decrees met with local resistance, as is shown by efforts to ensure that the villages did not keep the demoted holidays as they traditionally had. In 1785 the festive decoration of altars and churches on such days was proscribed, high mass could not be celebrated, and devotional exercises were forbidden, as were gambling and drinking in the local inn, at least before six in the evening.

The association of devotion and drinking, of church and inn, is revealing. The reformers were not altogether wrong when they saw in the eagerness with which the peasants clung to their processions and to their holidays, which often lasted two or three days, more than expressions of religious devotion. Leisure and devotion were inseparably intertwined. Both, at any rate, kept people from working, and it was industry above all that the reformers in Munich hoped to teach the Bavarian peasant. Given this emergent work ethic popular religion seemed mostly a refuge of laziness and superstition.

But it was not laziness that built the rococo churches and let the peasants cling to their saints and their holidays; it was a very different understanding of man's life on earth and the place of work in it. The peasant knew himself to be in the hands of higher powers, and this knowledge made him uneasy about attempts to use a merely human science to secure human existence (fig. 126). Lightning rods, for example, were often felt to be an arrogant interference on the part of man in a sphere that belonged to God.[17] The same mentality found expression in the tradition of ringing bells when a storm threatened, to drive away those evil and destructive spirits to which God had granted power to molest man. Again and again, in 1788, 1791, 1792, 1800, 1804, and 1806, the authorities forbade this superstitious practice.[18] Nature was still experienced as a spirit-filled presence, which could be benign or destructive. Abundant crops were not so much something that one could take credit for as a gift from God; and it was God's wrath that showed itself in famine, disease, or war. In the face of disasters that left the individual helpless, prayerful invocation of some saint, especially of the Virgin, for intercession on man's behalf seemed a more appropriate response than planning, which, no matter how careful, could never secure human existence. And was the effectiveness of such intercession not attested to by countless miracles?

Plate 16

One begins to understand why the peasant was so reluctant to give up his religious holidays and pilgrimages. They gave him a sense of security, of being in harmony with the earth and the powers that preside over it, that must elude those who have decided to pursue the Cartesian dream of rendering man the master and possessor of nature. This sense of attunement, this trusting turn to higher powers, is indeed the greatest obstacle to all human attempts to better man's lot. The reformers of the Enlightenment were quite right to see in this popular religion mingled with superstition the main obstacle to making Bavaria a modern state. What a waste of time that could have been spent so much more productively.[19]

Today we have become ambivalent enough about modernity and its project of securing human existence by conquering nature to look back nostalgically to a culture that did not burden man with the task of securing his place. And it is a burden, made heavier by our knowledge about the final vanity of this attempt. We find it difficult to make peace with nature and time. As Nietzsche knew, the rancor against time is the deepest source of our inability to be at peace with ourselves and with nature; and part of our love of the rococo is a longing for what escapes us. In a church like Die Wies, which in spite of all its artificiality belongs to nature, more specifically to this landscape before the Alps, we recapture something of that sense of well-being that let abbot Marian Mayr of Steingaden, who with this church had nearly bankrupted his monastery, take the stone of his ring to etch these words into a windowpane of his summer quarters right next to the church: *Hoc loco habitat fortuna, hic quiescit cor.* "In this place fortune dwells; here the heart finds rest."[20]

126. Munich, Bürgersaal, *Guardian Angel*, by Ignaz Günther, 1763

What separates the Enlightenment from this popular religion is first of all its very different understanding of time. Precisely because he knew about the precariousness of human existence, because of his intimacy with disaster and death, the peasant experienced more strongly and thankfully the miracle of growth and life. The victory that light gained every morning over the forces of darkness, the yearly triumph of spring over winter, which hinted at the Immaculata's conquest of the devil, supported his trust in the final victory of life over death. The religious year, with its many holidays, attuned him to the spiritual order. What sense did it make to him to speak of a waste of time? The concept of wasting time presupposes a very different understanding of life. Time is now seen as a scarce resource that, like money, must be spent prudently. Inseparable from this understanding is the emphasis on industry, on the glories of hard work. To this rhetoric the peasant was deaf. It was to open his ears that the Enlightenment attacked so relentlessly the religious year with its many holidays. And yet work has its end outside itself; it is for the sake of something else. Because of this, a life reduced to work becomes itself a waste of time. It is with good reason that Martin Heidegger, whose philosophical work has some of its roots in the Catholic baroque, can make the seemingly curious assertion that the authentic man always has time.[21] But this is just to say that to be truly at one with ourselves we cannot oppose ourselves to time as if it were a resource to be used ill or well. The specific beauty of the rococo church is inseparable from the fact that it speaks of freedom from the rancor against time.

The Critique of Opera

When the elector's mandate attacked the elaborate decoration of the rococo church, demanding "a noble simplicity appropriate to the veneration of the sanctuary," its point was not simply that such decoration is unnecessary, but that it fosters a false religiosity; that by focusing the worshiper's attention on what he can see, it obscures the real content of religion, which can be grasped only by the spirit. The tie between religion and theatrical spectacle, so crucial to the rococo church, is to be broken. To the Enlightenment this still baroque theatre, whether claiming to serve the majesty of the ruler or the majesty of God, had become mere theatre, detached from the reality that it professed to serve, offering only an empty shell, not the kernel; a highly artificial entertainment that led man away from the real business of life.

The antitheatrical attitude of the reformers in Munich expressed itself in a mandate that preceded the mandate against the rococo church by only a few months. Passion plays (a distorted echo of this tradition has survived in the passion play of Oberammergau) and the unusually elaborate Good Friday processions were forbidden. The injunction was renewed in 1788, 1792, and 1793.[22] The two reasons given hardly come as a surprise. For one, it was argued that the mysteries of religion are no proper subject matter for the stage. True devotion is hindered rather than fostered by productions that focus attention on what is superficial and external. There was also the second reason, that such plays kept people from more productive work and led to other excesses. The orders were soon extended to forbid all plays with a religious content; and, when in their passion for the theatre the peasants turned to secular plays, theatre was forbidden altogether.

These were hardly unusual or idiosyncratic measures. The baroque theatre had long been one of the main targets of enlightened guardians of the arts. Opera, which had played such a central part in the festive culture of the baroque, was found especially objectionable. The critique of opera is of interest here because many of the reasons advanced against it apply equally to the rococo church. Perhaps the most respected of its German critics was Johann Christoph Gottsched, who, as he himself wrote, had been taught by the rationalist philosopher Christian Wolff "to see order and truth in the world, which before had seemed to him like a labyrinth or a dream."[23] Typical of the Enlightenment is the way Gottsched appeals to reason and nature to support the demand that the artist confine himself to representations of what is probable. This insistence on probability is taken for granted by most of the theoreticians of the time. *Unnatural* and *irrational* are perhaps the most popular terms in the critical vocabulary of the Enlightenment. Once this emphasis on nature and reason has been granted, the attack on opera or, for that matter, on the rococo church is easy enough. If popular religion is attacked for being superstitious, opera is attacked for having drawn too much from "old romances and bad novels," which, while they cater to our longing for the marvelous and exotic, have very little to do with life. The artificiality of opera is a particular target: "Our operas have made everything musical. Persons have to laugh, cry, cough, and sniff according to notes, nobody dares to say good morning to another without keeping time. And the angriest person is forced to bite his tongue as long as his adversary is not finished with his trill."[24] Indeed, who could deny that in opera people "think, speak, and act very differently from the way one does in common life"? It is not truth that we gain from opera. Its artificial charms have more to do with magic.

There were other charges. Opera was rightly said to have disregarded the Aristotelian unities—although one may wonder to what extent these unities, particularly as expounded by Aristotle's French students, are compatible with nature. But the Enlightenment was not so much for nature as for nature subjected to reason, nature made manageable. It is possible to argue that the baroque theatre with its endless variety and change offers us a better figure of life than a play such as Gottsched's once-much-praised *The Dying Cato*, timidly based on plays by Addison and Deschamps.[25]

More serious was the charge that opera could not be used to improve morals. Gottsched saw art first of all as a teaching tool. Art should moralize. The reason opera is unlikely to make us better persons is, according to Gottsched, that the soul of opera is love—one thinks of Kierkegaard's much later discussion of Mozart's *Don Giovanni*—and love is the enemy of morality, a "dangerous and tyrannical passion" that does not let us keep to the path dictated by reason.[26] With it an irrational force manifests itself and claims the individual. To understand the opposition between rococo and Enlightenment, it is well to remember Sedlmayr's claim that the culture of the rococo centered on Venus. Gottsched might have agreed. And here we come to the heart of the struggle. It is not so much the unnatural, artificial character of the rococo that is objectionable—surely, if anything is natural, love is. But nature manifests itself here as a force that does not easily accommodate itself to the reason and morality of a Gottsched. Despite all its artificiality, the rococo may well be closer to nature than the Enlightenment. To make the test, compare paintings by Greuze and Fragonard. Fragonard's art may be theatrical and artificial, but precisely because we cannot take this theatre too seriously we come under the spell of the goddess that presides over this art. A similar point is made by a comparison of Die Wies in its self-conscious theatricality with the serene simplicity of a classicistic church like D'Ixnard's St. Blasien in the Black Forest (figs. 127 and 128). The almost natural and at times irrational spontaneity of the rococo church contrasts with the cool rationality of an architecture that looks back to the Roman Pantheon. To be sure, the parallel should not be pushed too far: it is not Venus that presides over the Bavarian pilgrimage church, whose altar shelters the miraculous image of Christ bound to the column, somewhat in the way the Virgin, whom we see above in the painting of the upper altar, holds her child. Theatre and artifice, no doubt. But they do not prevent this architecture from becoming as natural as architecture can become.

Architecture and the Demands of Reason

A comparison of Die Wies and St. Blasien is instructive because the two churches are in some ways quite similar. Both join a long rectangular choir to a circular or oval nave; in both cases the architecture of the choir and the nave could be said to hark back to Gothic hall churches, although the open expanse of the nave, which reduces the aisles to

127. St. Blasien, Benedictine abbey church (1768–83), exterior

128. St. Blasien, abbey church, interior

a mere mantle, distances the eighteenth-century churches from such antecedents. But this similarity makes the different character of the two churches all the more apparent. As the exterior already makes clear, D'Ixnard's St. Blasien contrasts simple, and therefore easily grasped, geometric shapes. In no case is an attempt made to soften these contrasts with mediating ornament. Geometric forms are allowed to retain their elemental force. The nave is a simple circle, the choir a strongly articulated rectangle. Dominikus Zimmermann, on the other hand, generates his oval out of two interlocking circles and uses ornament to obscure the spatial organization of the choir. The same contrast shows itself when we compare D'Ixnard's twenty white columns with their Corinthian capitals and the curious paired pillars that Dominikus Zimmermann used in Die Wies (fig. 129). Or compare the strong modillioned cornice that rings the clearly articulated dome of St. Blasien with the much weaker cornice in Die Wies, where the fresco helps to take away any sense of definite boundary. In St. Blasien architecture has regained its priority. Fresco and ornament play only a very minor part. We have a splendid example of that serenity demanded by the elector's mandate.[27]

The mandate's demand for simplicity and its invocation of the model of Italy suggest where we have to look for the spiritual sources of its critique of the rococo church: to Rome, where in opposition to baroque architecture Winckelmann had called for a return to the "noble simplicity and quiet grandeur" of the ancients. But it would be a mistake to

129. Die Wies, pilgrimage church, ambulatory (detail)

place too much emphasis on Winckelmann and the group of artists and theorists that had gathered in Rome, and to view neoclassicism as a style that was to replace the rococo. In many ways rococo and neoclassicism are parallel developments, presenting competing claims, deriving their strength from different social strata, which helps to explain their different reception in different countries. If the rococo has both an aristocratic and a truly popular base, neoclassicism is very much associated with the bourgeoisie. Thus it is more strongly represented in the Protestant countries of Europe than in the Catholic south. It is not at all surprising that most of the group of neoclassicists that had gathered in Rome did not come from Italy.

Never did France carry the rococo to such extremes as did Bavaria. By the time rocaille triumphed in Bavaria it had ceased to be a very important artistic force in France, where classicistic and antibaroque sentiments had a long tradition. Thus before Winckelmann Boffrand and Blondel had demanded noble simplicity and had insisted that the bizarre not be confused with genius.[28] The *Encylopédie* only sums up widespread tendencies.

> Baroque, adj., in architecture, is a nuance of the bizarre. It is, if one wishes, its refinement or, if that is possible, its superlative. The idea of baroque carries with it that of the ridiculous carried to excess. Borromini has provided the greatest models of the bizarre and Guarini can pass as the master of the baroque.[29]

The article is directed against the Italian baroque. But the same key words recur in critiques of the rococo.

Inseparable from this repudiation of what was then still an ongoing architectural tradition was the search for new foundations, which reason and nature were to furnish. To exhibit these foundations the ex-Jesuit Marc Antoine Laugier, perhaps the most widely read architectural theorist of the age, attempted to reconstruct the primitive hut.[30] It is supposed to be the archetypal building, born only of man's need for shelter. Laugier's thinking here is close to political philosophers like Hobbes or Locke, who in their attempt to establish the foundation of political authority imagine the natural condition of man in order to generate the state from it. In similar fashion Laugier assumes a state of nature. Guided only by his needs and his reason, forced to find shelter in a world that is not always friendly to him, primitive man builds his hut. Four supports are laid out in a rectangle, other pieces of wood are laid across them, then a roof is erected and covered with leaves. It is this house, which, according to Laugier, furnishes all architecture with its basic vocabulary.

The authority of the primitive hut does not depend on whether there ever has been such a hut, just as the authority of the social contract does not require there ever to have been such a contract. Regardless of the testimony of history, it is an idea at which reasonable human beings, open to nature and especially to their own nature, must arrive.

> The little hut which I have just described is the type on which all the magnificences of architecture are elaborated. It is by approximating to its simplicity of execution that fundamental defects are avoided and true perfection attained. The upright pieces of wood suggest the ideas of columns, the horizontal pieces resting on them, entablatures. Finally the inclined members which constitute the roof provide the idea of a pediment.[31]

On Laugier's account, too, the building is legitimated by being interpreted as a reenactment of an archetypal structure. This recalls interpretations of the Christian church as a repetition of such structures as Solomon's temple. But while these structures gained their authoritative status because they were thought to have been divinely inspired, Laugier's hut is supposed to derive its authority from human reason. Given this claim, it is remarkable how much this hut turns out to look like a Greek temple, which may make Laugier's reflections seem more like a rationalization of neoclassicistic aesthetics than the product of unalloyed reason.

On this point we have to agree with Laugier's Italian critic, Carlo Lodoli.[32] Lodoli, too, felt that architecture had lost its way, that it was basing itself on preconceptions that constituted a perversion of true architecture. The weight of the past had gotten the better of common sense. Even the ancients should not be copied slavishly. Sanmicheli and Palladio are accused of having followed them unthinkingly, without first inquiring into whether this architecture really served human needs. And for Lodoli it is function that should govern architectural form. The requirements of this functionalism even Laugier's hut could not satisfy, and it mattered little to Lodoli that Laugier could claim the canonic testimony of Vitruvius in support of his views. Is Laugier's claim that only column, entablature, and pediment are essential to architecture really reasonable, even if one adds, as Laugier did, walls, windows, and doors? Why rule out arches and arcades? According to Lodoli the Vitruvian conception of architecture was unduly hampered by thinking that all building must have its origin in wood construction. Do Etruscan and Roman architecture not teach us better? Indeed, if Greek architecture translates a timber vocabulary into stone, do we not have here architecture that in a very obvious way violates the demands of functionalism, and thus of reason? Lodoli demands of a truly functional architecture truth to materials.

Here we have come to another demand that leaves no room for rococo architecture with its love of masquerade, of the architectural lie. Think of Egid Quirin Asam's high altar at Rohr, where the Virgin seems to rise heavenward, defying gravity, supported by a carefully concealed metal rod. Or of the vision of heaven Cosmas Damian Asam conjured on the vault of Weltenburg: the church's dome seems to float above us without any visible support. In Die Wies, too, the vault possesses a tentlike lightness, made possible by the construction of the vault of timber, lath, and plaster rather than of stone. Given expectations formed by masonry vaults, the columns that support the vault seem much too weak, more ornament than architecture. The architect's "deception" creates the illusion of an almost weightless, immaterial construction. This repudiation of architectural values is carried through the entire church. Thus the unusual shape of the columns—a combination of round column and square pillar that is particularly sensitive to changes of light—helps to dematerialize the architecture, as does the bizarre shape of the windows. We have seen how essential such play is to the Bavarian rococo church. To insist with Lodoli on what we can call a realism of materials is to leave no room for this architecture.

But it matters little whether we follow Laugier or Lodoli. Once architecture is seen as a reasonable answer to natural needs, its symbolic function is denied. This denial rules out an architecture that still seriously considers the demand that the church building signify the Church. This denial also denies any place for a symbolic function of ornament. Ornament, if tolerated at all, becomes something added to architecture, at best a pretty dress thrown over a functional body. The building becomes a decorated shed, a formulation that invites criticism by those who would reduce architecture to what is essential.

The Impropriety of Rocaille

Rocaille and its unruly freedom particularly provoked the enlightened critics of the time. We meet with such criticism almost as soon as rocaille makes its first appearance in Germany. The reviewer of Cuvilliés's first book of engravings, writing in 1742 in Gottsched's *Neuer Büchersaal der schönen Wissenschaft und freien Künste*, speaks of "wild and unnatural shapes," lamenting that these ornamental fantasies delighted in presenting what was improbable and impossible. What made matters worse, he complained, was that these ornaments were imitated, that their offspring could be seen on important buildings, a disgrace both to art and to his own "so enlightened age."[33]

Reiffstein, the author of this review, who could count Winckelmann among his friends, expanded his critique four years later in a discussion of recently published collections of ornamental engravings by Karl Pier, Cuvilliés, and Lajoue (fig. 130).[34] Even Reiffstein could not dispute the technical excellence of these engravings, and he was sensitive to the

130. Jacques de Lajoue, *Naufrage*

spontaneity of the designs. But this very spontaneity made them guilty of what Reiffstein took to be the cardinal fault of all such art: its improbability. An unfettered imagination here outstrips nature and reason. How, for example, can children, weighed down with flower garlands or a huge cornucopia, float in the air even though they lack wings? How can a heavy cannon be suspended in space as if it had no weight? Again and again the engraver fails to obey the law of gravity. And Reiffstein is right: these engravings do indeed present us with "concrete impossibilities." John Canaday used that phrase to describe René Magritte's *Castle in the Pyrenees.*[35] The Belgian surrealist's castle rests firmly on a huge boulder, but despite its obvious solidity, this rock floats, somewhat like a balloon, in a sunny sky over an academically painted sea. The rococo engravers offer similar surprises, although the ornamental quality of their creations makes us more ready to accept their impossibilities.

Reiffstein also objects strongly to creatures that look as if they were products of an illicit union between man and fish. In these ornaments an imagination no longer restrained by reason gives birth to monsters: almost anything found in nature or art can serve the artist as material for combinations that follow no rule. Traditionally such monstrous creations have been associated with the demonic. The natural order is subverted by human willfulness. The Romanesque monsters condemned by St. Bernard come to mind, or the devilish creatures of a Bosch or a Grünewald, as do their successors in twentieth-century surrealism. The latter especially invite us to ask whether it is indeed just willfulness that is at work here. Could it be that a more profound understanding of reality is groping for expression (fig. 131)?

But are we not taking the ornamental engravings of the rococo too seriously when we place them in this company? To be sure, there is a certain similarity. But these eighteenth-century designs do not demand to be taken seriously as pictorial representations. In them the logic of ornament playfully competes with that of pictorial representation; or, one might say, ornament usurps the more dignified place of painting.

This play helps to account for the disregard of proper scale in these engravings, another target of Enlightenment criticism.[36] How can an entire landscape find place within a single shell? But to make this point is of course to refuse to deal with these creations on their own terms and to overlook the way the shell is not only an object represented in the engraving, but functions also as frame. No one would think of measuring the ornament of a frame by the spatial logic of the framed picture. The difficulty is, however, that these engravings deliberately obscure the boundary between frame and framed picture. The frame, we can say, has entered the picture. This willful confusion of framing and pictorial function is particularly clear in *Neues Caffehaus* (1756), a work by Johann Esaias Nilson, professor at the academy at Augsburg (fig. 132).[37] A rather ordinary gabled house is framed by rocaille, but this rocaille not only spreads out and becomes the earth that supports the house; it also envelops the house with a vinelike growth, curling around its corners. The ornament of the frame thus enters and becomes part of the picture. To obscure the relationship between frame and framed picture still further Nilson places the flag on top of the coffeehouse in such a way that it appears to be in front of the rocaille frame.

Even more revealing is a later engraving, created by Nilson after he had accommodated

131. François de Cuvilliés, design from *Livre nouveau de morceaux de fantaisie*, ca. 1750

himself to the change in taste and exchanged his rocaille for a more classicizing vocabulary. In *Der liebe Morgen* (fig. 133) of 1770, cow and cowherd are placed before a stone structure that looks like the slightly cracked base of some monument. Behind or on top of this monument—the spatial relationship is left ambiguous—we see a small house. Out of an open window a girl looks at the cowherd who has come with his horn to offer her a morning greeting. The spatial organization is further complicated by a broken octagonal frame, placed on top of the stone block in such a way as to frame window and girl. In spite of the difference in vocabulary, the ambiguity of the rococo engraving is retained, indeed made more striking. The ruined monument together with the broken frame has taken the place of rocaille (see fig. 131). The new vocabulary adopted by Nilson made it impossible to let the frame enter into the picture as easily as in the earlier engraving: instead the frame is represented quite literally. This representation lets it become an object in the picture. Its essence—and, if we take aesthetic distance to be constitutive of the aesthetic, the essence of the aesthetic—becomes the theme of the picture. Art becomes a self-conscious preoccupation with art. It is this aestheticism which accounts for the playfulness, the lack of seriousness in the engraving.[38]

Reiffstein would no doubt have deplored such play as lacking in the truth and moral significance that art must possess to be more than frivolous entertainment. And we may well wonder what place similarly playful ornament has in a church. We have seen that it is precisely its ambiguous status between ornament and picture that allows rocaille to play the mediating role between architecture and fresco assigned to ornament by the rococo church. Reiffstein wants no part of this. He is of course aware of the framing function of rocaille. But, he asks, how can such a disorderly ornament provide an effective frame? A painting can hardly present itself properly "locked into such disorderly borders."[39]

Reiffstein is of course right. As pointed out in the second chapter, the irregular concave and convex curves of rococo frames cannot frame as effectively as a simple rectangle or a circle. And this ineffectiveness is increased by the pictorial quality of an ornament that has to lessen the distance between frame and what is framed. But, as we have seen, the Bavarian rococo church turns to rocaille precisely because the fresco is not to "present itself properly." The impossibility to which a Reiffstein would object in the name of reason and nature is indeed present already in the fresco. The symbolic landscapes that rococo churches conjure up above us are as impossible as their perspective. Their creators

132. Johann Esaias Nilson, *New Coffee House*, before 1756

133. Johann Esaias Nilson, *The Dear Morning*

lightly disregard what proper perspective demands. These "improper" paintings demand "improper" frames. It is clear that such impropriety cannot be defended by someone who understands the demands of reason and nature as the enlightened critics of the time did. But this is not to say that it must be understood as a merely aesthetic game, although again and again the Bavarian rococo church will invite such interpretation. When the Bavarian rococo church plays with perspective it remains bound, although precariously, by a higher perspective that demands that we *see through* natural things and derive from them a significance that eludes the probabilities of human reason.

Reiffstein objects to the ornamental art of the rococo not only because of its disregard of the probable and possible, but also because of its affinity for the lower elements, for the sphere of earth and water and its creatures, mollusk, fish, and snake. Another Saxon critic of rocaille, F. A. Krubsacius, makes this criticism with a caricatured rocaille (fig.

134) made up of such things as withered flowers and straw, shell fragments and fish scales, hair and feathers, the whole inhabited by dragons, snakes, and other vermin.[40] Once again the criticism points to something important and again the parallel with surrealism suggests itself. Rocaille is the product of a fantastic chemistry. Its creators are alchemists who break nature into fragments, distill from them a new matter, which in turn generates not only familiar plants and animals, but also altogether new forms and shapes. This character becomes more striking when we turn from engravings to the work of a stuccoer like Anton Landes or Dominikus Zimmermann. Nowhere can it be studied better than in the ornament of the choir of Die Wies; nowhere do we find rocaille in more imaginative variations, now shell-like or plantlike, now assuming the look of earth, fire, and water. Out of this protean matter grow leaves and flowers. The stucco reaches a climax in those strangely beautiful, but also disturbing, almost threatening forms that suggest giant caterpillars (fig. 90).

Reiffstein remarks quite correctly on the origin of rocaille in the forms of certain sea-shells, but he is also quick to point out that there is little concern about truth to nature. The creators of rocaille are so free in their use of these forms that this origin is obscured. Indeed, instead of a distinctly shell-like material we have a substance that can have the look of water—the pulpit at Oppolding or Landes's doorframe at Maria Medingen offer good examples—but also of earth, or even, as Die Wies shows, of fire. But we should not make too much of such likeness: most of the rocaille found in Bavarian rococo churches is quite abstract.

As pointed out in the first chapter, the strength of this ornament is such that it tends to shed its merely ornamental role and to assert itself as a self-sufficient aesthetic object. We can observe the same tendency in the ornamental engravings that Augsburg produced in such profusion. Following French examples, ornament here becomes the *subject matter* of art, becomes an object in a picture. But given the period's understanding of painting as essentially representational, what room is there for this abstract ornamental matter in the

134. Johanna Dorothee Philipp, rocaille parody (after Krubsacius)

picture? If we accept the Enlightenment's interpretation of the way the authority of nature and reason had to rule the visual arts, there is no room at all. Even the Augsburg engravers attempt to interpret rocailles increasingly as more or less natural objects. Rocailles are made to look as if they were bizarre formations of earth, stone, or wood. The Enlightenment's understanding of painting as essentially representational leads here to what we can call a naturalization of rocaille. Bauer points to an engraving by J. W. Baumgartner, one of a series devoted to the elements.[41] The earth here raises itself in a fantastic archlike structure. This structure is of a substance with the earth that supports it (fig. 135). Rocaille is presented literally as earth. To be sure, the identification of earth and rocaille is motivated here by the task that Baumgartner had set himself. But even where there is not such motivation we find rocaille acquiring this earthlike appearance. Bauer points out that by the middle of the century earth rocaille had become the dominant form. "The most significant Augsburg engraver, J. E. Nilson, knows in his oeuvre only this form, which preserves hardly a trace of the old shell-matter."[42] Nilson gives his rocailles the look of curious objects that nature might have produced. Although perhaps not probable, they do at least have the look of being possible (fig. 136).

Even more naturalistic are the inventions of Gottlieb Leberecht Crusius, whose rocailles look like the surfaces of broken tree trunks (fig. 137).[43] Rocaille here appears like organic matter in a state of decay, like rotten or splintered wood. Given such engravings, Krub-

135. Johann Wolfgang Baumgartner, *Earth*, 1752

136. Johann Esaias Nilson, *The Play of Nature*, 1752

sacius would not seem to be altogether off the mark with his suggestion that rocailles turn not simply to the organic sphere, but to objects that are the products of disintegration and decay. That this cannot be said of the rocailles of the Bavarian rococo church has already been noted. Here rocaille seems more like an abstract figure of nature in spring.[44] Yet the association of rocaille and decay does make sense given designs like those of Crusius.

In chapter 5 I spoke of the relationship between the Bavarian rococo church and the ruin architecture of the period. The work of the Augsburg engravers helps to support the suggestion that there is a deep link between rocaille and decayed matter. This also raises a question. Architecture in ruins may be said to recall man to nature as to his real home. But in many of these engravings nature presents a rather sinister face. No longer do we think of the realm of Venus, of love and of birth. Why does rocaille, which may be considered a metaphor of life, approach matter in a state of disintegration as it becomes less abstract and more representational? The turn to representation is easy enough to understand. The aesthetics of painting at the time simply had no place for a nonrepresentational art. As the Augsburg designers claimed for their ornaments the kind of self-sufficiency associated with paintings, it must have seemed only natural to them to give to

137. Gottlieb Leberecht Crusius, *Capriccio*, ca. 1760

initially abstract forms the look of natural objects. But this does not explain why the pictorialization of ornament should show this preference for nature in a state of decay. To understand this preference it is necessary to keep in mind the demand that the artist represent, if not what is probable, at least what is possible, what nature might conceivably have produced. But when does nature come closest to producing abstract organic forms resembling rocaille, objects which, while no longer organisms, yet have the look of being organic? The answer is obvious: when organisms disintegrate. Subjected to the reasonable aesthetics of the Enlightenment the springlike beauty of rocaille has to approach that caricature of it that Krubsacius offers to us.

The artists associated with the Augsburg academy could not long disregard what had been happening in the larger world of art. After 1750 the distance that had separated designers like Cuvilliés from critics like Reiffstein began to narrow. As if to prove this point, just at the time the elector issued his general mandate Nilson published an engraving that shows a man standing next to a classicistic urn, tearing a rocaille (fig. 138). "It is," in Bauer's words, "a public 'peccavi' by which the professor of the Academy

138. Johann Esaias Nilson, engraving, ca. 1770

distances himself from his life's work."[45] Even in the Academy of Augsburg, which had trained so many rococo painters, the Enlightenment had triumphed.

Little concerned about theory, the stuccoers of Wessobrunn were more resistant to such developments. But they could not escape them. Neither the elector's decree nor other political events destroyed the Bavarian rococo church. They were only aspects of a larger development that permitted its flowering and necessitated its death.

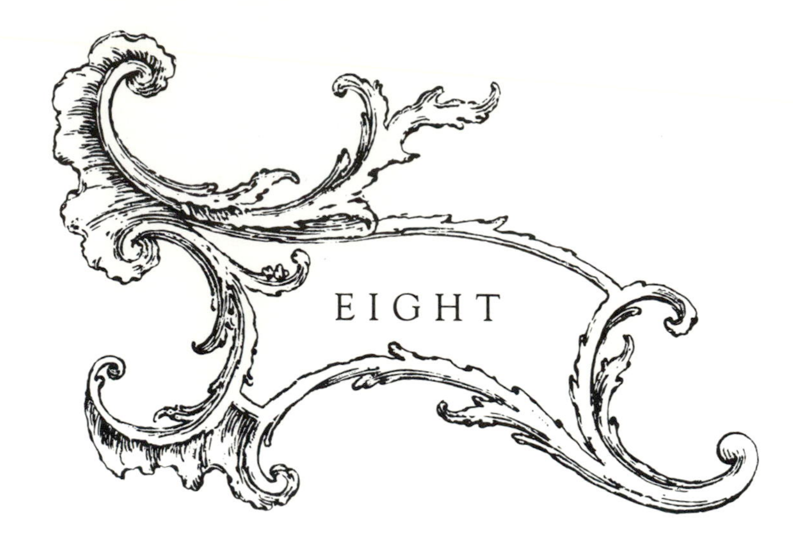

THE DISINTEGRATION OF THE ROCOCO CHURCH

Transition and End

It is striking how church building activity ebbs in the last third of the eighteenth century. Long before the secularization of 1802 and 1803 destroyed the monasteries, the economic base of the Bavarian church, increasing financial pressures and, perhaps more important, the prevailing spiritual climate made most monasteries hesitate to embark on large building projects. Johann Michael Fischer's touching but somewhat stiff and chilly Brigittine abbey church of Altomünster (1763–73) and the church Simon Frey built for the Augustinian canons of Suben (1766–70), an effective sequel to Schäftlarn, stand at the end of a development that had given Bavaria much of its best architecture. After 1770 examples become scarce: in 1780 Schlehdorf, poorer than such neighboring monasteries as Benediktbeuern and Rottenbuch, finally managed to finish the church that it had begun sixty years earlier, now in an uninspired style halfway toward neoclassicism. In Ebersberg a fire necessitated the reconstruction and redecoration of the central aisle. A comparison with the side aisles, where the rococo decoration from the middle of the century survived, illustrates not only the stylistic change that has taken place, but also the drop in quality (fig. 139). A much more successful example of this transitional style is provided by the choir of Ettal (1776). But these were all cases where an already existing structure had to be redecorated or completed. Only Asbach, a Benedictine monastery in a remote corner of Lower Bavaria, decided to replace its perfectly serviceable church with a more fashionable structure; only here we still find something of the building mania that had earlier produced churches like Die Wies. The younger Cuvilliés is credited with this coolly elegant structure (1771–84).[1] A somewhat different situation prevailed to the west, in Swabia, where political conditions were not yet so inhospitable to church architecture. Here the political independence of such abbeys as Neresheim, Oberelchingen, Rot an der Rot, and Wiblingen still allowed them to build churches that by this time had become impossible in Bavaria proper. Neresheim and Wiblingen are the grand finale of the South German rococo.

In the villages, too, few churches were built in the last two decades of the century. And indeed, what need was there for more churches? Were there not more than enough already? The secularization then tried its best to do away with what was thought to be an unreasonable excess. What earlier generations had built now began to be torn down, usually for economic reasons, to make some money by selling the furnishings of a church and anything else that would find a buyer—although the passion with which some officials tried to assure that a rococo masterpiece would be destroyed suggests ideological motivation.

The case of Rottenbuch is typical. On March 21, 1803 Franz Xaver Schönhamer, judge in Schongau, declared that the monastery had ceased to exist. The church was plundered—part of its inventory was sent to Munich, and what remained was put up for auction, although the judge complained that it was difficult to find buyers for the church itself, for its free-standing tower, and for the monastery buildings. That the small local parish should get such an expensive and splendid church seemed to him unreasonable. What would the parish do with it? Did it not already have its own, quite adequate church? Why

139. Ebersberg, St. Sebastian, two styles of decoration, ca. 1750 and 1783

should it even want the larger church, which would be much more difficult to maintain? But the parish did want the church and the government in Munich finally decided that its aesthetic merits were such that it should be preserved and become the new parish church. So it was the old parish church that was auctioned off, for 250 guilders. The judge still did not give up. In spite of local protests even valued relics were sold off to the highest bidder, and a buyer was found for the church's particularly splendid organ, which the judge felt drowned out the singing of the congregation. Fortunately that deal fell through, as did the plan to use the proceeds from the sale to tear down the church's side aisles and choir (Schönhamer thought them in need of repair and, given the size of the parish, quite unnecessary anyway).[2]

Only rarely did the Schönhamers get their way. Not only in Rottenbuch did popular protest help to preserve what enlightened yet blind officials wanted to destroy. At times this protest became so violent that it had to be met with force and the protesters jailed. But it did not go unheard. To it we owe the survival of churches like Fürstenfeld and Marienberg.[3] There were, however, serious losses, the destruction of the abbey church and of large parts of the monastery of Wessobrunn perhaps most saddening.[4]

After a visit to a place like Wessobrunn, where what remains—a quarter of the monastery buildings and the small parish church—still testifies so eloquently to what the secularization destroyed, it is tempting to dramatize and to claim that the Bavarian rococo was slain by a cultural invasion that, with the blessings of an enlightened court, gained control of the bureaucracy and imposed its middle-class values on a largely unsympathetic rural population. Given that view the mandate of 1770 assumes the significance of an ominous sign. There is some truth to this, but it certainly is not the whole story. Long before 1770 the Bavarian rococo church had begun to disintegrate, as is manifested by the churches that were being built. The Bavarian rococo died not violently but gradually, fading away to lead a kind of posthumous life in folk art. And while this slow process of disintegration makes for a less dramatic—and much more complicated—story, it is only when this story is told that we begin to understand that what ends with the Bavarian rococo church is not just another style, but an attitude to art and to life that lies irrecoverably behind us.

Autumnal Rococo

The rococo church dies when reflection on the essential difference between architecture and painting leads to the demand that the impure alliance between architectural and pictorial space be dissolved. Architecture is asked to reaffirm its own essence and to pursue tectonic rather than pictorial values. But, as we have seen, the latter are inseparable from the Bavarian rococo church. Not that it follows a strict illusionism and accepts the primacy of the picture. The irreducible tension between architectural and pictorial space is recognized, but only to become the object of a subtle play that both disguises and insists on it. The Bavarian rococo fresco does not let us forget that what may at first seem like an illusionistic extension of architectural space into a heavenly beyond cannot really be that. These landscapes above us, with their trees and streams, oceans and ships, become impossible when seen illusionistically. But the rococo church does not take the step that to neoclassicism will seem so inevitable: it will not treat the fresco simply as a picture. Rather, it assigns it a quasi-architectural function. By its pictorial illusion the fresco denies us a sense of the vault, which is rendered tentlike, almost weightless. As we have seen, it is this ambiguous attitude to baroque illusionism that helps to account for the preference for weak, scalloped frames and for the way the Bavarian rococo church exploits the possibilities offered by rocaille to create a mediating ornamental zone joining architecture and picture in an endless play that now obliterates, now preserves the tension between them.

By the middle of the century there is a certain resistance to the ambiguities resulting from such interplay. A good example is furnished by Birnau (1746–50). Hitchcock does not hesitate to consider this "the highest rococo achievement of the mid-century," excepting only the fresco—he would have preferred a lighter, airier composition, by someone like Johann Baptist Zimmermann (fig. 140).[5]

Breathtakingly situated above Lake Constance, Birnau is indeed one of the greatest achievements of the international rococo. More questionable is its success as a church. Norbert Lieb wonders whether what he considers "a certain profanity" of the space should be considered a symptom of the impending end of the culture of the ecclesiastic baroque, while Hugo Schnell senses here the beginning of neoclassicism.[6] Given Hitchcock's criteria, there can be no doubt concerning Birnau's rococo character; it is equally clear that it does not fit criteria arrived at by an analysis of the Bavarian rococo church. This raises once more the question raised in the first chapter: How is what has been called the Bavarian rococo church related to the rococo? Schnell's suggestion that in Birnau we already sense something of the impending neoclassicism raises another: How are rococo and neoclassicism related? Is it perhaps the way it remains bound to the culture of the Counter Reformation that separates the Bavarian rococo church both from the secular rococo and from neoclassicism?

Birnau, of course, does not belong to the Bavarian rococo. To be sure, the stucco work is by Joseph Anton Feuchtmayer, a member of one of the leading families of the Bavarian Wessobrunn, while the large fresco is by one of the leading painters of Augsburg, Gottfried Bernhard Goez.[7] But its architect, Peter Thumb, is from the Austrian Vorarlberg, which, rivaling Wessobrunn, had sent hundreds of builders and decorators all over Southern Germany and beyond. Characteristic of their work is a preference for beautifully proportioned but often rather conventional variations of the wall-pillar scheme as it had been established by St. Michael and the Studienkirche in Dillingen. In Birnau, however, the wall-pillars have shrunk to mere pilasters. The nave resembles a large, flat-ceilinged room, expanding in the curved side chapels. The boundaries of this space seem much more definite than in a Bavarian rococo church. No longer is a mantle placed around a central space. The delightful gallery that encircles this space has a more purely ornamental function. The play of indirect light, so essential to the best creations of the Bavarian rococo, has yielded to direct illumination. Nor is there an ornamental zone that effectively mediates between fresco and architecture. Hitchcock considers this fresco, with its *quadratura* architecture that recalls much earlier work by Pozzo and Cosmas Damian Asam,

"retardataire." But we need only imagine one of Johann Baptist Zimmermann's in its place to realize that this fresco is at home in this church as much as are Zimmermann's frescoes in the churches of his brother. Not that in Birnau we have the same kind of interplay between architecture below and fresco above; it is discouraged by the roomlike space, which gives prominence to the windows. The fresco here is not the equal partner of the architecture, but first of all ornament—and how well Goez's browns and pinks, with their blue and green accents, serve this interior. The ornamentalization of the fresco is supported by the way the place of mediating stucco ornament is taken by a painted ornamental parapet in the fresco that provides something like an inner frame. This framing architecture in the fresco may recall Pozzo or Asam, but the lack of an effective relationship to the architecture makes it difficult to interpret it illusionistically; the difficulty is enhanced by the way the fresco is divided into two quite distinct parts, each governed by its own point of view, and separated by a painted rib-band.

Measured by future developments, Birnau has to be considered a more advanced church than Die Wies. This becomes particularly clear when we look back to the organ. The nave presents itself to us as a splendidly decorated box (fig. 141). At the same time the Swabian character of the church is brought out. The dissolution of spatial boundaries sought by the Bavarians had always met with a certain resistance in Swabia. The point could be illustrated by a comparison of the way the wall-pillar scheme was adapted by Bavarian architects like Johann Michael Fischer with its adaptation by architects from the Austrian Vorarlberg. But it is better supported by a comparison of village churches in the two areas: the Swabian rococo interior tends to be more like a flat-ceilinged room. That once again we have to do with deep-seated spatial preferences is suggested by the fact that large late Gothic churches in Bavaria tend to be hall churches, while in Swabia we find a preference for the basilica, and that means for more clearly bounded spaces. This preference for clear boundaries makes the transition to neoclassicism seem much more natural in Swabia than in Bavaria. How easy it is to move from a church like Birnau to neoclassicism is shown by a comparison of Birnau with a village church that Peter Thumb's student, Johann Georg Specht, built (1797–1806) in Scheidegg in the Allgäu (fig. 142).[8]

But if we find in Birnau the first signs of a turn to neoclassicism, we also have to agree with Hitchcock: this turn at the same time leads to an architecture that may be considered a purer realization of an essentially secular rococo than any of the great Bavarian rococo churches that were being built at the same time. In comparison, they seem still baroque. Decisive is the different treatment of walls and ceiling, which at Birnau are experienced once more as the boundaries of the space in which we stand. At the same time ornament gains a new freedom and exuberance. There is a sense in which the South German rococo church not only has its origin in the essentially secular French rococo, but returns to this origin as the precarious synthesis it had fashioned disintegrates.

In Bavaria, too, the move toward classicism announces itself first of all in a reassertion of the primacy of architecture and the tectonic at the expense of the interplay between fresco and architecture. It is not surprising that the mason Johann Michael Fischer shows himself more receptive than the decorator Dominikus Zimmermann to the changing spiritual climate. (We also should remember that Fischer worked out of the capital and had

140. Birnau, pilgrimage church, interior

141. Birnau, pilgrimage church, interior, looking back toward the organ

142. Scheidegg, parish church of St. Gallus, interior

links to the world of the court, while Zimmermann had made his home in provincial Landsberg.) Consider the difference between Die Wies and Rott am Inn (figs. 84 and 103). In Rott am Inn forms have become more simple and sharply defined. The circle of the fresco frame contrasts with the right angles of the pillars that define the central octagon (fig. 143). The rococo has begun to freeze. In keeping with Fischer's emphasis on the tectonic, stucco now plays a much reduced part. No longer is there a mediating ornamental zone. Only the four large cartouches, binding the fresco to the arches below, hint at it. No attempt is made to carry the movement of the rising pillars into the fresco representing the glory of the Benedictine order, one of Matthäus Günther's best efforts. The cartouches themselves, by the Wessobrunner Jakob Rauch, act rather like giant clamps that force together what is really quite separate, in spite of their pink putti-populated clouds that recall Aldersbach. But how discrete, tame, and decorative they have become!

As the floor plan suggests, in spite of a new clarity that goes along with the hardening of forms and separation of functions, with Rott am Inn Fischer offers us yet another brilliant solution to the problems that had preoccupied the Bavarian rococo: an octagon, framed symmetrically by square spaces, is enveloped by a mantle that obscures spatial boundaries and provides for a wonderfully bright light, mostly indirect. Although in Rott am Inn the rococo has begun to freeze, such freezing does not mean in any way a quali-

143. Rott am Inn, abbey church, interior

tative decline; quite the opposite. More than any other rococo church this one recalls the words of *Revelations*: "like a most rare jewel, like a jasper, clear as crystal."

Rott am Inn stated themes that were to dominate the autumn of the Bavarian rococo church, which still produced a number of beautifully clear yet subtle village churches. The most prolific architect of the last decades of the eighteenth century was Leonhard Matthias Giessl. His churches at Starnberg (1763–70), Bettbrunn (1774), and Schwindkirchen (1782) demonstrate the continuing strength of this late rococo.[9] Reminiscences of Fischer's Rott am Inn and Altomünster are particularly evident in the octagons Franz Anton Kirchgrabner created in Eschenlohe (1765) and Egling (1767).[10] The latter has a façade of almost cubist simplicity (fig. 144). Still unburdened by theory, it has a distant affinity with the new aesthetic that manifests itself in the visionary utopian designs of a Ledoux. My favorite among these churches is Inning (1765–67), with its wonderfully elegant tower and exquisitely furnished bright interior that ranks with the best of the Bavarian rococo (fig. 145).[11] The carved supports of the organ gallery are unforgettable. I would like to think that Brancusi admired their form during his walk from Munich to Paris.

144. Egling, parish church St. Vitus, façade

145. Inning, parish church St. Johann Baptist, interior

A remarkably successful example of a very late rococo church is Kirchgrabner's church in Lippertskirchen, like so many of Bavaria's better rococo churches a centralized wall-pillar church, decorated only in the late nineties.[12] The out-of-the-way location of this small pilgrimage church at the foot of the Alps may account for the fact that here we still encounter rocaille forms in that green that is so characteristic of the last phase of this ornament; elsewhere, where artists were more susceptible to the changing fashion, ornament had by this time become neoclassical. Schwindkirchen, Maria Dorfen (1782–86), and Albaching (1790) effectively represent this classicizing rococo.[13]

In all of these churches one senses the approaching end. The *Gesamtkunstwerk* of the rococo church disintegrates as architecture reclaims its dominant role. Delivered from its mediating function ornament at first gains a new freedom and claims for itself the self-sufficiency and autonomy of a work of art; but this is a quickly passing phase. After 1760 ornament tends to become increasingly thin and anemic. Often it is replaced with painted rocaille. Content to serve the architecture, it has no longer the power to transform space or to mediate between architecture and picture. Indeed, such mediation is no longer desired.

As architecture gains a new purity, painting, too, becomes autonomous. Given the central part played by the adaptation of Italian illusionism in shaping the Bavarian rococo church, this shift back to clearly framed paintings needs to be considered more carefully.

The Secularization of Light and Landscape

Ecclesia ecclesiam significat. As we have seen, the Bavarian rococo church still can be understood as a symbolic representation of the Church, where the burden of establishing it as such a symbol falls first of all on the painter. Perhaps his most obvious strategy is to represent the Church in heaven. The glory compositions of the baroque thus return in the rococo church: circling the Deity, attended by angels and led by the Virgin, we see patriarchs and prophets, apostles and saints assembled on cloud banks whose golden hues hint at the transcendent. First of all it is the choir fresco that offers such sights. The main fresco is more likely to present historical events, demanding a terrestrial setting.[14] More often than not it will also include some representation of the heavenly sphere: the glory compositions of the baroque return, much reduced, in the fresco's center. The tension between earth and heaven, which finds one expression in the tension between earthbound architecture and light, airy frescoes, is iterated in the main fresco, where special care is taken not only to show that these two spheres are linked, but to exhibit the part played by the Church in effecting this linkage, and not simply by the Church in the abstract, but very concretely: by a particular order and its founder, or by a particular saint, where this work of mediation needs to be completed by the Virgin and finally and centrally by her Son. The rococo fresco thus represents the ladder of Jacob's dream; it invites us to understand the church as a new Bethel. But it is this new Bethel only because of its history. To represent this meaning of the church this history has to be made visible. Here we have one reason for the refusal of the Bavarians to adopt a rigorous illusionism and for their turn to the terrestrial sphere.

In the fifth chapter I tried to show that this turn is also supported by the Bavarians' Marian piety, which links Christian devotion to an appreciation of the divine presence in nature. A church like Steinhausen signifies the Church by signifying the Virgin. The Virgin in turn is signified by images suggested by the Song of Songs and its evocation of a garden in May. This organic character of the rococo church, with its intimation of the endlessly recurring miracle of the return of light and life, of the defeat of darkness and death, touches even the modern nonbeliever with its promise of an existence free from the rancor against time. Yet the turn to the organic, which is also a turn to landscape, is not without its problems. I am not thinking now of the impossibilities of these landscapes above the observer to which rationalist critics objected. What renders the rococo church problematic, at least as long as one insists that a church should be a sign of the Church, is rather that a concern with what is represented should overshadow concern with the fresco's symbolic function. The turn toward historical and landscape painting is one of the key aspects of the waning of the Bavarian rococo church.

The prolific Christian Winck's frescoes in the parish church of Inning may stand for countless others (fig. 145). The main fresco (1767) shows John the Baptist preaching in a charming sylvan setting. The greens, grays, browns, and blues of Dutch landscape painting dominate. In keeping with this is the handling of light and shade. Winck paints a particular event. The same is true of the choir fresco, showing the Baptism of Christ. Unlike the emblematic frescoes of a Zimmermann, these works preserve the unity of time and place. In them there is no room for even a residual glory composition. Bauer speaks of the painterly quality of the work of Winck and of his greater contemporaries Maulbertsch and Zick, where by a painterly approach he understands not simply one that emphasizes the play of light, shade, and color more than outline, but one that insists on the autonomy of the painting.[15] Although Winck's frescoes still take into account the observer's point of view, we no longer see these paintings in any way as illusionistic extensions of architectural space. They have become self-sufficient aesthetic objects, which rule out that interplay between fresco and architecture so important to the Bavarian rococo church.

A particularly striking example of this turn to landscape are the frescoes that Johann Wolfgang Baumgartner, once the leading artist in Augsburg, created for the chapel of Baitenhausen. Spiritually and geographically close to Birnau, this chapel too shows that the disintegration of the ecclesiastic rococo yields phenomena that may be considered more purely rococo than even Die Wies. Like the pilgrimage church in Steinhausen, the chapel owes its existence to a miraculous late Gothic image of the Virgin. To this image Marquard Rudolph von Rodt, prince bishop of Constance, attributed his escape from a storm that had surprised him and his companions journeying across Lake Constance. In thanksgiving he ordered a new chapel to be built. Franz Conrad von Rodt, his nephew and successor, completed the work with the present late rococo decoration, dating from 1760.[16]

As one would expect, the frescoes develop a Marian program. Representations of the Nativity in the choir and the Pietà in the nave frame the main fresco, which celebrates the Assumption and Coronation of the Virgin. Of special interest are two frescoes in the transept of the cruciform church. Here the painter was given the quite traditional task of illustrating lines from the Song of Songs which were referred to the Virgin, who is "fair as the moon" and "bright as the sun." In the painting to the left we see the moon rising over Lake Constance (fig. 146). Superimposed on it is the monogram of the Virgin. In boats and on the shore men point to and gaze at the wondrous sight. The city is obviously the nearby Meersburg, which still looks much as it did then; in the distance we see Constance and the chain of the Alps dominated by the Säntis. It is of course possible to understand Constance still as a sign of the Heavenly Jerusalem, as has been suggested.[17] The boat that we see in the distance, making its way toward the city, can then be understood as a symbol of man's precarious journey toward heaven. But even if such an interpretation is perhaps intended, the literalism of the representation makes it seem farfetched. Similarly, the fresco on the right shows the sun, again with the superimposed Marian monogram, over a landscape that quite faithfully represents what we still see as we step out of the chapel (fig. 147).

Are we to understand this landscape as a symbol of the Virgin? Perhaps. But instead of giving us a symbolic landscape such as Zimmermann painted in Steinhausen, Baumgartner literally represents sights familiar to all those entering the church. The painted sky is

146. Baitenhausen, pilgrimage church, fresco (*Fair as the Moon*)

precisely that, a painted representation of the sky that can in no way be read as a representation of heaven. The symbolic function of the fresco has been reduced to the superimposition of the Marian monogram on the heavenly body. The garden that is indeed a familiar symbol of the Virgin has become a quite terrestrial landscape. The light that illuminates this landscape is very much a natural light.

The secularization of light and landscape is also found in the main fresco. It might at first seem that Baumgartner offers us here just another variation on a familiar theme, which had found its most spectacular realization in the high altar of Rohr. Behind an altar we see the bishop of Constance praying to the Virgin: "Hear the prayer of your people!" Very much like stage props, architectural elements provide the setting. Above, the Virgin is about to be crowned. Putti carry ribands with inscriptions taken from the Lauretanian litany, commending Mary to those in need. Of particular interest are the fragmentary landscapes that occupy the sides of the painting and underscore the theatrical artificiality of the central representation which, like the Marian monograms on moon and sun, seems superimposed on the landscape in the background. The mother to the left with her newborn Child refers us to the Nativity represented in the choir, although this is a peasant woman, the house an ordinary farmhouse; the mountain in the background is once more the Säntis. To the right men and women implore the Virgin for help. Perhaps

147. Baitenhausen, pilgrimage church, fresco *(Bright as the Sun)*

it is the ship caught in the storm that we see in the background that prompts these prayers. Undoubtedly we are also to think of the bishop, who, having been saved from just such a storm, vowed to build the Virgin a new house. It has been suggested that we see this same bishop also in the closest boat of the Meersburg fresco and once more in the companion fresco to the right, kneeling at just the place where he was to build the new chapel.

If in Steinhausen we can speak of a Marian naturalism, such talk is even more justified in Baitenhausen. Peaceful and fruitful nature offers a symbol of the Virgin, as the four medallions surrounding the choir fresco make clear. The rising sun, rain falling on the earth, Noah's ark, and a fruit-bearing tree furnish symbols of the life and peace that Mary grants. Both Steinhausen and Baitenhausen establish a metaphoric link between nature and the Virgin. But in Steinhausen it is nature that speaks of the Virgin. In Baitenhausen the Marian theme offers the painter an occasion to represent nature. We are on the threshold of the transformation of the Marian piety of the rococo into a romantic naturalism. This should not surprise us. From the very beginning an undercurrent of a pre-Christian naturalism had been present in Marian devotion. (I remind the reader of the Marian poetry of Jakob Balde.) As the contents of religion become ever more spiritual and abstract, this undercurrent reasserts itself, until finally, when these contents evaporate altogether, only this naturalism remains. Consider once more the monogram of the Virgin superimposed on moon and sun. How close this is to the sun discs with the Marian monogram so popular especially at the beginning of the Bavarian baroque! And yet, now the sun in the fresco has become a literal representation of the sun, making it difficult for us to accept what we see as a symbol. To be sure, the monogram imposed on the sun forces the representational and the symbolic functions together. But the strength of the representation lets us see this imposition as forced. Baumgartner's sun and moon are still presented as metaphors, but the vehicle emancipates itself from the tenor and becomes the real center of our attention The secularization of Marian symbols leaves us with representation of the *maternal earth.*

Along with this process goes a secularization of light. The light of sun and moon has become very much terrestrial illumination. How different is the quality of the light in Zimmermann's main fresco in Steinhausen! What lets us refer his Arcadian landscape and the blue surrounding the glory composition at the fresco's center to heaven, even if the heavenly sphere here encompasses nature, is not just the idealization to which he subjects his landscape, but more important, his use of light. Direct illumination incarnates what it strikes; it gives substance and solidity. This is as true of painting as it is of architecture. Compare how differently Zimmermann and Baumgartner render the clouds swirling around the Virgin. Admittedly, Baumgartner is simply the better painter. But Zimmermann is less interested in painterly values than in the symbolic and architectural values of his frescoes. In Steinhausen the divine name is not superimposed on the sun, but is the light that illuminates the fresco; and unlike terrestrial light, it does so not from without, casting clear shadows, but from within. It would have been strange for Zimmermann to have worried about what shadows are cast by his clouds.

If the symbolic function of the rococo fresco is beginning to evaporate in Baitenhausen, so is its architectural function. Much more than Zimmermann's frescoes, we experience Baumgartner's frescoes as painted on the vault. The integrity of the vault is no longer threatened by the fresco; it becomes difficult to speak of an interplay between architecture and fresco. One would expect this development to announce itself in a changed attitude to ornament and frame. And indeed, in Baitenhausen we no longer find ornament mediating between architecture and fresco. But this is not to say that we have once again firmly framed autonomous paintings. Quite the reverse—the smaller landscape frescoes have no closed frames at all. In each case a fragmentary frame is provided by a stretched-out earth rocaille merging with the painted landscape and providing something like a base; the separate functions of picture and frame have been deliberately blurred. The inscribed ribands above provide additional closure. One is reminded of painted china of the period. The close connection of the fresco to contemporary Augsburg ornamental engravings, for which Baumgartner was well known (fig. 135), is obvious enough. Like these engravings, Baumgartner's frescoes oscillate between being picture and ornament. A new appreciation of the bare wall corresponds to this more ornamental approach to the fresco. Once more one senses the affinity between rococo and neoclassicism.

Just as Hitchcock discusses Birnau as an almost perfect example of rococo art, it is possible to consider Baumgartner's frescoes in Baitenhausen as such examples. It would be easy to come up with a definition of rococo that would justify such a judgement. But once again we have to remind ourselves that the Bavarian rococo church, at any rate, aims at something quite different. It tries to fashion frescoes and architecture into genuine partners, with ornament assigned the task of mediating between the two. In Baitenhausen the ornamentalization of the picture does not effect such mediation. By reducing the picture to a mere ornament, it reasserts the integrity of the ornament bearer. The priority of the architecture is no longer challenged. When ornament is experienced as ornament, as something added to the architecture, the call for a purer architecture is not far away.

A somewhat different analysis is demanded by Baitenhausen's main fresco. Here a simple molding forms an effective frame, despite its rather complicated shape. There are echoes of the past: the inscribed riband at the top weaves in and out of the picture in a way that may recall Aldersbach. The hand of the beggar on the left overlapping the fresco frame had become a standard device, here used rather timidly, to break its closure. Some integration between architecture and fresco is achieved by the way the curves of the frame follow that of the choir arch. But in spite of such reminiscences, fresco and architecture go their own ways. The fresco is beginning to assume the status of an independent aesthetic object.

These tendencies were in the air. Only one year later Winckelmann's friend Anton Raphael Mengs painted his insipid, yet epoch-making, *Parnassus* on the ceiling of the Villa Albani. Here we find a rigorous break with illusionism; the autonomy of the painting is affirmed without compromise. It is hardly surprising that the painters of the ecclesiastic rococo took their time with the new fashion. Even the classicizing Januarius Zick, who had studied in Paris and Rome and who in Wiblingen (1778–83) and Rot an der Rot (1784) still created works of real strength, made only a half-hearted adjustment to the new style he had come to admire. In Bavaria the transition from rococo to neoclassicism is illustrated by the frescoes in Maria Dorfen (1786). They are the work of Johann Joseph Huber, who in 1784 had become director of the academy in Augsburg. The frescoes—now firmly framed, one to each clearly articulated bay—represent scenes from the life of the Virgin. In spite of their perspective, still weakly illusionistic, these frescoes lack the strength to open the vault of the church to a higher dimension. Nor is this intended. Each fresco has become an autonomous painting. No longer do we meet with that easy disregard of the unity of time and place in which the Bavarian rococo had delighted and to which rationalist critics objected with such vehemence. Huber's frescoes tell their story simply and directly. Nothing is left of the emblematic or hieroglyphic character of the rococo fresco. No longer does the church symbolically represent the church. We have come to the end of a tradition almost as old as Christian architecture itself.

Autonomous Ornament

With the disintegration of the rococo *Gesamtkunstwerk*, its elements regain their independence: architecture reasserts the priority of tectonic over pictorial values; the fresco gains pictorial autonomy as it sheds first its symbolic, then its decorative function. As architecture and painting go their separate ways that mediation between the two which rocaille had served so well is no longer wanted. In response to this changed situation rocaille evolves in two quite different ways: ornament acknowledges once more the hegemony of architecture, while on the other hand, it, too, claims autonomy.

The first development poses few problems. From the very beginning rocaille had been used to soften or obscure too sudden transitions. We tend to find it in the coves joining wall and ceiling, or where two moldings or different surfaces meet. Rocaille continues to be used in such places until the very end of the eighteenth century, although increasingly it loses much of its former life and plasticity. Outstanding examples of this late rococo are the exquisitely delicate decorations Franz Xaver Feichtmayr created for Elector Max III Joseph in the Residenz in Munich in the early sixties. Feichtmayr's ornament is much more sparse than Cuvilliés's had been. Compared to the doughy rocailles Johann Baptist Zimmermann had created a few years earlier in the Great Hall of Nymphenburg, it seems aristocratic, very elegant, and just a bit tired. This ornament still has an organic look, although the decoration of a corner of what was once a conference room hints more at decay and disintegration than at growth (fig. 148). The molding invites comparison with a broken branch, the rocaille itself with splintered wood. The fragile autumnal quality of this ornament recalls Augsburg engravings of the same period.

148. Munich, Residenz, conference room, stucco (detail)

It is unnecessary to trace here the history of this last phase of rocaille. How long this ornament retained its popularity, particularly in areas less in touch with and thus less subject to shifts in fashion, is shown by the ornamentation of Lippertskirchen (fig. 149). The Wessobrunner Franz Doll created these delicate, somewhat anemic rocailles in 1796. By this time an artist associated with the court would have long shifted to a classicizing vocabulary. The reedlike character of Doll's elongated rocailles is emphasized by their green color. Little is left of the breathtaking vigor with which a Johann Michael Feichtmayr had created his rocailles in the fifties. In no way does ornament now challenge the priority of the architecture; in its reticent way it only helps to articulate the structure of the space.

Far more interesting is another development: as rocaille matures in the fifties it increasingly claims our interest as a self-sufficient aesthetic presence. Artists like Johann Michael Feichtmayr, Üblhör, and Landes created in these years ornament on the threshold of abstract art. The beauty of this ornament has little to do with the context in which it appears. To be sure, we may find these free forms in churches, but what does their uninhibited spontaneity have to do with this? The aesthetic has always been on close but uneasy terms with the sacred. At the very height of the Bavarian rococo it threatens to divorce itself from it.

The elevation of rocaille from mere ornament to a self-sufficient aesthetic object is

149. Lippertskirchen, pilgrimage church, decoration of vault

intimately connected to that disintegration of the rococo synthesis that I outlined in the preceding pages. As genuine mediation of architecture and painting is no longer desired, ornament is granted a new independence. Rauch's cartouches in Rott am Inn thus possess more integrity than Feichtmayr's in Zwiefalten; which is not to make a qualitative judgment. More than Feichtmayr's stuccoes, Rauch's seem applied. To a much greater degree they make us aware of the difference between supporting architecture and applied ornament, a difference that is illustrated so charmingly in Nilson's *Neues Caffehaus* (fig. 132).

In the eighteenth century Europe was not yet ready to accept a totally abstract art. Only as long as rocaille presented itself as just ornament and as such dependent on the ornament bearer was it allowed to remain abstract. Sculpture and painting were thought to be representational in their very essence; which leads one to expect that as ornament begins to shed its dependence it, too, will turn from abstraction to representation. Such aspirations are evident in the work of Meissonier or Lajoue, whose rocailles acquire the look of objects in the world. The insistence that art represent only what is probable, i.e. things that nature might have produced, subjects ornament to that naturalization so characteristic of the work of engravers like Crusius or Nilson (figs. 136 and 137).

The decorations Cuvilliés created in the Amalienburg carried this pictorialized ornament into architecture. In the Bavarian rococo church, because rocaille had to remain a framing and mediating ornament, it could develop into a protean abstract substance. Only as the precarious synthesis achieved by the rococo church falls apart, only as architecture and painting strive for a new purity, does its ornament, too, gain independence. And as ornament moves toward autonomy in the fifties and sixties we also meet with a turn from abstraction to representation that parallels what was taking place in ornamental engravings.

I will give just two examples. Especially in smaller churches it had become customary to give the wooden framing architecture of altars the look of marble by painting it with abstract patterns suggesting the expensive stone. In a number of churches around Erding the painters who created this marbling—perhaps bored with their routine work, perhaps aspiring to the glory of "real" painters, at any rate unwilling to produce merely ornamental patterns—let little scenes, representations of landscapes, architectures, ships, even Christ on the Cross, emerge out of swirling abstractions (fig. 150).[18] Somewhat as Jackson Pollock toward the end of his life let abstraction generate representational elements, so here the play of abstract forms condenses into images. A similar desire to elevate ornament into a representational art led Mathias Obermayer, an unusually imaginative stuccoer from Straubing, to transform the framing of the side altars at Windberg into delightful representations of the attributes of their saints. The altar of St. Catherine, the patron of philosophers, for example, is framed with bookshelves, inkwells, and drawers (fig. 151).[19]

Plate 11

There are, however, also cases where decoration becomes almost autonomous and yet remains abstract. A clock, a stove, a vase; an altar or a pulpit; something had to be ornamented. Characteristic of the fifties and sixties is a tendency not just to ornament such objects, but to *turn them into ornaments*. As a result they tend to look rather like free sculptures.

A comparatively early example is the high altar that Dominikus Zimmermann created

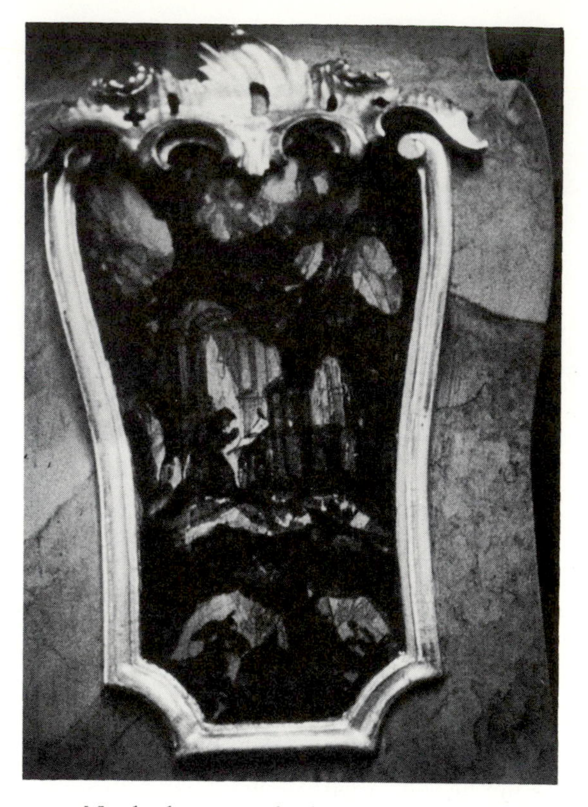

150. Niederding, parish church St. Martin, *Fassmalerei*, by Georg Andrä and Franz Xaver Zellner

151. Windberg, Premonstratensian abbey church, St. Catherine altar, 1756.

for his Johanneskirche in Landsberg am Lech (1752). Gone is the column architecture that since the beginning of the baroque had been standard in altar compositions, offering first a frame, later both frame and stageset; it has been replaced with free rocaille forms. The fantastic rocaille architectures of ornamental engravings have become three-dimensional reality. The color scheme suggests the precious artificiality of china. (The china factory at Nymphenburg had just been founded; Franz Anton Bustelli was about to create figurines that capture the essence of the aesthetic culture of the rococo.) In Landsberg aesthetic interest triumphs over the theatre of the baroque.

Plate 10

Although extreme, this is hardly a unique example. Much better known is the fantastic altar that Johann Michael Feichtmayr and Johann Georg Üblhör executed after a design by Küchel in the Franconian Vierzehnheiligen (1764). In Bavaria proper the little altar of the chapel in Kempfenhausen near Starnberg deserves to be mentioned. Its late date (1777) betrays itself in the way rocaille is yielding here to reedlike vines and flower garlands. More engagingly original are the altars that Johann Anton Bader created in Hörgersdorf, Eschlbach, and Rappoltskirchen, with their asymmetries and delightful surprises (fig. 152).[20] To this until recently unknown craftsman, working out of the provincial Dorfen, we owe one of the high points of the Bavarian rococo, the pulpit of Oppolding, which foams up in a rocaille of unusual strength and grace (fig. 124). A spontaneity unburdened by theory has here created an almost abstract work of art that has something of the inevitability that we associate with nature.

152. Eschlbach, parish church Mariae Geburt, right side altar

The pulpit of the little church in Oppolding is both a culminating achievement of the rococo and a sure sign of the disintegration of that synthesis which had been the goal of the Bavarian rococo church. In this respect it belongs with Peter Thumb's Birnau or with Baumgartner's frescoes in Baitenhausen. In all these works the aesthetic side of the rococo church threatens to overwhelm its sacred character. Sacred art approaches here the threshold of art for art's sake.

Has it crossed the threshold? We may want to insist that what prevents it from doing so is the continuing insistence that beauty not be created for beauty's sake. No matter how free it is permitted to become, ornament here still serves the traditional task of building a church hallowed, not simply by its use, but more essentially as a sign of the Church. The beauty of rocaille is still offered in praise, *ad maiorem Dei gloriam*, and still hints at a life unburdened by time.

And yet the beauty of the pulpit—like all beauty—is too ambiguous to let us give this answer with much conviction. Instead of presenting itself to us as a symbol of a life unburdened by time, its beautiful, self-sufficient presence may fascinate us so completely that for a time the burden of time seems to have been lifted.

CONCLUSION
THE DEATH OF ORNAMENT

The Ethical Function of Ornament

What dies with rocaille is not just another ornament, but ornament itself. As ornament emancipates itself from its merely ornamental function and gains aesthetic autonomy it becomes a kind of abstract art; but at the same time it loses its justification. In works like the pulpit of Oppolding ornament perishes of its own beauty.

Closely tied to an appreciation of the autonomous beauty of rocaille is the discovery of the beauty of the naked wall. A self-sufficient ornament can only stand in an accidental relationship to the ornament bearer. Like the ornamental skin of Nilson's *Neues Caffehaus*, it can be stripped off without serious loss to the supporting structure. How small the step is that separates the rococo church from a purer architecture that spurns the assistance of fresco or stucco is shown by Balthasar Neumann's Hl. Kreuz in the Franconian Etwashausen (1741–45). In accord with the wishes of the prince bishop of Würzburg, Friedrich Carl von Schönborn, Neumann left the white interior completely free of ornament (fig. 153).[1] Although still unmistakably rococo, architecture here has gained an almost classicistic purity. Neumann's church has its only somewhat less successful Bavarian parallel in the church that Ignaz Anton Gunetzrhainer built for the Carmelites of Reisach on the Inn (1737–39).[2] Here it was the ascetic Carmelite ethos, which shuns extroversion and ostentation, that led to the rejection of fresco and stucco. Both churches show how close the South German rococo could come to neoclassicism, how small the step is from superabundant ornament to a pure and naked architecture.

But even if the conceptual point is granted—if one admits not only that ornament cannot become a self-sufficient work of art and continue to function as ornament, but also that, especially in the fifties and sixties, rocaille approaches this point of autonomy, that ornament here negates itself—does this justify the claim that what dies with rocaille is ornament itself and that it is the aesthetic approach that is responsible for this death? Indeed, how can one claim that ornament dies in the eighteenth century? Do the facts not refute the assertion? In spite of the arguments of a Lodoli, in spite of the idea of a pure architecture projected by the designs of Boullée and Ledoux, nineteenth-century architecture once more relied heavily on ornament. And while it is true that the attack on

153. Kitzingen—Etwashausen, Hl. Kreuz, interior

ornament was renewed with greater vigor by some of the leading modern architects, we should not forget that most domestic architecture disregarded that attack and that there had always been a strong countercurrent, which in recent years has claimed increasing attention. Robert Venturi's call for a return to ornament has symptomatic significance.

There is a ready reply which can itself be stated as a question: Has the nineteenth century in fact produced a *living* ornament?[3] Labels like "neoclassicism," "neogothic," "neorenaissance," "neobaroque" make one wonder. To be sure, buildings continued to be decorated, but with borrowed forms. Most nineteenth-century ornament suggests the museum; this makes it difficult to speak here of living ornament. And has the twentieth century succeeded where the nineteenth failed? Even art nouveau does not provide a good counterexample. We do indeed have here decoration born of an attempt to create a new and distinctly modern ornament. But if this ornament owes less to the past than most of its nineteenth-century precursors, its aesthetic character, so removed from the realities of the day, made it artificial and arbitrary. It is difficult to dismiss Adolf Loos's remark: "The ornament that is manufactured today has no connexion with us, has absolutely no human connexion, no connexion with the world order. It is not capable of developing. What happened to Otto Eckmann's ornament, or van de Velde's? . . . Modern ornament has no parents and no progeny, no past and no future."[4]

With the rise of the aesthetic attitude ornament degenerates into mere decoration, and, as Hermann Broch observes:

> In all decoration, even in the most harmless, slumbers cynicism—itself the product of rationalist thinking—slumbers skepticism, which knows, or at least suspects, that what is being played is only a game of coverup. Where decoration is not naïve, but emerges from rationalism, it is not free creation, but pretense, sometimes successful, still pretense. And since it is also skeptical it has no support of its own, but needs examples. Rationalism belongs to this world and looks for the recipes offered by this world.[5]

To speak of ornament degenerating into mere decoration is to assume that we can draw a distinction between the two. Not that this distinction is easily justified by an appeal to ordinary language. We tend to use "ornament" in a way that makes it synonymous with "decoration" and opposes it to what is essential. Somewhat like a fancy dress, ornament is what we can really do without. But, as the *Oxford English Dictionary* reminds us, ornament can also be used in a different sense. When we speak of the ornaments of a church, we do not mean just its decoration, but "the accessories or furnishings of the Church and its worship." Such ornament would include chalice and vestments, organ and altars, and can include decoration, but placing it in a larger context. Decoration is ornament in this sense only if it exists not for its own sake, but stands in the service of the Church and its worship. Accordingly I would like to understand ornament as decoration that has a ceremonial and festal function. As St. Thomas observes, ornament helps to mark out special places and special times.

> Now man's tendency is to reverence less those things which are common, and indistinct from other things; whereas he admires and reveres those things which are distinct from others in some point of excellence. Hence, too, it is customary among men for kings and princes, who ought to be reverenced by their subjects, to be clothed in more precious garments, and to possess vaster and more beautiful abodes. And for this reason it behoved special times, a special abode, special vessels, and special

> ministers to be appointed for the divine worship, so that thereby the soul of man might be brought to greater reverence.[6]

A merely aesthetic approach cannot do justice to this function of ornament, which presupposes a recognition of what deserves to be ornamented, a sense of what is more and what is less significant. Ornament presupposes and helps to establish a rank order. Thus, the central part of a façade requires special ornament, as does the choir.[7] Ornament is appropriate only if the different parts of some larger whole are not of equal importance; if there are patterns of subordination, if one part governs the others. Like the human body, a baroque or rococo church may thus be said to have a head and a heart. Following Vitruvius, architects had long considered the proportions of the perfect human body—for the Christian the body of Christ—as a model.[8] Like the body, a building should be a hierarchically ordered organic whole. Ornament helped to articulate that hierarchy.

Toward the end of the eighteenth century this anthropomorphic approach to architecture "was abandoned by all progressive minds" and beauty was sought not in the *subordination* but the *coordination* of parts, the latter expressing itself in "simple repetition" or "dramatic antithesis."[9] But what function does this leave for ornament? *The death of ornament and the demise of the traditional theory of proportions belong together.* Both are granted a posthumous existence. Our own domestic architecture attests to this.

Rococo ornament still assumes that a successful building is a hierarchical order that assigns to each part its proper place, and it assumes that society is such an order. Ornament contributes to the articulation of that order. A palace should not look like a farmhouse; the House of God should not look like a house of men. In this sense ornament can be said to possess an ethical, not merely an aesthetic significance; ethical in the sense of helping to establish the ethos of a society, which assigns to persons and things their proper places. The transformation of ornament into mere decoration denies this ethical function.

Inseparable from the ethical function of ornament is its essentially public character. If it is to articulate the ethos of a society, ornament may not be the property of an individual or a particular group. Like ordinary language, it must be shared by the society in its entirety.

If ornament, in this sense at least, has indeed died, should we mourn this death? What I have said here should not be construed as a plea for ornament. If ornament loses its point to the extent to which society and life are no longer organized hierarchically, should we not accept its death as a necessary part of mankind's coming of age? Is hierarchical organization not an affront to humanity? We begin to understand the connection between the social revolution that overthrew the old order in the eighteenth century and the death of ornament.

The Case Against Ornament

No one has stated the case against ornament with more passion than the Viennese architect Adolf Loos in his notorious and revealing manifesto "Ornament and Crime."[10] The incompatibility between modern architecture and ornament here finds strident voice.

The title itself is a provocation. What does ornament have to do with crime? The association of the two must have seemed especially provocative in the Vienna of 1908, which still clung to its baroque heritage. Architecture at that time was caught between the *école polytechnique* and the *école des beaux arts*, between functional considerations and a concern for beauty that found its models in the past. Ruskin's insistence that we carefully distinguish between architecture and building, that the architect is an artist only when he concerns himself with what is useless and unnecessary but precisely because of this beautiful, points in the same direction, as do the widely imitated neobaroque and neorenaissance structures of Gottfried Semper: functional skeletons dressed up in borrowed garments.

But why associate ornament with crime? It may be possible to criticize nineteenth-century architecture's uneasy compromises between form and function on aesthetic grounds, and it is easy to sympathize with Gropius's demand that buildings once more be of a piece, complete. But does this justify the condemnation of all ornament? To call something a crime is to suggest that it constitutes a serious offense against the public welfare. Does ornament constitute such an offense? Loos insists that it does. Those enlightened officials who a hundred years earlier wanted to tear down masterpieces of rococo architecture in the name of reason expected understanding and thanks from the local peasants, for was it not their well-being that the officials had in mind? And did they not—does Loos not—have reason on their side? Is ornament not frightfully wasteful of time and money that would be better spent on food, medicine, and education? With malnutrition and illiteracy as widespread as they were in eighteenth-century Bavaria, how can ornament be defended? Indeed, what is ornament good for? Reason demands utility, and utility, as Ruskin knew, argues against ornament. Do gingerbread men or marzipan pigs provide more nourishment than plain bread? We can let children enjoy such things, but adults? Loos links architectural ornament to cookery exhibitions that value the ornate appearance of food over its nutritional value. Both, if Loos is right, have become anachronisms. They really have no place in the modern world and should have disappeared long ago.

Loos took it to be his great discovery, a discovery he was eager to pass on to the world, that "the evolution of culture is synonymous with the removal of ornament from utilitarian objects." This discovery, he felt, should bring joy to the world. When it met with a hostile reaction he was unhappily surprised. The message seemed so obvious. How could reasonable persons disagree? How could they cling to what Loos considered the unhappy inheritance of the eighteenth century, which weighed especially on Austria and helped to account for her comparative backwardness?

> If two people live side by side with the same needs, the same demands on life and the same income but belong to different cultures, economically speaking the following process can be observed: the twentieth century man will get richer and richer, the eighteenth century man poorer and poorer. I am assuming that both live according to their inclinations. The twentieth century man can satisfy his needs with a far lower capital outlay and hence he can save money.[11]

The point is difficult to deny. In the late eighteenth century similar arguments had been advanced, contrasting the increasing backwardness of Bavaria with a far more progressive Prussia. Loos found his shining examples of truly modern societies in England and even more in the United States. Even their culinary culture (or should we say their lack of one?) provided a valuable model. If we are to believe Loos, a person who is truly of the twentieth century should prefer his vegetables boiled in water, perhaps with a little butter; should prefer a slab of roast beef to boeuf bourguignon. Haute cuisine and ornament both are crimes that inflict "serious injury on people's health, on the national budget and hence on cultural evolution."[12]

Cultural evolution, as Loos understands it, is inseparable from economic success. Here we have the key to his attack on ornament. Given economic considerations ornament is simply wasteful. How could the Viennese ever catch up with the English as long as they remained caught up in their baroque love of ornament? Architecture should serve life. In this it resembles a machine. The builder should be governed by the same concerns as the engineer. But the engineer has no use for ornament. A functionalist approach to architecture demands the death of ornament.

Loos's emphasis on the economic argument against ornament does not fully explain his resistance to it, however. His writing communicates a more personal distaste. Loos finds ornament obscene. His comparison of ornament to graffiti smeared on lavatory walls is telling, as is the suggestion that the willingness to accept the naked wall provides us with a measure of cultural evolution. To find ornament obscene suggests a connection between it and the erotic sphere, and at least in the case of rocaille we can indeed trace such an affinity. Rocaille never loses all connection with the realm of Venus. Krubsacius was not altogether wrong when he sensed something obscene about it.

I cannot consider here the more general thesis of the erotic meaning of all ornament, but only suggest that Loos's claim that ornament should be considered the erotic "baby talk of painting" deserves to be taken seriously. The child's libidinous relation to itself and to its environment finds an expression in the way in which every empty wall invites spontaneous decoration. But while the child's sexuality remains polymorphous and unfocused, cultural progress demands focusing, demands repression. Loos can accept ornament when it is produced by children or persons who have not yet caught up with modern civilization, but otherwise it is said to betray either the criminal or the degenerate aristocrat. The vehemence of Loos's response to ornament suggests, however, that there is something that still has a hold on him. We consider obscene only what moves us, but in a way we think we should not be moved. The demands placed on us by our own nature conflict with our self-image and accepted morality. Precisely for this reason they need to be repressed.

Even though Loos claims that modernity leaves no room for ornament, he is not insensitive to the positive significance that ornament continues to have for many people and, as a self-proclaimed aristocrat, he does not want to impose his values on those not yet ready for them. It would be cruel to deprive them of something that they need. He claims to understand

> the Kaffir who weaves ornaments into his fabric according to a particular rhythm that only comes to view when it is unravelled, the Persian who weaves his carpet, the Slovak peasant woman who embroiders her lace, the old lady who creates wonderful things with glass beads and silk. The aristocrat lets them be; he knows that the hours in which they work are their holy hours.

The passage is telling. The creation of ornament is here said to give work something of the quality of worship. It attunes its creator to a larger order. Such attunement does not require justification. The activity justifies itself.

Traditionally aesthetic experience is discussed as experience that does not serve some other end, but justifies itself. There is, however, an important difference. Aesthetic experience is opposed to work. Loos's Kaffir or Persian, the Slovak peasant woman or the old lady, knowing no such opposition, can fashion their ornaments without giving it much thought. Genuine ornament occurs only where the aesthetic sphere has not yet been separated off from ordinary life—which is also to say where economic considerations have not yet gained that importance which they have for us—and in such cases the objection that the work is inefficient misses the point. The people who built Steinhausen or Die Wies could not have been expected to understand the charge that all this work was just a waste of time and money better spent on education.

But is this lack of understanding really a failure? Is it so clear that the Slovak peasant woman stands on a lower rung of the cultural ladder than the aristocrat Adolf Loos? What does he have to offer her? What did the enlightened reformers have to offer the Bavarian peasants who clung so tenaciously to their ornamented churches? To be sure, we can cite a great deal, above all better health and better education. And yet today, seventy years after Loos's attack on ornament, when modernity is coming under increasing critical scrutiny, it is difficult not to be disheartened by modern man's inability to generate once more a living ornament, for this inability betrays the fragmentation of our life. And with the whole we have lost the holy. For how many of us are the hours of work holy hours? The uneasiness that raises such questions is not laid to rest by the assurance that the national economy would be greatly strengthened by the willingness to abandon all ornament.

Loos recognized the force of such concerns. He knew very well that life would be empty without activities that are more than means to some end, activities that we engage in for their own sake. Here questions of efficiency are out of place. Loos also knew that our enjoyment of ornament is intimately tied to its superfluity, which challenges a thinking that approaches things only as means to some end. Ornament helps to lift the burdensome character of human existence. Thus the visual culture of the Bavarian rococo helped to transfigure lives shadowed by war, hunger, and disease. But do we not today have more effective ways of dealing with these old enemies? And, Loos would add, we have art.

> After the toils and troubles of the day we can go to Beethoven or to Tristan. . . . But anyone who goes to the Ninth Symphony and then sits down and designs a wallpaper pattern is either a confidence trickster or a degenerate. Absence of ornament has brought the other arts to unsuspected heights. Beethoven's symphonies would never have been written by a man who had to walk about in silk, satin, and lace. Anyone who goes around in a velvet coat today is not an artist but a buffoon or a house painter. We have grown finer, more subtle. The nomadic herdsmen had to distinguish themselves by various colors—modern man uses his clothes as a mask. So immensely strong is his individuality that it can no longer be expressed in articles of clothing. Freedom from ornament is a sign of spiritual strength."[13]

The passage invites challenge; it also demands to be taken seriously. Significant is the claim that for us an art that has separated itself from ordinary life has taken the place of ornament. Art for art's sake is the ornament of modern life. If Loos is right our highest experiences are of an aesthetic nature. Such experiences alone justify themselves and, where God is dead, there is no other justification. We work to have more time for art. Accepted is that disintegration of life which finds expression in phrases like "art for art's sake," "business is business," "war is war." *Art for art's sake is a splinter of the traditional value system that has become autonomous.*[14]

Important, too, is Loos's suggestion that the replacement of ornament with art for art's sake is inseparable from the introversion that characterizes modern man. In spite of ready counterexamples, there is truth to the claim that we use clothing or houses less to represent ourselves and our place to others than to hide behind their protection. And where a dress or an extravagant house does become a personal expression, it expresses the individual in his individuality, not his place in society. Along with the disintegration of life into autonomous spheres goes the disintegration of the community into atomic individuals.

Ornament both assumes and serves to strengthen a way of life that integrates rather than separates spirit and body, work and leisure, individual and society. It is easy to understand why it is so difficult, especially for a Viennese or a Bavarian, not to look back with nostalgia to the baroque and rococo. Such nostalgia finds its architectural expression in the borrowed ornaments of historicist architecture.

Aesthetic Purity

If we are to believe Loos, we no longer need ornament, because we have something better. Instead of ornament we have our art; and art could rise to its present height only because ornament had died. A provocative claim: the rise of modern art is linked to the death of ornament. I have argued for a related thesis: the aesthetic attitude that carries rocaille beyond its merely ornamental function toward artistic autonomy also lets it perish. But to show the essential incompatibility of that attitude with all ornament it is necessary to consider more carefully what it involves.

As pointed out in the preface, we owe the term *aesthetics* to Alexander Gottlieb Baumgarten. Like Gottsched a follower of Leibniz and Wolff, Baumgarten is another characteristic representative of the German Enlightenment. Modern aesthetics originated in the same circle that generated Reiffstein's and Krubsacius's attacks on rocaille. Our aesthetic understanding of art is part of the legacy left to us by the Enlightenment.

One of Baumgarten's similes helps to characterize this understanding: a successful poem is said to be like the world, more precisely like the world described by Leibniz. In that world nothing is superfluous, nor is anything missing; it is a perfectly ordered whole having its sufficient reason in the divine artist. The same ought to be true of the work of art: its integrity should be such that to add or subtract anything would be to weaken or destroy the aesthetic whole. Quite traditional in its suggestion that the artist is a second God, Baumgarten's simile seems innocent enough. After all, ever since Aristotle unity has been demanded of works of art. To be sure, to demand unity is not to deny complexity, tension, and incongruity, but in the end order should triumph. In a successful work of art what may at first appear to be discordant elements are in the end recognized as absolutely necessary, so that nothing is superfluous, while it is impossible to add anything without weakening or destroying the aesthetic whole. It is evident that such an aesthetic leaves little room for ornament. Certainly works of art do not tolerate additional ornament. Such an addition cannot be reconciled with the required unity. Nor can ornament become a work of art in its own right without casting off its subservience to the ornament bearer. Beauty, which Baumgarten understands in typical eighteenth-century fashion as sensible perfection, demands that art cast out ornament and that ornament become absolute. As we have seen, much rocaille is on the threshold of such emancipation. It is precisely the aesthetic character of rocaille that makes it ornament that *threatens the destruction* of ornament.

To the unity of the work of art corresponds the self-sufficiency of the aesthetic experience. We do not need art to survive. Art so understood does not so much serve life as it compensates for life's deficiencies. From this aesthetic view it follows that art cannot be the servant of religion or of the state and succeed as art. Emphasis on the self-sufficiency of the aesthetic experience leads to an assertion of the aesthetic sphere as an autonomous realm. Art is for art's sake.

If beauty demands aesthetic purity and if aesthetic purity denies a place to ornament, it is also difficult to see how architecture can ever be beautiful in this sense. A building has to be more than an object for aesthetic contemplation; the architect has to take into account the uses to which his work will be put, while those using it cannot keep their distance from it. To the extent that we measure buildings by the aesthetic conception of what constitutes a complete work of art, architecture has to be considered deficient and impure, a not quite respectable art. It is hardly an accident that with the rise of the aesthetic approach not only ornament, but architecture, too, enters a period of uncertainty and crisis. Both are essentially dependent art forms; the ideal of aesthetic self-sufficiency has to threaten their essence. Just as in the eighteenth century attempts are made to create ornament that approaches the self-sufficiency of a work of art, so there are attempts to elevate architecture to the status of a pure art. The designs of Ledoux offer the most obvious examples. The architect here has become an abstract artist who casts his forms, his cubes, pyramids, and spheres, into the void. Not surprisingly, Ledoux's most daring designs, like so many ornamental designs, remained on paper. The pursuit of purity leads the architect to utopian fantasies unlikely ever to be realized. Reality demands compromises; aesthetic vision has to be tempered by extra-aesthetic considerations. As long as the theory of architecture remains subject to the aesthetic approach, it is in no position to do justice to the essence of architecture.

This would be of little importance if it were only a matter of a few theoreticians speculating about the essence of architecture. But such speculation is only an aspect of a more deeply rooted change in sensibility that in the name of reason divorced pragmatic and aesthetic considerations and placed the architect uneasily between the two. On the one hand the uses of architecture were emphasized; on the other architecture was supposed to be beautiful. And who could quarrel with the demand that architecture be both practical and beautiful? Unfortunately, the hopes of functionalists notwithstanding, there not only is no assurance that an economical and efficient solution to a practical problem will also be aesthetically pleasing, but given the aesthetics of purity, there is no chance that the marriage of engineer and architect will be free of tension and compromise. What passes for such marriage is usually architecture that *has the look* of functionality rather than being truly functional. Given the aesthetic approach, beauty has to appear as something added on to what is dictated by necessity, decoration that is given a special value precisely by its superfluity. Seen in this context, Nilson's *Neues Caffehaus*, with its easily peeled-off skin of rocaille, points forward to iron skeletons that in the nineteenth century wore neorenaissance or neobaroque skins. The tensions that result from this mingling of pragmatic and aesthetic considerations are readily experienced and rule out aesthetic completeness. Aestheticians have thus tended to understand architecture as an impure art of compromise.[15] Indeed, subjected to the aesthetic approach architecture has to appear fundamentally incomplete. The demands of the aesthetic and of life are too heterogeneous to permit a synthesis.

Given the essential incompatibility between the aesthetic approach and the essence of both architecture and ornament, it may seem curious that just these two provide the first anticipations of the revolution that was to culminate in the abstract art of the twentieth century. That the revolution of modern art can be traced back to the architects of the French Revolution has been shown by Emil Kaufmann and, following him, by Hans Sedlmayr.[16] That this architectural revolution is anticipated by the evolution of rocaille has been shown by Hermann Bauer and, following him, by this study. In the eighteenth century ornament approaches the status of a completely free art. Only in the twentieth century were painting and sculpture to aspire to a similar freedom. The traditional understanding of both painting and sculpture as arts of representation helps to explain this time lag.

The aesthetic approach tends toward abstract art. Already in Kant's *Critique of Judgment*, which offers the most searching philosophical analysis of the aesthetic, the requirements of a completely free beauty and of representation are shown to be incompatible. To appreciate a free beauty we may have no concept of what sort of thing the beautiful object is supposed to be. The beautiful pleases by its form alone. The self-sufficiency demanded of the aesthetic experience implies the demand that there be nothing about the aesthetic object that refers the observer beyond itself; it may not represent or signify anything else, or even have a meaning. That such an approach leaves little room for an understanding of the church as an artwork signifying the Church is evident.

How much this view remains in force today is suggested by the way in which Frank Stella describes his artistic goals:

> I always get into arguments with people who want to retain the old values in painting—the humanistic values that they always find on the canvas. If you pin them down, they always end up asserting that there is something besides the paint on the canvas. My painting is based on the fact that only what can be seen *is* there. It really is an object. Any painting is an object and anyone who gets involved enough in this finally has to face up to the objectness of whatever it is that he's doing. He is making a thing. All that should be taken for granted. If the painting were lean enough, accurate enough, or right enough, you should be able to just look at it. All I want anyone to get out of my paintings, and all I ever get out of them, is the fact that you can see the whole thing without confusion. . . . What you see is what you see.[17]

Distancing himself from what he calls "the humanistic values" of a more traditional approach to painting—the parallel provided by the way the revolutionary architecture of the eighteenth century distances itself from an older, more humanistic approach should be noted—Stella projects the ideal of an art that would force us just to look at it, that would not allow us to "*avoid* the fact that it is supposed to be entirely visual."[18] The spectator is to be reduced to a pure eye, the work of art to an absorbing visual presence.

Why this fascination with presence? Why should, as Michael Fried claims, the authentic art of our time aspire to "presentness"?[19] That Fried speaks of "presentness" and not simply of "presence" is significant, for it suggests that the aesthetic experience is to deliver us not simply from meaning and representation, but from the burden of time. If the work of art is to be all there, if nothing is to be absent and lacking, it must place the observer beyond memory and expectation, beyond hope and fear, beyond interest and boredom.

> It is this continuous and entire presentness, amounting as it were to the perpetual creation of itself, that one experiences as a kind of *instantaneousness*: as though if only one were infinitely more acute, a single brief instant would be long enough to see everything, to experience the work in all its depth and fullness, to be forever convinced by it.[20]

Minimal art provides the most obvious examples, although Fried suggests that there is poetry and music that similarly lets time stand still "because *at every moment* the work itself is wholly manifest."[21] We begin to see more clearly what informs the aesthetic project: the hope to negate time within time. The pursuit of presence is born of the hope to create an art that would deliver us from the burden of time. "Presentness," writes Fried, "is grace."[22] The author of this grace is no longer God, but the artist. No longer able to turn to God or the Virgin to be freed from the dread of time, modern man turns to beauty to discover in it a fleeting substitute for that eternity for which he can no longer hope. But if presentness is indeed grace, grace is denied to man. Man cannot escape the temporality of his situation. The more singlemindedly art pursues presence and purity, the more decisively will it take its leave from reality.

If Kant's conception of free beauty can be argued to demand an abstract art, the art of Kant's day left this demand pretty much unmet. Searching for examples of a manmade free beauty all that Kant could come up with were instrumental music and (given the theme of this study this deserves special emphasis) ornament. "Delineations *à la grecque*, foliage for borders or wall papers, mean nothing in themselves; they represent nothing—no object under a definite concept—and are free beauties."[23] When Kant here brackets the architectural function of ornament, he follows as thinker the same aesthetic approach that had led to the creation of works like the pulpit of Oppolding. Such bracketing lets ornament appear as a self-sufficient aesthetic presence.

Insistence on the autonomy of the aesthetic sphere has to put into question the role of ornament in architecture. While Kant thus discusses ornament as an example of free beauty, he shares the Enlightenment's uneasiness about the function of ornament in architecture, especially in church architecture. "We could add much to a building which would immediately please the eye if only it were not to be a church. We could adorn a figure with all kinds of spirals and light but regular lines, if only it were not the figure of a human being."[24] Given Kant's conception of what constitutes the essence of a church or of man, such decorations seem not only inessential, but altogether out of place. If the essential autonomy of the aesthetic sphere demands an art free from all servitude, free even from all representation and thus abstract, the sacred character of a church or the moral dignity of a person are difficult to reconcile with decoration. Religion and morality must keep their distance from the aesthetic; the latter is denied what I have called an ethical function.

Historically speaking the late rococo of the pulpit of Oppolding leads nowhere. Given the aesthetics of the eighteenth century, no justification for such an autonomous art could be given; to the critics of the Enlightenment it had to seem irrational and frivolous. But if the pulpit represents a splendid dead end, this dead end can be read as a figure of modern abstract art. I have suggested that the aesthetic approach demands both the transformation of ornament into an autonomous art and the liberation of painting from its representational function. Here we have the twin roots of abstract art which may be understood either as the result of an ornamentalization of painting or as ornament developing into an independent aesthetic object.

A look at the development of painting in the years preceding the First World War supports this suggestion. To establish it would require a separate study; here I will only call attention to certain aspects of what happened in Munich at that time. The dominant figure is of course Kandinsky, but Kandinsky's achievement was not that of a genius working in isolation. His turn to abstract art has to be seen in the context of *Jugendstil* art. Endell especially had been calling for an art "with forms that signify nothing, represent nothing and recall nothing, but will be able to excite our souls as deeply as only music has been able to do with tones."[25] Before the turn of the century Adolf Hoelzel had begun to experiment with nonrepresentational forms; he called his creations *abstract ornaments*.[26] Just as Loos was trying to banish ornament from architecture, ornament became self-sufficient and autonomous. The parallel to developments in eighteenth-century art is evident.

More important than any possible causal relationship between these developments[27] is their inner affinity, which is explained by the logic of the aesthetic approach governing both. Just as ornament can become aesthetically pure only by shedding its dependent status, destroying itself as ornament, so art, to the extent that it submits to the rule of the aesthetic approach, has to strive for a purity incompatible first with representation and finally with all meaning. As Kant knew, an art offering completely free beauties is an impossibility. All art is essentially a more or less successful realization of some purpose or intention. The observer who approaches an object as a work of art has to assume such an intention—works of art, when seen as art, can never simply "be there," but always refer us beyond themselves to a governing intention, to intended meaning. But the loss of such meaning is demanded by that pursuit of purity and presence which characterizes so much modern art. Kant already wrote that beautiful art should look as if it were the product of nature; similarly, Clement Greenberg insists that what confers presence is "the look of non-art."[28] On such an interpretation modern art has its hidden telos in its own negation. The self-destruction of ornament in the eighteenth century would appear to prefigure the self-destruction of art for art's sake.

One may object that the account that has been offered here fails to justify talk of a death of ornament. Did ornament not survive by reaffirming its dependent status? The last stage in the development of rocaille, when it turns flat and anemic and the hegemony of architecture is reasserted, can be taken to illustrate the inevitable retreat from ornamental autonomy. Similarly in our day art seems to be retreating from the ideal of aesthetic purity. Thus there is increasing interest in representation. Here, too, one can speak of a reversal.

But as long as our attitude to art remains governed by the aesthetic approach, this reversal will lack conviction. For inseparable from the aesthetic approach is the severing of the aesthetic sphere from religious, ethical, and practical concerns. Given that approach ornament can be no more than something, perhaps beautiful, but inessential, added to a building. Ornament can regain its ethical function only if the architecture it serves reclaims that function for itself, and this is to say, only if the aesthetic approach is overcome. Similarly, as long as the aesthetic approach remains dominant, art can be no more than a perhaps beautiful, but nonessential, ornament of life. Here, too, a genuine reversal assumes an overcoming of the aesthetic approach.

Once again Kant is illuminating. As interesting as his recognition of the inevitable failure of man's search for a completely pure art is his reluctance to give to that art which comes closest to the creation of free beauty—instrumental music and ornament—a very high place. Art, Kant insists, should aim at more than just beauty; it should edify. Art should speak to man of his essence and vocation. If, liberated from this ethical function, the aesthetic sphere forms an autonomous province that fails to illuminate the world of human practice but only offers an escape from it, must we not repeat the criticism that the Enlightenment leveled against rocaille and direct it against all art? Kant's own analysis of the aesthetic makes it difficult to return to art its ethical function, although he struggles to do so.[29] The difficulty is indeed rooted in the nature of the aesthetic, where the autonomy granted to the aesthetic sphere needs to be understood as the other side of an interpretation of reason that makes it the sole custodian of reality.

Given that characteristically modern interpretation, art must seem to deflect man from his real vocation. Consider once more Adolf Loos's arguments against ornament. Must not these same arguments also challenge an art that exists for its own sake? Imagine two persons, living side by side, with the same income, but one of the two insists on satisfying a passionate interest in art—would that person not become poor and the other rich? Loos did not see that his attack on ornament is easily rephrased to put into question his aristocrat's support of a purer art. Is the pursuit of such an art not a crime in a world where millions continue to suffer from hunger, war, and disease? This is not to deny the charms of an art for art's sake, the lure of its promise to lift, if only fleetingly, the burden of time. But we may well wonder whether that promise does not lead man out of reality. And if his vocation is to realize himself in this world, this would make it a temptation to be resisted.

Art and the Sacred

There is today a widespread suspicion that the arts have lost their way. In such situations it makes sense to review the direction in which one has been traveling; in this case that means to rethink the aesthetic approach, its presuppositions and its implications. The

Bavarian rococo church can help us with such reflections. Not that it furnishes a paradigm inviting reappropriation. It never had much of a future; it presents itself to us as a splendid anachronism incapable of development. The Bavarian rococo church still presupposes an almost medieval figural understanding of reality that in the more progressive parts of Europe had been rendered impossible by the Reformation and by the new philosophy and science;[30] its beauty can still be understood as a symbol of the beauty of heaven or of that bride of whom the Song of Songs and the Book of Revelation speak and who is identified with the Virgin. But if it permits such understanding, it does not demand it; someone committed to the aesthetic approach is likely to insist on its irrelevance. And would not the phenomenon presented by the rococo church support him? What sense can we still make of talk of beauty as a symbol or sign of a transcendent beauty? We may try to recover the historical context that will open up the figural dimensions of the rococo church for us, but can such recovery ever become genuine appropriation? Must it not reduce the rococo church to an occasion for a scholarly hermeneutic game threatening to replace what is actually experienced with cerebral construction?

But if the Bavarian rococo church captivates us by its seemingly self-sufficient aesthetic presence, surely it also points beyond itself, not only to the intentions of those who built it, but to something that still moves and concerns us—even if we can no longer accept the way in which the rococo, following the tradition, interpreted this meaning, where the playfulness of these interpretations shows that even their authors did not take them too seriously. Is there not a way in which what is articulated when the beauty of the church is likened to the beauty of a bride or of a garden in May still claims us, even if we are unable to translate it into a clear and distinct discourse? If so, does this not suggest that the aesthetic approach cannot do full justice to our experience with art? Does not all genuine beauty capture our attention by its sensuous and seemingly self-sufficient presence, only to be experienced as a figure of a reality that transcends us and assigns us our place? That view, at any rate, has a long tradition. Already the Greeks understood the beautiful as both a captivating presence and as a sign of man's true home. Similarly, Christian thinkers interpreted the pleasure granted by the beautiful as a foretaste of paradise, a taste so sweet that it easily lets one forget what is signified and promised. Threatening such forgetting, beauty tends to obscure its tie to the sacred. The Bavarian rococo church especially can teach us that beauty invites its own secularization. That the concept of secularization does in fact provide a key to the aesthetic approach is suggested by Fried's pronouncement that "presentness is grace." The rhetoric here still hints at the traditional understanding of the beautiful as a figure of the sacred, but at the same time it refuses such an interpretation. Aesthetic presence is given a dignity that does not belong to it, and the attempt to seize it shows only an empty silence.

But to suggest that beauty tends toward its own secularization is to give only a very one-sided interpretation of the rise of the aesthetic approach. That tendency goes unchecked only when man no longer turns to art to articulate his place, when his understanding of reality and of his vocation has become such that reason alone is thought to provide proper access. The age of reason was to loosen the bond that once had tied the aesthetic, the ontological, and the ethical function of art together.

154. Osterhofen, abbey church, north side of the nave

The Bavarian rococo church invites us to rethink this development, its rewards and its price. At the same time our own response to it gives us some understanding of where we stand in the process (fig. 154). In this sense it may become for us a picture or a mirror of our condition and destiny.

NOTES

Introduction

1 See Karsten Harries, *The Meaning of Modern Art: A Philosophical Interpretation* (Evanston, Ill.: Northwestern University Press, 1968) and "Hegel and the Future of Art," *The Review of Metaphysics* 27, no. 4 (June 1974): 677–96.

2 The term *Bavarian* is somewhat misleading; most of the churches discussed are located within Bavaria as it existed in the eighteenth century and in the adjacent Swabian territories. The religious centers of this region were Augsburg and Freising, although Salzburg, Eichstätt, Regensburg, and Passau, were also important; its political center was Munich; its artistic centers were Augsburg and Munich. I am not concerned with the larger region that makes up modern Bavaria, which includes Franconia. But Franconia forms an artistic landscape with its own identity. The Franconian rococo, which culminates in the work of Balthasar Neumann, invites independent treatment. See maps, p. 274 below.

3 Emil Kaufmann, *Architecture in the Age of Reason: Baroque and Post-Baroque in England, Italy, France* (New York: Dover, 1968), pp. 141–80.

4 For this view of the rococo as a last style, as also for the view of rocaille as the last living ornament, I am indebted to Hans Sedlmayr's *Verlust der Mitte* (Frankfurt/M: Ullstein, 1959). See especially pp. 141–46. Sedlmayr's suggestive remarks have been developed by Hermann Bauer in *Rocaille: Zur Herkunft und zum Wesen eines Ornament-Motifs* (Berlin: De Gruyter, 1962). Those familiar with this study will recognize the extent of my debt to it.

5 The comparison is Arnold Hauser's. See *The Philosophy of Art History* (Cleveland and New York: Meridian Books, 1963), p. 210.

6 See Hans Tintelnot, "Zur Gewinnung unserer Barockbegriffe," *Die Kunstformen des Barockzeitalters*, ed. Rudolf Stamm (Bern: Francke, 1956), pp. 13–91.

7 Fiske Kimball, *The Creation of the Rococo* (New York: Norton, 1964), p. 5. See pp. 3–7 for a more extended discussion of the term *rococo*.

8 Arnold Hauser, *The Social History of Art*, vol. 3 (New York: Vintage, 1951), p. 34.

9 Kimball, *Creation of the Rococo*, pp. 172–73, 179n, 227–32.

10 See Bauer, *Rocaille*, p. 76.

11 One might object that someone who thinks that a negative answer must be given to this question should look for a different term to describe what has been called "the Bavarian rococo church." S. Lane Faison has suggested, somewhat facetiously as he admits, *barococo*, "to describe a creative amalgamation of two styles: Roman-Viennese Baroque and Parisian Régence-Rococo." But by now "Bavarian rococo church" has become so well established that attempts to replace it with another label are likely to fail. See Faison's review article in *Journal of the Society of Architectural Historians* 29, no. 2 (May 1970): 198.

12 See Norbert Lieb and Franz Dieth, *Die Vorarlberger Barockbaumeister* (München, Zürich: Schnell & Steiner, 1960), p. 60 for a full discussion of various proposals for the chronology of baroque and rococo architecture. For an English paraphrase of that discussion, see Henry-Russell Hitchcock, *Rococo Architecture in Southern Germany* (New York: Phaidon, 1968), pp. 4–5.

13 Bernhard Rupprecht, *Die bayerische Rokoko-Kirche, Münchener Historische Studien, Abteilung Bayerische Geschichte*, ed. Max Spindler, vol. 5 (Kallmünz: Lassleben, 1959), pp. 55–56. Some of Rupprecht's

basic insights are anticipated in Adolf Feulner, *Bayerisches Rokoko* (München: Wolff, 1923), which, despite its early date, remains the best introduction to the Bavarian rococo.

14 See Rupprecht, *Rokoko-Kirche*, pp. 42–46 and Hitchcock, *Rococo Architecture*, pp. 192–97.

15 Hitchcock, *Rococo Architecture*, pp. 12–13.

16 Kimball, *Creation of the Rococo*, p. 6.

17 *Summa theologiae*, III, 83, 3 ad 2m.

Chapter 1. The Pictorialization of Ornament

1 In the seventeenth century "rocaille" is used to refer to those heavy incrustations of rocks and shells that decorated grottoes and fountains. Already in 1734 we find the term used to characterize the work of Meissonier. By 1736 it has become well enough established to appear in the title of a series of ornamental engravings by Jean Mondon fils, his *Premier livre de forme rocaille et cartel* of 1736. See Hermann Bauer, *Rocaille: Zur Herkunft und zum Wesen eines Ornament-Motifs* (Berlin: De Gruyter, 1962), pp. 16–19, and Fiske Kimball, *The Creation of the Rococo* (New York: Norton, 1964), pp. 3–4 and 160.

2 See Kimball, *Creation of the Rococo*, pp. 109–11.

3 Henry-Russell Hitchcock, *Rococo Architecture in Southern Germany* (New York: Phaidon, 1968), p. 175.

4 Friedrich Wolf has suggested, not altogether convincingly, that it is indeed de Groff who has to be considered the leading artist at the court of Max Emanuel. Effner, according to Wolf, was mainly an administrator, and much of what has been considered his work should actually be credited to de Groff. See "Francois de Cuvilliés (1695–1768)," *Oberbayerisches Archiv* 89 (1967): 25–28 and "Wilhelm de Groff (1676–1742). Der Dekorkünstler des Kurfürsten Max Emanuel," *Oberbayerisches Archiv* 90 (1968): 52–61.

5 See Sixtus Lampl, *Johann Baptist Zimmermanns Schlierseer Anfänge. Eine Einführung in das Bayerische Rokoko* (Schliersee: Sixtus Lampl, 1979), pp. 40–66.

6 Hitchcock, *Rococo Architecture*, p. 131 and p. 125.

7 Hugo Schnell, "Die Wessobrunner Baumeister und Stukkatoren," *Wessobrunn. Kunstführer, Grosse Ausgabe*, 13, 2nd ed. (München, Zürich: Schnell & Steiner, 1960), p. 20.

8 Christina Thon seems to me right when she considers the adoption of French bandwork by decorators from Wessobrunn a development initially independent from but paralleling that of the court art of Munich. See *J. B. Zimmermann als Stukkator* (München, Zürich: Schnell & Steiner, 1977), pp. 230, 233, and 234.

9 Luisa Hager, *Nymphenburg* (München: Hirmer, n.d.), p. 16. Georg Hager, "Die Bauthätigkeit und Kunstpflege im Kloster Wessobrunn und die Wessobrunner Stuccatoren," *Oberbayerisches Archiv* 48 (1893–94): 380. Norbert Lieb, *München. Die Geschichte seiner Kunst* (München: Callwey, 1971), p. 149, and Max Hauttmann, *Der kurbayerische Hofbaumeister Joseph Effner* (Strassburg: Heitz, 1913), pp. 9–10.

10 Hauttmann, *Effner*, p. 13.

11 L. Hager, *Nymphenburg*, p. 15, and G. Hager, "Wessobrunner Stuccatoren," 399.

12 Georg Hager already demonstrated that the acanthus ornament of the Wessobrunners owed as much to French as to Italian models. The ceiling decorations of the *Aula Tassilonis* in Wessobrunn (ca. 1700), often taken as the paradigm of Wessobrunn stucco, have French antecedents. Thus, the way the acanthus vines play over hare and hound derives from Jean Lepautre's series of trophies, published in 1680 and widely known in Bavaria. See "Wessobrunner Stuccatoren," 379.

13 Hitchcock, *Rococo Architecture*, p. 131.

14 Bauer, *Rocaille*, p. 39.

15 Kimball, *Creation of the Rococo*, p. 110.

16 For an excellent discussion of these rooms see Thon, *Zimmermann*, pp. 44–46, 85–87. The balustrade motif in the corner frescoes of the library in Ottobeuren recalls the ceiling of the Great Hall of the Palazzo Costabili in Ferrara (after 1500). In Bavaria it had made an early appearance in the illusionistic painting above the Kaisertreppe in the Residenz in Munich (1616), now destroyed.

17 Compare Bauer, *Rocaille*, p. 47.

18 Kimball, *Creation of the Rococo*, p. 179 n.

19 Henry-Russell Hitchcock, *German Rococo: The Zimmermann Brothers* (Baltimore: Penguin, 1968), p. 60.

20 Ibid., p. 61.

21 Bauer, *Rocaille*, p. 40.

22 Ibid., p. 11.

23 Ibid., p. 40.

24 A review that appeared in the *Mercure* for March 1734 calls the new engravings (to describe them the reviewer speaks of *rocaille!*) "dans le goût d'Etienne la Belle." Since then the cartouches of Stephano della Bella have often been cited as one of the sources of the *style rocaille*. The mature rococo may be said to have combined the plasticity of the baroque cartouche with the ornamental logic of Mannerist and *régence* grotesques.

25 See Thon, *Zimmermann*, p. 102.

26 Thon suggests that his decorations in Benediktbeuern and Steinhausen make it likely that Zimmermann not only executed, but influenced, Cuvilliés's designs. See *Zimmermann*, pp. 125 and 214.

27 The Fürstäbtliche Zimmer were decorated from 1732 to 1735. They are thus roughly contemporary with the Reiche Zimmer of Munich's Residenz. Some details suggest that the decorators of Kempten were very familiar with Cuvilliés's most recent work. We do not know who was in charge of the decoration of the Kempten rooms; the prince abbot's court painter, Franz Georg Herman, has been suggested. Johann Georg Schütz, a student of Dominikus Zimmermann, appears to have been the leading stuccoer. The quality of the decoration and some details suggest Johann Georg Üblhör, who is said to have worked under Cuvilliés's direction in the Residenz and who is known to have been the author of the decoration of the splendid Throne Room. See Michael Petzet, *Stadt und Landkreis Kempten. Bayerische Kunstdenkmale, Kurzinventar* (München: Deutscher Kunstverlag, 1959), pp. 26–34. Also Hugo Schnell, *Die fürstäbtliche Residenz in Kempten* (München: Schnell & Steiner, 1947), pp. 14–15, and Kornelius Riedmiller, *Führer durch die Prunkräume der ehemals fürstäbtlichen Residenz in Kempten (Allgäu)* (Kempten, 1968), p. 10.

28 Schnell, *Die fürstäbtliche Residenz*, p. 57. See n. 16.

29 Hugo Schnell points out the similarity to altar compositions by Dominikus Zimmermann. See *Die fürstäbtliche Residenz*, p. 42.

30 Bauer, *Rocaille*, p. 39.

31 For a discussion of this church see Hitchcock, *Rococo Architecture*, pp. 191 and 192.

32 G. Hager, "Wessobrunner Stuccatoren," 440–41.

33 Bernhard Rupprecht, *Die bayerische Rokoko-Kirche, Münchener Historische Studien, Abteilung Bayerische Geschichte*, ed. Max Spindler, vol. 5 (Kallmünz: Lassleben, 1959), p. 31.

34 How easily the gable motif could join rocaille is shown not only by a glance at French ornamental engravings of the thirties, but also by the Zimmermanns' Die Wies (1746–54). See also Cuvilliés's use of the same motif in the Reiche Zimmer of the Residenz.

35 Here the balustrade is only painted. See Thon, *Zimmermann*, p. 224, n. 114.

36 Ernst Guldan has shown that the author of these frescoes is not Innozenz Waräthi, whom Hitchcock cites, following the earlier literature. See *Wolfgang Andreas Heindl* (Wien, München: Herold, 1970), pp. 42–47.

37 Ibid., p. 44; see also Hitchcock, *Rococo Architecture*, p. 40.

38 We find these clouds already in Ensdorf (1714), Cosmas Damian Asam's first major work. Recalling Gaulli's fresco in Il Gesù, the main fresco here spills over the frame, offering the spectator a way into the composition, connecting the space in which he stands with the space above. The same device recurs in Munich's Dreifaltigkeitskirche (1715), at Michelfeld (1717) and at Weingarten (1718–19).

39 Hitchcock, *Rococo Architecture*, p. 43.

40 At Rohr, however, the presumably intended frescoes remained unexecuted. As a result the stuccoed clouds seem rather pointless.

41 Hitchcock, *Rococo Architecture*, p. 53.

42 Ibid., p. 54.

Chapter 2. Space and Illusion

1 The decoration of the Grüne Gallerie in the Residenz in Munich (1733), which includes frescoes, recalls the library and the Festsaal of Benediktbeuern. Most of this decoration was lost in World War II. The recently completed reconstruction did not extend to all of the frescoes. As a result some of the framing ornament now seems somewhat pointless.

2 Willi Mauthe, *Die Kirchen in Weilheim* (Weilheim: Kirchenverwaltung Mariä Himmelfahrt, 1953), pp. 8–11. Almost a hundred years earlier illusionistic frescoes made an appearance on the ceilings of the Bavarian dukes' Stadtresidenz in Landshut. But it is difficult to connect these frescoes (1542–43) by Hans Bocksberger the Elder from Salzburg, Luwig Refinger from Munich, and Hermann Posthumus, probably from Holland or Italy, with Greither's work. Influenced by the Palazzo del Té, they constitute an isolated if remarkable achievement, so remarkable indeed that they made Hans Tintelnot claim that the daring foreshortening of Hermann Posthumus's paintings "anticipates around 1545 already everything that we admire in Guercino's Ludovisi fresco." *Die barocke Freskomalerei in Deutschland* (München: Bruckmann, 1951), p. 25. See also Hans Thoma, Herbert Brunner, and Theo Herzog, *Stadtresidenz Landshut. Amtlicher Führer* (München: Bayerische Verwaltung der Staatlichen Schlösser, Gärten und Seen, 1969), pp. 8–9.

3 Ernst Bassermann-Jordan, *Die dekorative Malerei der Renaissance am bayerischen Hofe* (München: Bruckmann, 1900), p. 130, pl. 88, and p. 134, pl. 90. Tintelnot, *Freskomalerei*, pp. 26–31.

4 Werner Horstmann, *Die Entstehung der perspektivischen Deckenmalerei* (München: UNI-Druck, 1968), p. 4.

5 See Margarete Baur-Heinhold, *Süddeutsche Fassadenmalerei vom Mittelalter bis zur Gegenwart* (München: Callwey, 1952).

6 A dependence on Weilheim is suggested by the octagonal dome over the choir, not over the crossing, here nonexistent. The model provided by the cathedral in Salzburg would seem to be more distant. From 1645 to 1654 the artist's father, Hans Konrad Asper, was court architect in Munich. See Norbert Lieb, *Münchener Barockbaumeister* (München: Schnell & Steiner, 1941), p. 46.

7 Karl Mindera, *Benediktbeuern. Kunstführer, Grosse Ausgabe*, no. 23 (München: Schnell & Steiner, 1957), p. 25. See also Mindera, "Die Frühzeit des Hanns Georg Asam in Benediktbeuern und sein Erstlingswerk," *Das Münster* 3, no. 5/6, (1950): 145–56 and Engelbert Baumeister, "Zeichnungen von Hans Georg Asam," ibid., 156–61. For a discussion of the church in Garsten see Josef Perndl, *Pfarrkirche in Garsten. Kleine Führer*, no. 503 (München: Schnell & Steiner, n. d.)

8 This was discovered in the course of a thorough restoration of the church (1962–73). Hans Georg Asam's first fresco is the Nativity above the high altar. The fresco is unusual also for its perspective, which anticipates later work by Cosmas Damian Asam. See Leo Weber SDB, *Benediktbeuern. Kleine Führer*, no. 34, 3rd ed., (München, Zürich: Schnell & Steiner, 1974).

9 Mindera, *Benediktbeuern*, p. 26.

10 Mindera, "Die Frühzeit des Hanns Georg Asam," 146–47.

11 See, for example, A. M. Zendralli, *I Magistri Grigioni* (Poschiavo: Menghini, 1958), p. 122, where both churches are attributed to Antonio Riva. This mistake is repeated by Henry-Russell Hitchcock, *Rococo Architecture in Southern Germany* (New York: Phaidon, 1968), p. 22. The architect in Benediktbeuern was in all probability Caspar Feichtmayr. See Mindera, *Benediktbeuern*, p. 22. For a good illustration see Hitchcock, pl. 16.

12 See Erika Hanfstaengl, *Cosmas Damian Asam* (München: Neuer Filser Verlag, 1939) and Bernhard Rupprecht, *Die Brüder Asam: Sinn und Sinnlichkeit im bayerischen Barock* (Regensburg: Pustet, 1980), the latter accompanied by superb photographs by Wolf Christian von Mülbe. For a good account in English see Hitchcock, *Rococo Architecture*, pp. 19–88.

13 The award-winning picture, recently discovered by Helene Trottmann (see "Die Zeichnungen Cosmas Damian Asams für den Concorso Clementino der Accademia di San Luca von 1713," *Pantheon*, 38, [1980]: 158–64) is excellently reproduced in Rupprecht, *Die Brüder Asam*, p. 59.

14 See Hans Zitzelberger, *Ensdorf. Kleine Führer*, no. 721, 2nd ed. (München, Zürich: Schnell & Steiner, 1968); Hanfstaengl, *Cosmas Damian Asam*, pp. 28–31; and Rupprecht, *Die Brüder Asam*, pp. 60–65.

15 Asam's clouds recall the work of Gaulli. Similar devices, however, were not unknown to the older Asam. See Mindera, "Die Frühzeit des Hanns Georg Asam," p. 150.

16 Hermann Bauer, *Der Himmel im Rokoko. Das Fresko im deutschen Kirchenraum des 18. Jahrhunderts* (Regensburg: Pustet, 1965), p. 55, now also available in Hermann Bauer, *Rokokomalerei* (Mittenwald: Mäander, 1980), pp. 81–91. See also Bernhard Rupprecht, *Die bayerische Rokoko-Kirche, Münchener Historische Studien, Abteilung Bayerische Geschichte*, ed. Max Spindler, vol. 5 (Kallmünz: Lassleben, 1959), pp. 25–26.

17 In St. Jakob in Innsbruck Asam similarly reiterated the architecture in the fresco. See Hanfstaengl, *Cosmas Damian Asam*, pp. 42–43, and Rupprecht, *Die Brüder Asam*, pp. 70–74; also Tintelnot, *Freskomalerei*, p. 60.

18 Rupprecht interprets the reiteration of the architecture below as an important step preparing for the autonomous existence of the fresco space, which he takes to be characteristic of the Bavarian rococo church. *Rokoko-Kirche*, p. 5 and *Die Brüder Asam*, p. 33.

19 Already in Benediktbeuern Hans Georg Asam employs a similar perspective, attempting a first fusion between the panel tradition and Italian illusionism.

20 The Aldersbach fresco has a precursor in Johann Michael Rottmayr's ceiling fresco in the Jesuit church St. Matthias in Wroclaw (Breslau) (1704–1706). See Eberhard Hempel, *Baroque Architecture in Central Europe* (Harmondsworth: Penguin, 1965), p. 114, pl. 66 A. Born in Laufen on the Salzach, then belonging to Salzburg, Rottmayr (1654–1730) went to Venice, where he studied with Carl Loth, son of the Weilheim painter Ulrich Loth. On his return from Italy he established himself as the leading painter active in Austria. Although it unites the nave even more forcefully than Asam's fresco in Aldersbach, a very different approach to space governs Rottmayr's work. The fresco in Wroclaw is very much a baroque work, closer to Pozzo than to Asam.

21 The following analysis is indebted to Rupprecht's searching discussion. See *Rokoko-Kirche*, pp. 6–8, and *Die Brüder Asam*, pp. 82–83. Also Michael Hartig and Hugo Schnell, *Aldersbach. Kleine Führer*, no. 698, 5th ed. (München, Zürich: Schnell & Steiner, 1970), and Hanfstaengl, *Cosmas Damian Asam*, pp. 49–52.

22 Hanfstaengl, *Cosmas Damian Asam*, p. 50.

23 Rupprecht, *Rokoko-Kirche*, p. 7.

24 Ibid.

25 Hitchcock, *Rococo Architecture*, p. 6.

26 Ibid., p. 7. Since Aldersbach was founded by monks from Ebrach (1146), its connection to the Franconian monastery was particularly close. Still, I doubt whether the Franconian examples Hitchcock mentions had any influence on Asam's work. Nor do we need to postulate such influence to account for the scalloped frame in Aldersbach. By this time the scalloped frame was very much "in the air."

27 Kuno Bugmann, *Einsiedeln. Kleine Führer*, no. 538 6th ed. (München, Zürich: Schnell & Steiner, 1981); also Hanfstaengl, *Cosmas Damian Asam*, pp. 70–76, and Rupprecht, *Die Brüder Asam*, pp. 37, 144–55. For an illustration see Hitchcock, *Rococo Architecture*, pl. 50.

28 The reconstruction of this interior has returned to Munich its most beautiful rococo interior. For a full account see Dominikus Lutz, OFM, *Die Klosterkirche St. Anna in München* (München: Franziskanerkloster St. Anna, 1977).

29 In spite of the fact that it was consecrated only in 1737, four years after Steinhausen, St. Anna has a slight priority. The foundation stone of the Munich church was laid in 1727, one year before work began in Steinhausen. The vault was decorated in 1729, antedating the decoration of the vault in Steinhausen by two years. There is, however, one key element present in Steinhausen and lacking in St. Anna: Cosmas Damian Asam's *St. Anne in Glory* lacks the landscape elements, so striking in Johann Baptist Zimmermann's large fresco in Steinhausen, that were to become a standard part of Bavarian rococo interiors.

30 P. C. Cannon-Brookes, *Great Buildings of the World. Baroque Churches* (London, New York, Sydney, Toronto: Paul Hamlyn, 1969), p. 181.

31 Founded in 1710, the Art Academy of the free imperial city of Augsburg became the center of fresco painting in Southern Germany. From 1730 its director was Johann Georg Bergmüller, who had received his training from Johann Andreas Wolff in Munich, then from Carlo Maratti. Among his students we find such accomplished painters as Johann Evangelist Holzer, whose early death put an end to a career of unusual promise, and Gottfried Bernhard Göz. Matthäus Günther, Cosmas Damian Asam's best student, settled here, as did Christoph Thomas Scheffler. But the list is much longer. Together with the engravers and the publishing houses of Augsburg these painters made Augsburg, even more than Munich, the real center of the decorative arts of the Bavarian rococo. See Herbert Schindler, *Grosse Bayerische Kunstgeschichte*, vol. 2 (München: Süddeutscher Verlag, 1963), pp. 294–301.

32 See Edelstetten (1710), the Carthusian monastery church in Buxheim (1711), Schliersee (1714) (fig. 4), the cloister of the cathedral in Freising (1716), Maria Medingen (1719–22). For plates and descriptions, see Henry-Russell Hitchcock, *The Zimmermann Brothers* (Baltimore: Penguin, 1968).

33 Amigoni, however, had already entered the elector's service in 1717. From Munich he was called to Ottobeuren in 1719, where he worked, with many interruptions, until 1729. See Hugo Schnell, *Ottobeuren. Kunstführer, Grosse Ausgabe*, no. 2 (München, Zürich: Schnell & Steiner, 1955), p. 21. Christina Thon suggests that it was Amigoni who, impressed by what he saw of Zimmermann's work in Ottobeuren, recommended him to Effner (*J. B. Zimmermann als Stukkator* [München, Zürich: Schnell & Steiner, 1977], p. 17). From Ottobeuren Amigoni went to London. In 1736 he moved to Paris. Three years later he returned to Venice. He spent the last years of his life in Madrid, as court painter of the king of Spain. Amigoni's work in Schleissheim was preceded by a large fresco covering the ceiling of the Hall of the Badenburg in the park of Nymphenburg. Unfortunately it was almost completely destroyed in World War II. The present reconstruction is unsatisfactory.

34 From 1720 to 1725 J. B. Zimmermann received 6680 guilders for his work in Schleissheim. He had ample opportunity to observe the work of the two painters. See Johannes Mayerhofer, *Schleissheim, Deutsche Bibliothek*, vol. 8 (Bamberg: Buchnersche Verlagsbuchhandlung, 1890), p. 58, and Thon, *Zimmermann*, pp. 302–07.

35 Although a strict illusionism forbids the appearance of landscape on the ceiling, the violation of this rule has a long history. Pietro da Cortona did not hesitate to paint a naval battle on the ceiling of the Sala di Marte in the Palazzo Pitti (1646)—a theme that became popular in eighteenth-century Bavaria, which liked to glorify the Virgin with representations of the victory over the Turkish fleet at Lepanto, which was attributed to her assistance. Still closer to the spirit of the Bavarian rococo church is Luca Giordano's *Triumph of Judith* (1704) in S. Martino in Naples. In this connection the frescoes Amigoni painted in the Benediktuskapelle and the Abstkapelle in Ottobeuren (1725–28) must be mentioned. That the fresco of the Bavarian rococo church—more especially its refusal of a rigorous illusionism, inseparable from the attempt to represent not just a second world but landscape on the ceiling—has its roots in Italy, more especially in Venice, is suggested also by the fresco the young Tiepolo painted in the Palazzo Sandi in Venice (1724–25). Bauer, *Der Himmel im Rokoko*, p. 56, and Rudolf Wittkower, *Art and Architecture in Italy, 1600–1750* (Harmondsworth: Penguin, 1973), pp. 254 and 324.

36 See Rupprecht, *Rokoko-Kirche*, pp. 24–25, 32–37.

Chapter 3. Architecture Against Architecture

1 Bernhard Rupprecht *Die bayerische Rokoko-Kirche, Münchener Historische Studien, Abteilung Bayerische Geschichte*, ed. Max Spindler, vol. 5 (Kallmünz:

Lassleben, 1959), pp. 55 and 56. See p. 4 above.

2 See, e.g., Erika Hanfstaengl, *Cosmas Damian Asam* (München: Neuer Filser Verlag, 1939), p. 2; Carl Lamb, *Die Wies* (München: Süddeutscher Verlag, 1964), pp. 99 and 109; Georg Lill, *Deutsche Plastik* (Berlin: Wegweiser, 1925), pp. 127–36; and Adolf Feulner, *Bayerisches Rokoko* (München: Wolff, 1923), p. 67.

3 Ried's vaults look back not so much to Bohemian as to Franconian and Bavarian antecedents; more important than the Parler tradition is that of Hans von Burghausen and Stefan Krumenauer. It has been suggested that Ried came from a village of that name in the Innviertel, then still Bavarian. Duke Hans Georg the Rich of Landshut may well have recommended the brilliant young architect to his royal brother-in-law in Prague. See Götz Fehr, *Benedikt Ried: Ein deutscher Baumeister zwischen Gotik und Renaissance* (München: Callwey, 1961) and James H. Acland, *Medieval Structure: The Gothic Vault* (Toronto: University of Toronto Press, 1972), pp. 209–15.

4 Acland, *Medieval Structure*, p. 221.

5 See Hans Jakob Wörner, *Architektur des Frühklassizismus* (München, Zürich: Schnell & Steiner, 1979), pp. 43–48.

6 See pp. 107–114 below.

7 St. Petri in Münster, the first Jesuit church in the Rhineland (1590–97), has a significance for Rhenish Mannerism that parallels that of St. Michael. The Jesuit churches in Koblenz, Aachen, Cologne, Münstereifel, Coesfeld, Bonn, and Siegen followed its model. The most impressive example of Franconian Mannerism, the Julius-Stil—named after Julius Echter von Mespelbrunn, prince bishop of Würzburg and a leader of the Counter Reformation in Germany—is the pilgrimage church at Dettelbach (1610–13).

8 See Acland, *Medieval Structure*, pp. 178–81. Here also a good discussion of how the building material, in Bavaria usually brick, limits and directs the architect's imagination.

9 See p. 103 below.

10 The Gothic cathedral in Albi and such Catalan churches as St. Catherine in Barcelona come to mind. A remark Nikolaus Pevsner makes about Il Gesù remains suggestive when applied to St. Michael: "The extreme width of the nave under the powerful tunnel-vault degrades the chapels into mere niches accompanying a vast hall, and it has been suggested that the choice of this motif was due to Francesco Borgia, the Spanish General of the Jesuit Order, and thus ultimately to the tradition of the Gothic style in Spain as already presented in Rome by the Catalan church of S. Maria di Monserrato (1495). If the suggestion is accepted, there is here yet another instance of post-renaissance return to medieval ideals." *An Outline of European Architecture*, 5th ed. (Harmondsworth: Penguin, 1958), p. 172. The Jesuits in Munich had very close connections with both Rome and Spain. We can assume that these helped to influence the architecture of their church.

11 Hauttmann speaks of it as a *Verlegenheitslösung*, a substitute for the basilical solution which the German builders did not dare. Max Hauttmann, *Geschichte der Kirchlichen Baukunst in Bayern, Schwaben und Franken 1550–1780* (München: Weizinger, 1923), p. 113.

12 Norbert Lieb sees in Sustris the creator of the entire church. See *Münchener Barockbaumeister* (München: Schnell & Steiner, 1941), pp. 13 and 219 n. 10, and *München. Die Geschichte seiner Kunst* (München: Callwey, 1971), p. 94. Supporting Hauttmann, Erwin Schalkhausser's analysis of the nave denies Sustris a decisive role in either its construction or its decoration. See "Die Münchener Schule in der Stuckdekoration des 17. Jahrhunderts," *Oberbayrisches Archiv für vaterländische Geschichte*, 81–82 (München, 1957): 5–27.

13 The decoration of St. Michael—after the destruction of the Second World War it is only now (1981) being reconstructed—is not of one piece. We can easily distinguish four quite different vocabularies: (1) The decoration of the nave vault recalls the wooden coffered ceilings of the Renaissance. (2) A different decorative system is employed in the somewhat later choir. If the geometric panels of the nave appear rather like wooden panels fixed to the vault, leaving empty strips between them, here the stuccoed bands look applied to the vault, somewhat in the way the rib-bands of the nave separate the different bays. (3) A third decorative scheme appears in the intrados of the transeptal arches. Here we find *Beschlagwerk*, an ornament which, as the German term suggests, derives from bandlike metal fittings. (4) The characteristic Wessobrunn stucco in the Maria Haar Kapelle dates from 1697.

14 The architect of the nave remains unknown. See Herbert Schade, *St. Michael in München. Kleine Führer*, no. 130, 6th ed. (München, Zürich: Schnell & Steiner 1971), pp. 8–9.

15 For the importance of the Dillingen church for the *magistri grigioni*, that remarkable group of architects from the Italian-speaking Grisons that dominated architecture in Southern Germany for the better part of the seventeenth century, see A. M. Zendralli, *I magistri grigioni—architetti e crostuttori, scultori, stuccatori e pittori—dal 16° al 18° secolo* (Poschiavo:

Menghini, 1958). Hans Alberthal (Giovanni Albertalli), to whom the Studienkirche is usually credited, belongs to this group, although it is not clear whether he was born in Roveredo or in Eichstätt. Friedrich Naab and Heinz Jürgen Sauermost call attention to the fact that a series of small wall-pillar churches was built in the vicinity of Bellinzona in the seventeenth century. They suggest a connection with Pellegrino Tebaldi's S. Fedele in Milan. See "Möglichkeiten des Wandpfeilersystems," *Vorarlberger Barockbaumeister* (catalogue of the exhibition in Einsiedeln and Bregenz, 1973), pp. 85–86. None of these wall-pillar churches, however, antedates the Studienkirche.

For an account of the importance of the Studienkirche for the work of the architects from the Austrian Vorarlberg, who in the second half of the seventeeth century came first to rival and then to replace the *magistri grigioni*, see the above and Norbert Lieb and Franz Dieth, *Die Vorarlberger Barockbaumeister* (München, Zürich: Schnell & Steiner, 1960), pp. 28–33.

16 Three artists associated with Augsburg, Matthias Kager, Joseph Heintz, court painter to Emperor Rudolph II, and Elias Holl, the leading German architect of the period, have been suggested. See *Vorarlberger Barockbaumeister*, p. 147.

17 Fürstenfeld provides an important link between St. Michael and the wall-pillar churches of Johann Michael Fischer. Fischer's treatment of cornice and attica in Diessen recalls Fürstenfeld, as does the column motif of Zwiefalten.

18 See p. 4 above.

19 For an overview of the development of the hall choir see Kurt Gerstenberg, *Deutsche Sondergotik. Eine Untersuchung über das Wesen der deutschen Baukunst im späten Mittelalter* (Darmstadt: Wissenschaftliche Buchgesellschaft, 1969), pp. 152–62.

20 Better known as Hans Stethaimer. The latter was in fact the nephew of Hans von Burghausen; he succeeded his uncle as architect of St. Martin in Landshut.

21 That association determined the hall character of the Hofkirche in Neuburg on the Danube built by the Protestant duke Philipp Ludwig of Neuburg as an answer to Munich's Catholic St. Michael. The church council criticized the plans submitted by Joseph Heintz for their many "angles," which, while perhaps appropriate in a Catholic church with its proliferation of altars, were felt to conflict with the spirit of the Protestant service. The hall church of the nearby Lauingen was to provide the example. The church's anti-Catholic rhetorical stance was lost when Philipp Ludwig was succeeded by his son Wolfgang Wilhelm, who had converted to Catholicism and entrusted the new church to the Jesuits. See Albert Lidel, *Hofkirche Neuburg/Donau, Kleine Führer*, no. 989 (München, Zürich: Schnell & Steiner, 1973), and Hauttmann, *Geschichte*, pp. 119–20.

22 See Lamb, *Die Wies*, p. 65, and Hauttmann, *Geschichte*, p. 124.

23 The church in Gars, too, was built by the Augustinian Canons. Why this Augustinian preference for the hall choir? Hauttmann suggests that a similar solution had already been found in the Augustinian Hl. Kreuz in Augsburg (1492–1508). Hauttmann, *Geschichte*, pp. 123–24.

24 Lieb and Dieth, *Die Vorarlberger Baumeister*, p. 35.

25 See Michael Hartig, *Wallfahrtskirche Vilgertshofen, Kleine Führer*, no. 484, 2nd ed. (München, Zürich: Schnell & Steiner, 1965) and Henry-Russell Hitchcock, *Rococo Architecture in Southern Germany* (New York: Phaidon, 1968), p. 128.

26 The most obvious precursor of this not-altogether-successful experiment is provided, not by the cathedral in Salzburg, often mentioned in this connection, but by the Kreuzkapelle of St. Michael in Munich (1592). In that chapel, too, we find the narrow choir arch that separates as much as it joins the nave and the centralized choir with its dark submerged dome. The Weilheim dome found an impressive successor in Michael Beer's exciting if strangely barbarian choir dome in St. Lorenz in Kempten (1652–56). See Hugo Schnell, *Stadtpfarrkirche St. Lorenz in Kempten, Kleine Führer*, no. 423, 3rd ed. (München, Zürich: Schnell & Steiner, 1971).

27 The comparison of St. Jakob with Herkommer's St. Mang in Füssen (1701–17) is instructive. In Füssen, too, there is tension between expectations raised by the basilical plan and the devaluation of the crossing with its lightless hemispherical dome, which forces the eye forward to the brightness of the choir and prevents the crossing from functioning as the center of the interior. This devaluation of the crossing invites its elimination or its transformation into a dark antechoir joining altar room and nave.

28 See pp. 54–66 above.

29 The choir of Diessen recalls the choirs of Johann Georg Fischer's churches, for instance his slightly earlier St. Katharina in Wolfegg. But, as Heinz Jürgen Sauermost points out, it would be a mistake to conclude from the obvious similarities that Johann Michael Fischer owed the solution found in Diessen to Johann Georg. Such solutions lay in the air. See Heinz Jürgen Sauermost, *Der Allgäuer Barockbaumeister Johann Georg Fischer* (Augsburg: Verlag der schwäbischen Forschungsgemeinschaft, 1964), p. 156.

30 Good examples are provided by three village churches, now within the city limits of Munich: Schwabing (1654–60), Forstenried (1672), and Oberföhring (1680).

31 See Michael Hartig, *Kloster Holzen. Kleine Führer*, no. 452, 3rd ed. (München, Zürich: Schnell & Steiner, 1970).

32 Rarely visited, although on the outskirts of Munich, this small, beautiful church, attributed to Philipp Köglsperger, deserves to be better known. As Hitchcock points out, in Kreuzpullach we find not only the ovalized rectangle, but also the scalloped fresco frame (*Rococo Architecture*, pp. 49 and 115). Here already the ovalization of the nave answers a certain centralization of the choir. But the originality of the church should not be exaggerated. Once again we are dealing with tendencies that were in the air. Ovalized rectangles are a characteristic feature of the churches the Erding architect Anton Kogler built in the second decade of the eighteenth century. Bockhorn (1712 ff.) and Tading (1714–19) are characteristic examples. In Itzling (1716) such centralization is coupled with a centralization of the choir that anticipates the Asam brothers.

33 Hitchcock, *Rococo Architecture*, p. 116.

34 Ibid., p. 115.

35 Norbert Lieb, *Murnau Obb.*, *Kleine Führer*, no. 476, 3rd ed. (München, Zürich: Schnell & Steiner 1961).

36 Viscardi's pilgrimage church in Freystadt (1700–1708) and his Dreifaltigkeitskirche in Munich (1711–15) must be mentioned. The impact of the latter is felt in Johann Baptist Gunetzrhainer's remarkable Schönbrunn (1723–24), although the way the plan of this church joins cross and ellipse recalls Austrian churches as well. Hitchcock mentions it as perhaps the first church to employ the oval (*Rococo Architecture*, p. 117), while Feulner claims that here, for the first time, we meet with that dissolution of a central space that was to become characteristic of the mature rococo. After such advance notice, one is likely to be somewhat disappointed by Schönbrunn. Schliersee, although architecturally much less ambitious, already has a much more pronounced rococo character.

37 Hitchcock, *Rococo Architecture*, p. 180.

38 See Lieb, *Barockkirchen*, p. 93.

39 Hans Jantzen, *Kunst der Gotik* (Hamburg: Rowohlt, 1957), pp. 71–73.

40 Compare, for example, the handling of the wall-pillars in the Studienkirche in Dillingen or in Maria Steinbach.

41 Cf. Sixtus Lampl, *Johann Baptist Zimmermanns Schlierseer Anfänge: Eine Einführung in das Bayerische Rokoko* (Schliersee: Sixtus Lampl, 1979) pp. 49–50.

42 Rupprecht, *Rokoko-Kirche*, p. 40. In this respect, too, Die Wies invites comparison with Johann Schmuzer's Vilgertshofen.

43 S. Lane Faison, review of Hitchcock, *Rococo Architecture*, and of Hempel, *Baroque Art and Architecture in Southern Europe, Journal of the Society of Architectural Historians*, 29, no. 2, (1970):198.

44 Arthur Schopenhauer, *The World as Will and Representation*, vol. 1, tr. E. F. Payne (New York: Dover, 1969), p. 215.

45 See Bernhard Rupprecht, *Die Brüder Asam: Sinn und Sinnlichkeit im bayerischen Barock* (Regensburg: Pustet, 1980), pp. 176–99. Alastair Laing minimizes Fischer's role in the decoration of his churches, especially of St. Anna im Lehel and Osterhofen ("Central and Eastern Europe," in Anthony Blunt, ed., *Baroque and Rococo Architecture and Decoration* [New York and London: Harper & Row, 1978], pp. 219–52). Osterhofen, in particular, is said to appear "to be wholly the work of the Asams who decorated it, rather than of Fischer, who built it" (p. 228). Rupprecht, on the other hand, emphasizes Fischer's contribution (*Die Brüder Asam*, p. 178). A comparison of St. Anna im Lehel as it looked after the first reconstruction after the war with its appearance before the war or today not only demonstrates the crucial contribution made by the decoration, but also strongly suggests that Fischer must have had some such decorative scheme in mind when he designed the church. A comparison of St. Anna and Osterhofen with the more modest church in Unering supports that suggestion.

46 Christian F. Otto, *Space into Light: The Churches of Balthasar Neumann* (Cambridge: The Architectural History Foundation and M.I.T. Press, 1979), pp. 44–45.

Chapter 4. Theatrum Sacrum

1 Richard Alewyn and Karl Sälzle, *Das grosse Welttheater. Die Epoche der höfischen Feste in Dokument und Deutung* (Hamburg: Rowohlt, 1959), p. 16.

2 Eberhard Straub, *Repraesentatio Maiestatis oder churbayerische Freudenfeste. Miscellanea Bavarica Monacensia*, vol. 14 (München: Neue Schriftenreihe des Staatsarchivs, 1969), pp. 191–96.

3 Ibid., pp. 299–300.

4 Messerer denies that the sculptor Johann Baptist Straub had done anything improper. He explains that three archangels were to be represented in the high altar, not scenes from the life of the Virgin. The putto expresses only an attribute of the angel. And yet it is difficult to imagine this playful transformation of traditional representations of the Annunciation before the rococo. See Wilhelm Messerer, *Kinder ohne Alter: Putten in der Kunst der Barockzeit* (Regensburg: Pustet, 1962), pp. 33–34.

5 Rudolf Wittkower, *Gian Lorenzo Bernini: The Sculptor of the Roman Baroque* (London: Phaidon, 1966), p. 27.
6 Bernhard Rupprecht, *Die bayerische Rokoko-Kirche, Münchener Historische Studien, Abteilung Bayerische Geschichte*, ed. Max Spindler, vol. 5 (Kallmünz: Lassleben, 1959), p. 17.
7 Hermann Bauer, *Der Himmel im Rokoko: Das Fresko im deutschen Kirchenraum des 18. Jahrhunderts* (Regensburg: Pustet, 1965), pp. 9–14.
8 Thirty years before Bergmüller Cosmas Damian Asam had already used this device in his Christmas fresco at Aldersbach. See p. 62 above.
9 Cf. Sigfrid Hofmann, *Die Kirchen der Pfarrei Steingaden* (Steingaden: Katholisches Pfarramt, 1960), pp. 6–8.
10 For a survey of the changing approaches to the high altar in Bavaria see Richard Hoffmann, *Der Altarbau im Erzbistum München und Freising in seiner stilistischen Entwicklung vom Ende des 15. bis zum Anfang des 19. Jahrhunderts. Beiträge zur Geschichte, Topographie und Statistik des Erzbistums München und Freising*, ed. Martin von Deutinger, vol. 9 (München: Lindauersche Buchhandlung, 1905).
11 In 1620 Candid painted his enormous *Assumption* for the high altar of Munich's Frauenkirche, where it remained until 1858. It now hangs above the entrance to the sacristy.
12 It is important to keep in mind that this elaborate high altar composition is essentially incomplete. This incompleteness finds expression in the empty choir stalls. The dramatic scene presented by the sculptor demands the fulfillment provided by the dramatic celebration of the liturgy. See Johannes Zeschick OSB, *Benediktinerabtei Rohr, Keine Führer*, no. 1015 (München, Zürich: Schnell & Steiner, 1974).
13 Henry-Russell Hitchcock, *Rococo Architecture in Southern Germany* (New York: Phaidon, 1968), p. 45.
14 The high altar compositions at Rohr and Weltenburg are just about contemporary. By 1724 both appear to have been completed. See Norbert Lieb, *Barockkirchen zwischen Donau und Alpen*, 2nd ed. (München: Hirmer, 1958), pp. 33–46, 149–50.
15 See Hermann Schmidt and Hugo Schnell, *Landsberg: Stadtpfarrkirche und Johanneskirche, Kleine Führer*, no. 88, 2nd ed. (München, Zürich: Schnell & Steiner, 1961), and Henry-Russell Hitchcock, *German Rococo: The Zimmermann Brothers* (Baltimore: Penguin, 1968) pp. 78–79.
16 S. Lane Faison, review of Anthony Blunt, ed., *Baroque and Rococo: Architecture and Decoration*, *Journal of the Society for Architectural Historians* 39, no. 1, 72.
17 My interpretation is indebted to that found in Jakob Mois, *Die Stiftskirche zu Rottenbuch* (München: Schnell & Steiner, 1953), pp. 81-85. See also Hugo Schnell, *Rottenbuch, Kleine Führer*, no. 8, 15th ed. (München, Zürich: Schnell & Steiner, 1964).
18 See Ernst Guldan, *Eva und Maria* (Graz, Köln: Böhlaus, 1966), pp. 39–41.
19 John Donne, *Annunciation*, in *The Poems of John Donne* (London, New York, Toronto: Oxford University Press, 1951), p. 290.
20 As a device to facilitate the transition from nave to choir the stuccoed curtain was first used in Bavaria by the brothers Asam in the cathedral of Freising (1724). This paradigm, unfortunately later destroyed, was soon picked up by other decorators. Christina Thon's suggestion that formally considered the curtain motif functions as a device to join different spatial compartments must be accepted; at the same time it is impossible to overlook the reference to the theatre. See Thon, *J. B. Zimmermann* als Stukkator (München, Zürich: Schnell & Steiner, 1977), pp. 110 and 255, n. 466.
21 See Alewyn and Sälzle, *Das grosse Welttheater, p.* 62.
22 I am following Rupprecht's analysis. See especially *Rokoko-Kirche*, p. 42.
23 Bauer, *Der Himmel im Rokoko*, p. 35.
24 Arnold Hauser, *The Social History of Art*, tr. Stanley Godman, vol. 2 (New York: Vintage, n. d.), p. 189.
25 Ibid.
26 See Carl Lamb, *Die Wies* (München: Süddeutscher Verlag, 1964), pp. 23–25.
27 Jacques Maritain, *Art and Scholasticism and the Frontiers of Poetry*, tr. Joseph W. Evans (New York: Scribner, 1962), p. 52.
28 Leon Battista Alberti, *On Painting*, tr. John R. Spencer (New Haven: Yale University Press, 1956), p. 64.
29 *Republic* X, 602 c and d, tr. B. Jowett.
30 Quoted in Frances A. Yates, *Theatre of the World* (London: Routledge & Kegan Paul, 1969), p. 30.
31 See Jurgis Baltrušaitis, *Anamorphoses ou perspectives curieuses* (Paris: Olivier Perrin, 1955).
32 For illustrations see the catalogue of the exhibition *Anamorphoses: Games of Perception and Illusion in Art* (New York: Abrams, 1976), plates 23–26.
33 S. Lane Faison has suggested to me that we think of Egid Quirin's portrait of his brother as we would of Dürer's self-portraits in some of his altarpieces. But the specific theatricality of this church with its many levels of reality, its play with aesthetic distance, needs to be considered when interpreting this image of its creator. Cosmas Damian presents himself to us as a magician who delights in his creation. He seems more real than the figures of the fresco, among whom

he included his younger and more devout brother, whom he painted as an angel. Visually this sculpture belongs with the princess of the high altar who needs to be saved from the dragon. To insist on the playfulness of this art is not to question its seriousness.

34 Albrecht Schöne, *Emblematik und Dramatik im Zeitalter des Barock* (München: Beck, 1964), p. 227.
35 Stephen Orgel, *The Illusion of Power: Political Theatre in the Renaissance* (Berkeley and Los Angeles: University of California, 1965), p. 17.
36 See Edmund Stadler, "Raumgestaltung im barocken Theater," in *Die Kunstformen des Barockzeitalters*, ed. Rudolf Stamm (Bern: Francke, 1956), p. 191.
37 Margarete Baur-Heinhold, *Theater des Barock: Festliches Bühnenspiel im 17. und 18. Jahrhundert* (München: Callwey, 1966), p. 118.
38 Besides the already-mentioned works by Stadler and Baur-Heinhold see also Donald C. Mullin, *The Development of the Playhouse* (Berkeley and Los Angeles: University of California, 1970).
39 Rupprecht, *Rokoko-Kirche*, pp. 12–13. On the Bibienas see Rudolf Wittkower, *Art and Architecture in Italy 1600–1750* (Harmondsworth: Penguin, 1973), p. 574, n. 47. Adolf Feulner calls attention to Ferdinando Bibiena's S. Antonio at Parma as a precursor of Weltenburg: *Bayerisches Rokoko* (München: Wolff, 1923), p. 23.
40 Orgel, *Illusion of Power*, p. 30.
41 Baur-Heinhold, *Theater des Barock*, p. 180.
42 Orgel, *Illusion of Power*, p. 39.
43 Straub, *Repraesentatio Maiestatis*, p. 84.
44 Ibid., p. 99.
45 Orgel, *Illusion of Power*, p. 39.
46 Benno Hubensteiner, *Bayerische Geschichte* (München: Pflaum, n. d.), p. 191.

Chapter 5. Time, History, and Eternity

1 Louis Dupré, *The Other Dimension* (Garden City: Doubleday, 1972), p. 1.
2 See Karsten Harries, "The Dream of the Complete Building," *Perspecta* 17 (1980): 36–43.
3 The following account relies heavily on P. Herbert Schade S. J., "Die Berufung der Jesuiten nach München und der Bau von St. Michael," *Der Mönch im Wappen: Aus Geschichte und Gegenwart des katholischen München* (München: Schnell & Steiner, 1960), pp. 209–57. See also P. Herbert Schade S. J., *St. Michael in München. Kleine Führer*, no. 130, 6th ed. (München, Zürich: Schnell & Steiner, 1971).
4 Fischer von Erlach's Karlskirche in Vienna (1715 ff.) can be cited as a distant successor. See Hans Aurenhammer, *J. B. Fischer von Erlach* (Cambridge: Harvard University Press, 1973), p. 136.
5 Schade, "Berufung der Jesuiten," p. 239. See Otto von Simson, *The Gothic Cathedral* (New York and Evanston: Harper & Row, 1964), p. 141.
6 Lengthy excerpts in Schade, "Die Berufung der Jesuiten."
7 Unlike its Romanesque predecessors, however, and unlike most baroque and rococo churches, St. Michael faces south instead of west. In this willingness to sacrifice the traditional orientation of the church for the sake of a dramatic presentation of the façade, a modern, secular understanding of space betrays itself.
8 Schade, "Die Berufung der Jesuiten," p. 247.
9 Ibid., p. 238.
10 Ibid., p. 249.
11 See Lieb, *Barockkirchen zwischen Donau und Alpen* (München: Hirmer, 1953), pp. 60–66 and Ills. 61–81 and *Diessen/Ammersee. Kleine Führer*, no. 30, 6th ed., (München, Zürich: Schnell & Steiner, 1973).
12 See, for example, St. Clare in Cheb, illustrated in Christian Norberg-Schulz, *Late Baroque Architecture* (New York: Abrams, 1971), ill. 113.
13 Henry-Russell Hitchcock, *Rococo Architecture in Southern Germany* (New York: Phaidon, 1968), p. 182.
14 Ibid., pp. 189 and 256.
15 Lieb, *Diessen*, p. 11.
16 Bernhard Rupprecht *Die bayerische Rokoko-Kirche, Münchener Historische Studien, Abteilung Bayerische Geschichte*, ed. Max Spindler (Kallmünz: Lassleben, 1959) pp. 21–23.
17 Jakob Biedermann, *Cenodoxus*, ed. Rolf Tarot (Tübingen: Niemeyer, 1963). The play had its first performance in Augsburg in 1602. In 1625 Joachim Meichel translated the popular play into German (München: Hanser, 1957).
18 Messerer, *Kinder ohne Alter: Putten in der Kunst der Barockzeit* (Regensburg: Pustet, 1962), p. 69.
19 Bauer, *Rocaille: Zur Herkunft und zum Wesen eines Ornament-Motifs*, (Berlin: De Gruyter, 1962), pp. 26–27.
20 Luisa Hager, *Nymphenburg* (München: Hirmer, n.d.), pp. 26–27.
21 Johann Doerig, "Die spanische Barockliteratur," *Die Kunstformen des Barockzeitalters*, ed. Rudolf Stamm (Bern: Francke, 1956) p. 299.
22 See Gaston Bachelard's discussion of "nests." *The Poetics of Space*, tr. Maria Jolas (Boston: Beacon Press, 1969), pp. 90–104.
23 Bauer, *Rocaille*, pp. 71–74.
24 The affinity of the Magdalenenklause and its "wild setting" with the English park and its picturesque architecture forces one to question Emil Kaufmann's claim that Robert Morris's views on landscape archi-

tecture "show him far ahead of his continental contemporaries." When Morris writes of natural surroundings, where "in the *cooler Hours* of Reflection, a Man might retire, to contemplate the Important *Theses of Human Life*," he expresses a sentiment well known to the continental baroque and rococo (see *Architecture in the Age of Reason: Baroque and Post-Baroque in England, Italy, France* (New York: Dover, 1968), p. 27). One wishes that Dora Wiebenson, *The Picturesque Garden in France* (Princeton: Princeton University Press, 1978), had included a fuller account of its early history.

Chapter 6. Ecclesia and Maria

1 *Summa theologiae*, III, 83, 3 ad 2m. See Dagobert Frey, "Der Realitätscharakter des Kunstwerkes," *Kunstwissenschaftliche Grundfragen: Prolegomena zu einer Kunstphilosophie* (Darmstadt: Wissenschaftliche Buchgesellschaft, 1972), p. 115, and Günter Bandmann, *Mittelalterliche Kunst als Bedeutungsträger* (Berlin: Mann, 1951), p. 11.
2 Although by no means the only one. An obvious response is tied to the understanding of the church as the body of Christ, which can lead to attempts to relate its proportions to those of the perfect man. Important especially to Renaissance theorists of architecture, this fusion of Christian and Vitruvian ideas had, as far as I can tell, little impact on the Bavarian rococo church. See Otto von Simson, *The Gothic Cathedral* (New York and Evanston: Harper & Row, 1964), p. 36, n. 38, and Joseph Rykwert, *On Adam's House in Paradise: The Idea of the Primitive Hut* (New York: Museum of Modern Art, 1972), pp. 118–20.
3 See Simson, *Gothic Cathedral*, p. 8.
4 On the importance of the Solomonic Temple see Simson, *Gothic Cathedral*, pp. 37–38, 95–96 and Rykwert, *Adam's House*, pp. 121–40. It is worth noting that only after the Middle Ages are attempts made to discover how exactly the Temple of Solomon must have looked. To be sure, the understanding of this temple as a figure of heaven and as the archetypal church was common throughout the Middle Ages, but only in the baroque do we find attempts to actually reconstruct it, beginning with Juan Bautista Villalpanda's highly influential attempt to recover that lost archetype of the church, supposedly based on a plan that God Himself had authored. Not too surprisingly, given Villalpanda's association with Philip II of Spain and his architect Juan de Hererra, Solomon's temple turns out to look in some ways rather like the Escorial, and serves to legitimate this residence-monastery of the Spanish king, who (resembling Solomon in this respect too) bore the title "king of Jerusalem" (Rykwert, *Adam's House*, p. 122). Not everyone was convinced by the efforts of the Spanish Jesuit. But the vigor and duration of the discussion that ensued show that Villalpanda was not alone with his concern about how the temple really looked, a concern that is foreign to the Middle Ages. Just as Luther insisted on the simple sense of God's word, so Villalpanda appeals to an unfortunately lost divine plan, a plan that, he reasoned, could be recovered by interpreting the clues found in the Bible in the light of Vitruvius, that is, in the light of reason. The long-lasting authority of this reconstruction is suggested by the fact that when the great Austrian architect Johann Bernhard Fischer von Erlach illustrates the Solomonic temple in his *Entwurff einer historischen Architectur* (Wien 1721) he follows Villalpanda. In such attempts a quite modern literalism betrays itself, which, as one would expect, had more of an impact on the theory of architecture than on its practice. The Bavarian rococo church, at any rate, shows no trace of it.
5 Bernhard Rupprecht, *Die bayerische Rokoko-Kirche, Münchener Historische Studien, Abteilung Bayerische Geschichte*, ed. Max Spindler (Kallmünz: Lassleben, 1959), pp. 20–21.
6 Worth noting is that in those cases where we know which building provided the model, there is little resemblance. The popular Loreto chapels provide an obvious exception, but usually one is content with allusions that help to place the church in a particular context. While these allusions do not lead to literal imitation they can have considerable architectural significance. For instance, only if we keep in mind that in Bertoldshofen the model of St. Anthony in Padua was prescribed do we understand the otherwise inexplicable proliferation of domes. That the architect, Johann Georg Fischer, and his patron were content with what seems to us a superficial resemblance shows that what was wanted was not a literal representation, but some feature that, reappearing in the successor church, allowed it to be interpreted as a sign of its model.
7 Bandmann, *Mittelalterliche Kunst als Bedeutungsträger*, p. 89.
8 Simson, *Gothic Cathedral*, p. 9.
9 Hans Sedlmayr, *Die Entstehung der Kathedrale* (Zürich: Atlantis, 1950).
10 Simson, *Gothic Cathedral*, p. 37.
11 Ibid.
12 Rupprecht, *Rokoko-Kirche*, pp. 20–21.
13 See pp. 146–50 above.
14 P. Herbert Schade S. J.,"Die Berufung der Jesuiten nach München und der Bau von St. Michael," *Der Mönch im Wappen: Aus Geschichte und Gegenwart des katholischen München* (München: Schnell & Steiner, 1971). For Schade's discussion of the analysis of St.

Michael advanced by Gisela Deppen in "Die Wandpfeilerkirchen des deutschen Barock. Unter besonderer Berücksichtigung der baukünstlerischen Nachfolge von St. Michael in München," unpublished diss., München 1953, esp. pp. 244–45.

15 J. P. Migne, *Patrologiae cursus completus, Series Latina*, vol. 210, 579 A.

16 Albrecht Schöne, *Emblematik und Drama im Zeitalter des Barock* (München: Beck, 1969), pp. 34–42.

17 W. A. P. Smit, "The Emblematic Aspect of Vondel's Tragedies as the Key to Their Interpretation." *The Modern Language Review* 52, (1957): 555. Schöne, *Emblematik und Drama*, pp. 205–14.

18 Erwin Schalkhausser, "Die Münchener Schule in der Stuckdekoration des 17. Jahrhunderts," *Oberbayerisches Archiv für vaterländische Geschichte* 81–82 (1957): 28–38. The decoration of the nave is by Hans Krumpper (1614). That of the choir (1630) is, according to Schalkhausser, the work of a lesser artist.

19 Benno Hubensteiner, *Vom Geist des Barock: Kultur und Frömmigkeit im alten Bayern* (München: Süddeutscher Verlag, 1967), pp. 115–22.

20 Kurt Pfister, *Kurfürst Maximilian von Bayern und sein Jahrhundert* (München: Ehrenwirth, n. d.), p. 208.

21 Hubensteiner, *Vom Geist des Barock*, pp. 86–88.

22 Ibid., pp. 154–55.

23 Ibid., p. 101.

24 Schalkhausser, "Die Münchener Schule," 50–53, 75–78, 82–89.

25 See pp. 68–69 above.

26 Rupprecht speaks of a "Rokoko der Hermeneutik," *Rokoko-Kirche*, p. 24.

27 Ibid.

28 See pp. 170 and 182 above.

29 Rupprecht, *Rokoko-Kirche*, p. 19.

30 See p. 168 above.

31 Hans Sedlmayr, "The Synthesis of the Arts in Rococo," in the catalogue of the exhibition, *The Age of Rococo* (München: Rinn, 1958), p. 26.

32 Jakob Balde, *Dichtungen. Lateinisch und Deutsch.* Ed. and tr. Max Wehrli (Köln und Olten: Hegner, 1963). See Hubensteiner, *Vom Geist des Barock*, pp. 159–172.

33 Balde, *Dichtungen*, pp. 117–18.

34 My translation is indebted to Wehrli's German translation (pp. 92–95). In my selection of these three stanzas I follow Hubensteiner.

35 Sedlmayr, "Synthesis of the Arts in Rococo," p. 26.

36 Friedrich Ohly, "Die Geburt der Perle aus dem Blitz," *Schriften zur mittelalterlichen Bedeutungsforschung* (Darmstadt: Wissenschaftliche Buchgesellschaft, 1977), pp. 274–311.

37 A. A. Barb, "Diva Matrix," *Warburg Journal* 16 (1953): 205–7.

Chapter 7. Rococo Church and Enlightenment

1 The text in Norbert Lieb, *Münchener Barockbaumeister. Leben und Schaffen in Stadt und Land* (München: Schnell & Steiner, 1941), p. 11.

2 Benno Hubensteiner, *Bayerische Geschichte* (München: Pflaum, n. d.), pp. 233–37.

3 See Richard Benz, *Deutsches Barock. Kultur des achtzehnten Jahrhunderts*, part 1 (Stuttgart: Reclam, 1949), pp. 307–40.

4 Dorette Hildebrand, *Das kulturelle Leben Bayerns im letzten Viertel des 18. Jh. im Spiegel von drei bayerischen Zeitschriften. Miscellanea Bavarica Monacensia*, vol. 36 (München, 1971), p. 19.

5 Hubensteiner, *Bayerische Geschichte*, p. 238.

6 See Georg Hager, "Die Bauthätigkeit und Kunstpflege im Kloster Wessobrunn und die Wessobrunner Stuccatoren," *Oberbayerisches Archiv* 48(1893–94): 195–521 and Hugo Schnell, "Die Wessobrunner Baumeister und Stukkatoren," *Wessobrunn* (München, Zürich: Schnell & Steiner, 1960) pp. 13–21.

7 See Hubensteiner, *Vom Geist des Barock* (München: Süddeutscher Verlag, 1967), pp. 139–58.

8 Baur-Heinhold, *Süddeutsche Fassadenmalerei vom Mittelalter bis zur Gegenwart* (München: Callwey, 1952) and Alois J. Weichslgartner and Wilfried Bahnmüller, *Lüftlmalerei* (Freilassing: Pannonia, 1977).

9 For a discussion of the Bavarian enlightenment see Hans Grassl, "Münchener Romantik," *Der Mönch im Wappen, Aus Geschichte und Gegenwart des katholischen München* (München: Schnell & Steiner 1960) pp. 223–360 and Richard van Dülmen, "Zum Strukturwandel der Aufklärung in Bayern," *Zeitschrift für bayerische Landesgeschichte*, vol. 36, no. 2, (1973): 662–79.

10 Anita Brittinger, *Die bayerische Verwaltung und das volksfromme Brauchtum im Zeitalter der Aufklärung*, diss. München, 1938, p. 8.

11 Norbert Lieb, *Barockkirchen*, p. 111.

12 Hugo Schnell, *Die Wallfahrtskirche Wies. Kunstführer*, Grosse Ausgabe, no. 1, 10th ed. (München, Zürich: Schnell & Steiner, 1960), p. 5.

13 Hugo Schnell, *St. Martin/Garmisch. Kleine Führer*, no. 20, 3rd. ed. (München, Zürich: Schnell & Steiner, 1964), pp. 3–4.

14 Hugo Schnell, *Bertoldshofen. Kleine Führer*, no. 647 (München, Zürich: Schnell & Steiner, 1957), pp. 3–4.

15 Fintan Michael Phayer, *Religion und das gewöhnliche Volk in Bayern in der Zeit von 1750–1780. Miscellanea Bavarica Monacensia*, vol. 21 (München, 1971), pp. 20 ff.

16 Brittinger, *Die bayerische Verwaltung*, pp. 49–54.
17 Ibid., p. 16.
18 Ibid., pp. 14–15.
19 As Phayer points out, the Bavarian state correctly saw the incompatibility of Catholic baroque culture and capitalism. The secularization of everyday life was a necessary condition of Bavaria's entry into a recognizably modern world. An important part of this was the secularization of sexual life. Toward the end of the eighteenth century the traditional relation between property and children, which forced a high degree of abstinence upon the impecunious, was inverted, which invites an interpretation of the erotic character of the popular rococo—think of the cult of the Virgin—as a sublimation of what one was forced to repress. As a result of the Enlightenment these restraints collapsed. The number of illegitimate children increased dramatically. By the early nineteenth century from one-third to one-half of the children are illegitimate. It should be noted that in Bavaria, at least, the collapse of traditional morality appears not as a result, but as a presupposition of industrialization. The spiritual revolution here preceded the economic. See *Religion und das gewöhnliche Volk*, pp. 106–44.
20 Schnell, *Die Wies*, p. 8. According to Carl Lamb the words were inscribed by Gilbert Michel, the last abbot of Steingaden, who retired to Die Wies after the secularization had destroyed his monastery. *Die Wies* (München: Süddeutscher Verlag, 1969), p. 115.
21 Martin Heidegger, *Sein und Zeit*, 7th ed. (Tübingen: Niemeyer, 1953), p. 410.
22 Brittinger, *Die bayerische Verwaltung*, pp. 43–44. Increasingly it is no longer the village community that plays. The average person has become a mere spectator.
23 Cited in Benz, *Deutsches Barock*, p. 315.
24 Cited from Gottsched's journal *Vernünftige Tadlerinnen* by Benz in *Deutsches Barock* p. 235. See also Johann Christoph Gottsched, *Versuch einer critischen Dichtkunst* (Leipzig: Breitkopf, 1751), p. 740.
25 Benz, *Deutsches Barock*, p. 323.
26 Gottsched, *Versuch*, pp. 740–43.
27 Hans Jakob Wörner, *Architektur des Klassizismus* (München, Zürich: Schnell & Steiner, 1979), pp. 79–109, and P. Schleich SJ., *St. Blasien/Schwarzwald, Kleine Führer*, no. 555, 20th ed., (München, Zürich: Schnell & Steiner, 1973).
28 Emil Kaufmann, *Architecture in the Age of Reason* (New York: Dover, 1968), pp. 130–34.
29 Quoted in Tintelnot, "Zur Gewinnung unserer Barockbegriffe," *Die Kunstformen des Barockzeitalters*, ed. Rudolf Stamm (Bern: Francke, 1956), p. 19.
30 See Joseph Rykwert, *On Adam's House in Paradise: The Idea of the Primitive Hut* (New York: Museum of Modern Art, 1972) pp. 43–48.
31 Cited in ibid., p. 44.
32 Ibid., pp. 49–51.
33 Cited in Bauer, *Rocaille: Zur Herkunft und zum Wesen eines Ornament-Motifs* (Berlin: De Gruyter, 1962), pp. 63–64. This section depends on Bauer's searching analysis.
34 Ibid., pp. 42–45.
35 John Canaday, *Embattled Critic* (New York: Farrar, Straus, and Cudahy, 1962), p. 107.
36 Bauer makes this "micromegalic structure" constitutive of rocaille and relates it to the way the rococo plays with the different modes of reality that belong to ornament and picture. Such play creates the impression of "an irony, that in the final analysis is a play with the possibilities of art, with art pure and simple." *Rocaille*, p. 21.
37 Ibid., pp. 56–57 and 66–68.
38 Applied to the work of engravers like Crusius or Nilson Bauer's analysis of the aesthetic character of this art is completely convincing. More questionable is its extension to the ornament of the rococo church. Still, we cannot deny that again and again its ornament carries the rococo church to the threshold of aestheticism.
39 Bauer, *Rocaille* p. 42.
40 Extensive excerpts of the text ibid., pp. 65–66.
41 Ibid., p. 52.
42 Ibid.
43 Ibid., pp. 53–55.
44 See p. 195 above. Ornamental engravings from the thirties and forties carry the same association, although spring is here tied to Venus rather than to the Virgin. Designs by Jacques de Lajoue, Jean Mondon fils, and François Boucher offer good examples.
45 Bauer, *Rocaille*, p. 63.

Chapter 8. *The Disintegration of the Rococo Church*

1 See Hans Jakob Wörner, *Architektur des Frühklassizismus in Süddeutschland* (München, Zürich: Schnell & Steiner, 1979), pp. 112–15 and plates 56–59.
2 Jakob Mois, *Die Stiftskirche zu Rottenbuch* (München: Schnell & Steiner, 1953), pp. 55–62.
3 Fürstenfeld was declared structurally unsound, and closed. To save demolition costs cannons were assembled on a nearby hill. Only the initiative of the citizens of Bruck saved the church. See Lorenz Lampl, "Zur Geschichte von Fürstenfeld," *700 Jahre Fürstenfeld, Kunstführer, Grosse Ausgabe*. no. 39 (München, Zürich: Schnell & Steiner, 1963), p. 28.

The events at Marienberg paralleled those in Rottenbuch. Here, too, a judge fought for the destruction of the church with a zeal that today is difficult to understand. The opposition of the local population led to the imprisonment of fourteen men. Only a visit by Crown Prince Ludwig finally assured the survival of the church. See M. Jordan, *Marienberg* (Neuburg: Oefele, n. d.), p. 6. The desire to drag the local population into a more enlightened age that filled Montgelas and his officials made these very common occurrences.

4 Norbert Lieb, Hugo Schnell, J. Klem. Stadler, *Wessobrunn: Geschichte, Bedeutung. Führung, Kunstführer*, Grosse Ausgabe, no. 13, 2nd ed. (München, Zürich: Schnell & Steiner, 1960).

5 Henry-Russell Hitchcock, *Rococo Architecture in Southern Germany* (New York: Phaidon, 1968), p. 165.

6 Norbert Lieb, *Barockkirchen zwischen Donau und Alpen* (München: Hirmer, 1953), p. 134 and Hugo Schnell, *Birnau am Bodensee, Kunstführer, Grosse Ausgabe*, no. 16, 2nd ed., (München, Zürich: Schnell & Steiner 1955), p. 9.

7 While Hitchcock speaks of the "retardataire character of Goez's frescoes," Schnell sees Goez as the most modern of the major artists associated with Birnau. Like Lieb, he emphasizes that it was Goez who decided the color scheme of the entire church. Credit for the interior belongs at least as much to him as it does to Thumb or Feuchtmayer. From Moravia, but a Bergmüller student, Goez carried the decorative approach associated with Augsburg engravings (he was himself well known as a creator of ornamental fantasies) into fresco painting. The advanced rococo character and unusually high quality of his art is shown by the frescoes he painted two years after Birnau in Schloss Leitheim. They rank with the very best created by the Bavarian rococo.

8 Alfred Volkert and Hugo Schnell, *Scheidegg-Allgäu, Kleine Führer*, no. 871 (München, Zürich: Schnell & Steiner, 1967).

9 See Wörner, *Architektur des Frühklassizismus*, pp. 59–60, 129–31, 147–48, 260.

10 Ibid., pp. 60–63.

11 Kirchgrabner is documented as *Palier*; Giessl is usually listed as the architect, an attribution that is strengthened by the fact that the frescoes are by Christian Winck, who often collaborated with Giessl. See Hermann Bauer and Bernhard Rupprecht, *Corpus der barocken Deckenmalerei in Deutschland* (München: Süddeutscher Verlag, 1976), p. 327.

12 Given the late date it is not surprising that the newly enlightened church authorities in Munich refused to make funds available for side altars, stuccoes, and frescoes. The charming late rococo decoration was made possible by benefactors. See Joseph Vogt, *Lippertskirchen. Kleine Führer*, no. 830 (München, Zürich: Schnell & Steiner, 1965).

13 Wörner, *Architektur des Frühklassizismus*, pp. 146–148. Schwindkirchen is once again by Giessl. Maria Dorfen and Albaching are the work of Matthias Rösler. Wörner mistakenly attributes the former to Giessl.

14 As already mentioned, the situation was different in Austria, where one was less willing to accept the impossibilities so characteristic of the Bavarian rococo fresco. See Hermann Bauer, *Der Himmel im Rokoko. Das Fresko im deutschen Kirchenraum des 18. Jahrhunderts* (Regensburg: Pustet, 1965), p. 55. Perhaps it is worth noting that Zimmermann's fresco in Die Wies preserves a trace of landscape with the setting it provides for the gate of eternity.

15 Bauer, *Der Himmel im Rokoko*, pp. 65-71.

16 Elfriede Schulze-Battmann, *Baitenhausen. Kleine Führer*, no. 923, (München, Zürich: Schnell & Steiner 1969).

17 Ibid., p. 3.

18 Arthur Rümann, *Schlüssel zur unbekannten Heimat* (München: Süddeutscher Verlag, 1962), pp. 174–77.

19 P. Norbert Backmund O. Praem., *Prämonstratenserabtei Windberg, Kleine Führer*, no. 473, 2nd ed., (München, Zürich: Schnell & Steiner, 1963).

20 Valentin Niedermeier and Bernhard Schütz, *Hörgersdorf, Eschlbach. Oppolding, Kleine Führer*, no. 934 (München, Zürich: Schnell & Steiner, 1970). See also Josef Blatner, "Barock und Rokoko," *Im Zeichen des Pferdes: Ein Buch vom Landkreis Erding* (Erding, 1963).

Conclusion

1 Hans Reuther, *Die Kirchenbauten Balthasar Neumanns* (Berlin: Hessling, 1960) and Christian F. Otto, *Space Into Light: The Churches of Balthasar Neumann* (Cambridge: The Architectural History Foundation and M.I.T. Press, 1979), pp. 88–92. See also Neumann's parish church in Gaibach.

2 Hugo Schnell, *Kloster Reisach am Inn, Kleine Führer*, no. 154, 6th ed. (München, Zürich: Schnell & Steiner, 1978).

3 Hans Sedlmayr, *Die Revolution der modernen Kunst* (Hamburg: Rowohlt, 1955), pp. 46–48 and Bauer, *Rocaille*, p. 74.

4 Adolf Loos, "Ornament and Crime," *Programs and Manifestoes on 20th-century Architecture*, ed. Ulrich Conrads, tr. Michael Bullock (Cambridge: M.I.T. Press, 1975), p.22.

5 Hermann Broch, "Hofmannsthal und seine Zeit,"

Essays, vol. 1 (Zürich: Rhein, 1955), p. 44.

6 *Summa theologiac* I–II, 102, art 4, reply.

7 Fischer's use of columns in Diessen offers a good example. See p. 165 above.

8 Emil Kaufmann, *Architecture in the Age of Reason: Baroque and Post-Baroque in England, Italy, France* (New York: Dover, 1968), p. 91. See also Geoffrey Scott, *The Architecture of Humanism: A Study in the History of Taste* (New York: Norton Library, 1974), p. 159.

9 Kaufmann, *Architecture in the Age of Reason*, p. 141. The shift from patterns of subordination to patterns of coordination provides a key to the change in aesthetic sensibility in the late eighteenth century: It can be traced not only in architecture, but in the other arts as well. It found its philosophical justification in Kant's rejection of Baumgarten's analysis of the beautiful in terms of perfection (where perfection implies the governing role of a theme or purpose to which the different parts of an aesthetic object are subordinated), for which he substituted his own analysis of the beautiful as "purposiveness without a purpose."

10 Loos, *Programs and Manifestoes*, pp. 19–24.

11 Ibid., p. 21.

12 Ibid.

13 Ibid., p. 24.

14 See Hermann Broch, "Der Zerfall der Werte," *Essays*, vol. 2, pp. 5–43.

15 Immanuel Kant, e.g., discusses architecture as an essentially impure art. See *Critique of Judgment*, tr. J. H. Bernhard (New York: Hafner, 1951), par. 51, p. 166.

16 See Kaufmann, *Architecture in the Age of Reason*, p. 266, n. 439, where he discusses the relationship of Sedlmayr's work to his own. Also pp. 110–67 and Sedlmayr, *Der Verlust der Mitte* (Berlin: Ullstein, 1959) and *Die Revolution der modernen Kunst*, pp. 46–48.

17 Frank Stella, quoted by Bruce Glaser, "Questions to Stella and Judd," *Minimal Art: A Critical Anthology*, ed. Gregory Battcock (New York: Dutton, 1968), pp. 157–58.

18 Ibid., p. 158.

19 Michael Fried, "Art and Objecthood," in *Minimal Art*, pp. 146–47.

20 Ibid., p. 146.

21 Ibid., p. 145.

22 Ibid., p. 147.

23 Kant, *Critique of Judgment*, par. 16, p. 66.

24 Ibid.

25 Peg Weiss, *Kandinsky in Munich: The Formative Jugendstil Years* (Princeton: Princeton University Press, 1979), p. 34.

26 Ibid., pp. 40–47, and the catalogue of the exhibition *Adolf Hoelzel: Aufbruch zur Moderne*, 1 April–1 June, 1980 in the Museum Villa Stuck in Munich.

27 Arthur Rümann reports that Gabriele Münter told him of Kandinsky's interest in the curious painted marbling father and son Zellner created in several churches near Erding. See *Schlüssel zur unbekannten Heimat* (München: Süddeutscher Verlag, 1962), p. 177 and p. 304. (See fig. 150 of this book.) It would indeed have been curious if artists like Endell, whose work was condemned for its "rococo" character, had not been intimately familiar with the work of the Bavarian rococo.

28 Clement Greenberg, "Recentness of Sculpture," *Minimal Art*, p. 185.

29 See especially Kant's discussion of the "Ideal of Beauty" and of "Beauty as the Symbol of Morality." *Critique of Judgment*, pars. 17 and 59.

30 Even Kant considered this figural understanding of beautiful nature a fact requiring interpretation. His own interpretation relies on the analogy between aesthetic judgment and moral feeling, although he is quite aware that his account "seems far too studied to be regarded as the true interpretation of that cipher through which nature speaks to us figuratively in her beautiful forms" (*Critique of Judgment*, par. 42, p. 143).

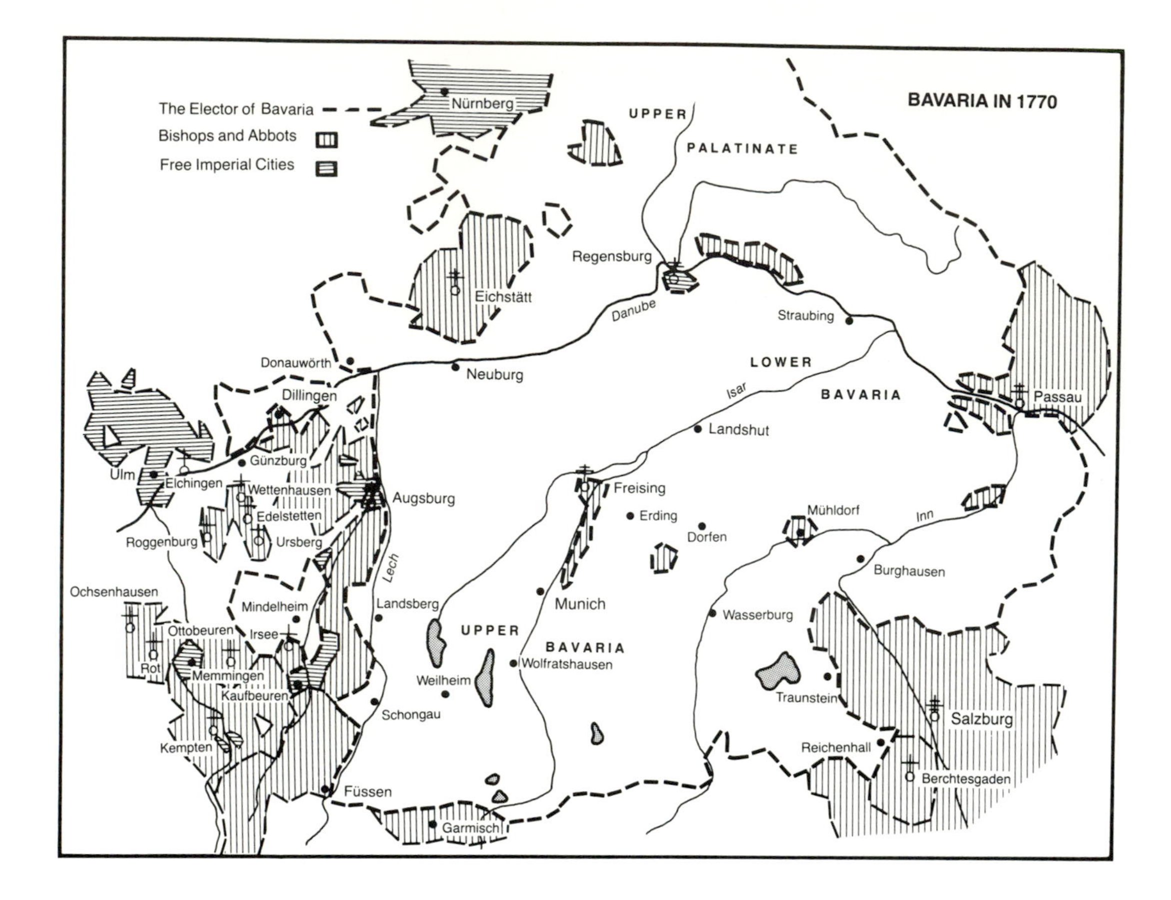
BAVARIA IN 1770
The Elector of Bavaria
Bishops and Abbots
Free Imperial Cities
Nürnberg
UPPER
PALATINATE
Regensburg
Eichstätt
Danube
Straubing
LOWER
BAVARIA
Passau
Donauwörth
Neuburg
Dillingen
Isar
Landshut
Ulm
Günzburg
Eichingen
Wettenhausen
Augsburg
Freising
Edelstetten
Erding
Dorfen
Mühldorf
Inn
Roggenburg
Ursberg
Burghausen
Lech
Ochsenhausen
Mindelheim
Landsberg
Munich
Wasserburg
Ottobeuren
Irsee
UPPER
BAVARIA
Rot
Wolfratshausen
Memmingen
Kaufbeuren
Weilheim
Traunstein
Salzburg
Schongau
Kempten
Reichenhall
Berchtesgaden
Füssen
Garmisch

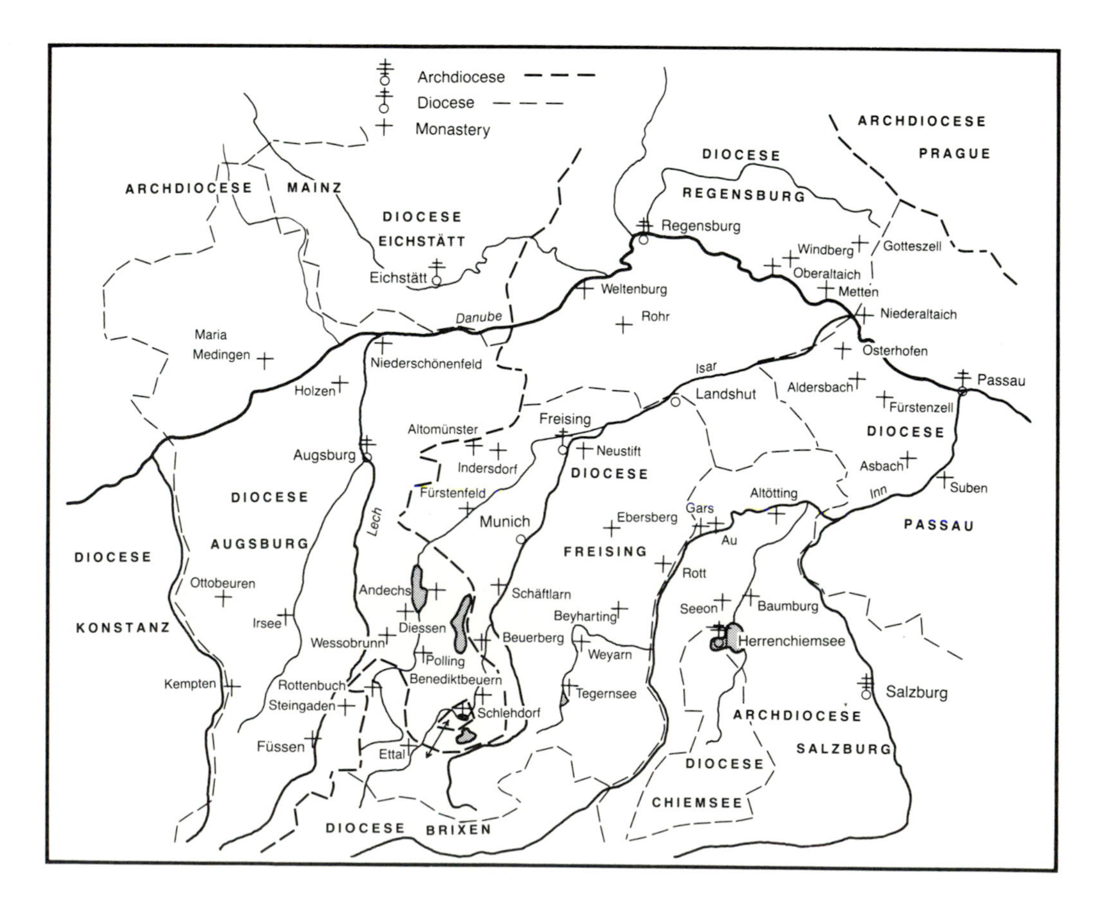
Archdiocese
Diocese
Monastery
ARCHDIOCESE
PRAGUE
DIOCESE
REGENSBURG
ARCHDIOCESE
MAINZ
DIOCESE
EICHSTÄTT
Regensburg
Windberg
Gotteszell
Oberaltaich
Eichstätt
Metten
Weltenburg
Rohr
Niederaltaich
Danube
Maria
Medingen
Niederschönenfeld
Osterhofen
Isar
Passau
Aldersbach
Holzen
Landshut
Fürstenzell
Altomünster
Freising
DIOCESE
Augsburg
Neustift
Indersdorf
DIOCESE
Asbach
Suben
DIOCESE
Fürstenfeld
Altötting
Inn
Gars
AUGSBURG
Munich
Ebersberg
Au
PASSAU
Lech
DIOCESE
FREISING
Rott
Ottobeuren
Andechs
Schäftlarn
Seeon
Baumburg
KONSTANZ
Irsee
Beyharting
Wessobrunn
Diessen
Beuerberg
Herrenchiemsee
Polling
Weyarn
Kempten
Rottenbuch
Benediktbeuern
Steingaden
Tegernsee
Salzburg
Schlehdorf
ARCHDIOCESE
Füssen
SALZBURG
Ettal
DIOCESE
CHIEMSEE
DIOCESE
BRIXEN

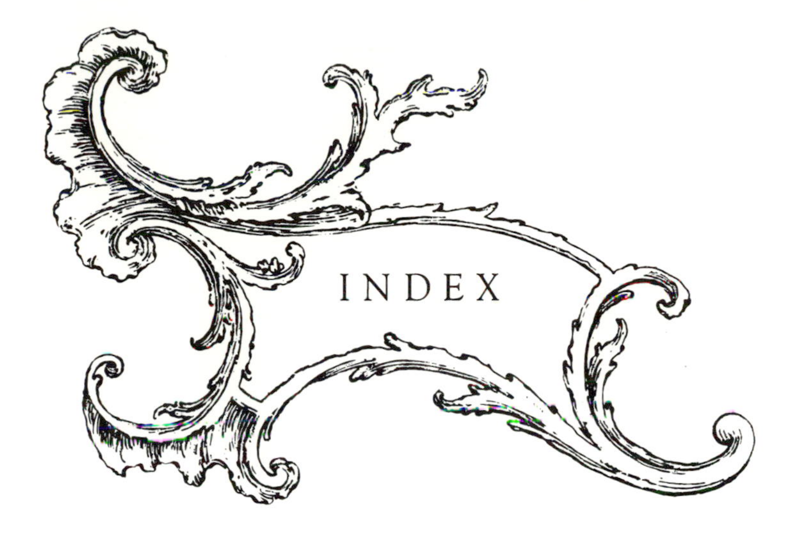

INDEX